John Erik Wittern

Modeling and Selection of Software Service Variants

Modeling and Selection of Software Service Variants

by

John Erik Wittern

KIT Scientific Publishing

Dissertation, Karlsruher Institut für Technologie (KIT)
Fakultät für Wirtschaftswissenschaften

Tag der mündlichen Prüfung: 14. Mai 2014
Referenten: Prof. Dr.-Ing. Stefan Tai, Prof. Dr.-Ing. Stefan Jähnichen

Impressum

KIT Scientific Publishing

Karlsruher Institut für Technologie (KIT)
KIT Scientific Publishing
Straße am Forum 2
D-76131 Karlsruhe

KIT Scientific Publishing is a registered trademark of Karlsruhe Institute of Technology. Reprint using the book cover is not allowed.

www.ksp.kit.edu

Print on Demand 2015

ISBN 978-3-7315-0349-1
DOI 10.5445/KSP/1000045936

Acknowledgments

First version

This thesis could not have been completed, had it not been for numerous people who supported and influenced me during the last 4 years.

Firstly, a big thank you to my supervisor, Prof. Dr.-Ing. Stefan Tai. He considerably shaped the way I think about research and computer science in particular. His contributions to both my work and my understanding of research always combined deep technical knowledge with the urge to motivate one's work based on relevant problems in relevant contexts. Stefan's approach to conducting research will always be the gold standard for me.

I further thank Prof. Dr.-Ing. Stefan Jähnichen, who kindly acted as my Korreferent and provided me with the opportunity to present and discuss especially the feature modeling aspects of this work with him and his team at TU Berlin. I also thank Prof. Dr. Rudi Studer and Prof. Dr. Ir. Marc Wouters, who completed the thesis committee.

Dr. Christian Zirpins helped me shape this work from the beginning. I thank him for the great time working in the COCKPIT project together, the fantastic journeys we undertook in this context, and his valuable advice and guidance that expanded beyond his time at our research group.

I started my time at eOrganization writing my Diplomarbeit in 2009. I thank my two supervisors, Robin Fischer and Dr. Ulrich Scholten, who invoked my scientific curiosity, ensured a smooth transition into my time as a doctorand, and became dear friends.

I thank my eOrganization colleagues in Karlsruhe, Dr.-Ing. David Bermbach, Bugra Derre, Dr. Christian Janiesch, Jörn Kuhlenkamp, Markus Klems, Tilmann Kopp, Michael Menzel, Steffen Müller, Dr.-Ing. Nelly Schuster, and Raffael Stein for providing such a great environment to work in and for the various, fruitful collaborations. I thank my FZI colleagues Dr. Gregory Katsaros, Luise Kranich, Alexander Lenk, David Müller, Prof. Dr.-Ing. Frank Pallas, and Mandy Schneider in Berlin, who made the Aussenstelle a great place to work and taught me a lot about Tischfussball. I further thank all my colleagues from AIFB, FZI/IPE, and KSRI. I am especially thankful for the great administrative support I received from Heike Döhmer and Rita Schmidt. I thank my collaborators from the COCKPIT project and the many students I had the pleasure to work with.

I thank my family and friends - they supported me throughout these years and gave me the strength and perseverance required to finish this work. I especially appreciated the inspiring discussions about my work and its context with my father, Prof. Dr. Klaus-Peter Wittern, and with Dr. Timm Gudehus.

Finally, I thank my great love Gesina.

Berlin, May 2014 *Erik Wittern*

Second version

The first version of this dissertation was published at the EVA STAR-catalog of the Karlsruhe Institute of Technology[1] in May 2014, rapidly, to adhere to the time constraints for completing my PhD. This second version primarily provides improved typesetting and layout, achieving higher readability throughout. It further includes minor improvements on the first version (making it a version, actually, rather than a variant): A new appendix B shows screenshots of an implementation of the SFM tool suite. References that had been under review when the first version was published have been updated to point to the now accepted publications. Finally, the consistency of the language used throughout this thesis has been improved.

New York City, Februrary 2015 *Erik Wittern*

[1] `http://nbn-resolving.org/urn:nbn:de:swb:90-411324`

Abstract

Providers and consumers have to deal with variants during the development and the delivery of software services. Variants are alternative instances of a service's design, implementation, deployment, or operation. Making decisions about variants is parts of any software service development activities. Providers need to deliver variants to address diverse or changing consumer needs, which are best served by a specific variant. Approaches to deal with variants from software product line engineering lack desirable capabilities for representing characteristics, collaboration in modeling, and (participatory) selection of variants, even among services. This thesis presents service feature modeling, a novel approach consisting of a variability modeling language and a set of methods to address these challenges in modeling and selecting software service variants.

The service feature modeling language extends standard feature modeling from software product line engineering. A typology of feature types differentiates their semantics with the goal to utilize service feature models (SFMs) in novel ways, like realizing comparability of variants across services. Attribute types represent concerns common to multiple attributes within an SFM to reduce modeling efforts and for attribute aggregation. A novel modeling method considers SFMs to be composed by services, addressing the collaboration of experts in modeling and the integration of dynamic or complex attribute values.

Making use of SFMs, a structured selection process flexibly combines a set of methods for decision-makers to determine which variant to develop or deliver. A configuration set determination method, extending existing approaches with attribute aggregation, produces all valid service variants represented by an SFM. Determined configuration sets are narrowed down with a novel, fuzzy requirements filter. Skyline filtering, adapted from database systems, dismisses service variants that are dominated by others. Preference-based ranking applies a well-known multi-criteria decision making approach to rank service variants based on their fulfillment of preferences. Through abstractions, it aims to enable participation by involving non-technical decision-makers in service variant selection.

This thesis presents an evaluation of the outlined concepts, consisting of multiple parts. A proof-of-concept implementation and a performance evaluation of a SFM tool suite show the realizability and applicability of service feature modeling, including the composition of SFMs from services and all outlined usage methods. A first use case concerns the development of public services under consideration of service variants, whose selection was driven by citizen participation. A second use case concerns the modeling and selection of Infrastructure as a Service (IaaS) variants and their automatic consumption and usage. Finally, an empirical evaluation indicates good usability, expressiveness, and usefulness and interpretability of service feature modeling.

Contents

1. Introduction

Software services[1] provide deployed capabilities, which are realized by software, and can be consumed on demand over networks. They play an ever-increasing role in businesses, culture, and personal life. For example, companies use software services to manage customer relationships [Sal], to run business processes like purchasing, production, human resources, or distribution [SAP], or to host their IT [Ama]. Public administrations provide software services to offer public services [U.S]. Or, end users use software services offered by social networks to communicate or share their private lives [Fac], they consume movies [Net] and music [Spo], or plan and book their holidays [Tri]. *Web services* are a common type of software services, which are consumed over the Internet. They enable interoperation and composition even across organizational borders [Pap03]. *Cloud services* are another common type of software services, which provision scalable, abstracted IT infrastructures, platforms and applications with a pay-per-use model [BKNT11].

Stakeholders, acting in the role of either *service provider* or *service consumer*, perform different activities across a software service's lifespan. *Service development* consists of specification, design, and implementation activities. In general, service providers perform these activities while consumers are only involved if participatory approaches are used [HJR$^+$10]. *Service delivery* is the combination of provision and consumption activities to fulfill a service request. Provision activities are performed by the service provider while consumption activities are performed by the consumer. In some business models, further roles exist associated with additional activities. For example, in Web service marketplaces a service broker intermediates between consumers and providers [BD06]. However, we focus here on the two fundamental roles involved in any type of software services.

Both, in the development and the delivery of software services, providers and consumers have to deal with *variants*. Variants are alternative instances of a service's design, implementation, deployment, or operation. Variants exist in parallel and do not supersede each other, in contrast to versions which are ordered in time [ABKS13] and are thus often subsumed as part of change manage-

[1] In the following, we use the term *service* interchangeably for the term *software service*.

ment [Som11][2]. Related to the notion of versions, software configuration management (SCM) focuses on the development and evolution of a system [CW98], whereas variants are about multiple instances existing in parallel. Making decisions about variants is part of any software service development activities. There are alternative designs to evaluate, different technologies exist for implementing a software service, or it can be deployed in different ways. The definition and subsequent selection of variants, supporting decision-making regarding the realization of a service, is therefore essential. Neglecting to assess variants during development in a structured way tempts developers to use the first alternative that comes to mind [Sha12] and increases the risk of causing cost for reversing faulty design decisions later on [Bos13]. Providers need to deliver variants to address diverse or changing consumer needs, which are best served by a specific variant [MMLP09, NCTH11]. If providers would just deliver a single variant, they risk addressing only a limited target customer group. Reversely, consumers need to select suitable variants for consumption that match their specific needs [SM10]. Neglecting this step can cause (costly) over-delivery [LNSJ12] or risks service delivery to deviate from needs [RA11]. Businesses, thus, cannot neglect dealing with software service variants.

Modeling can be used to define, communicate, experiment, or decide about aspects of a system [Lud03, Rot89], in this case a service's variants. This thesis proposes a modeling language, allowing to represent service variants, and a set of methods that, utilizing the modeling language, select a single or a subgroup of variants based on stakeholder requirements and preferences.

1.1. Examples for Variants in Software Services

Within this section, we provide three examples to illustrate that software service variants exist and are relevant in different contexts. These examples provide furthermore a basis to, in the following sections, discuss benefits and motivate challenges of variants.

1.1.1. Public Service Design

The *Citizens Collaboration and Co-Creation in Public Service Delivery (COCKPIT)* project presents the challenge to define and select variants regarding the

[2]Note: Versions which are branches of a software service may exist in parallel and may thus be referred to as variants [CW98]. Reversely, variants existing in parallel may have a version history and may thus be referred to as a version. The important notion for us to denote variants is that they are intended to exist in parallel, cf. section 2.3.

design of public services [KKKP10]. The project aims to enable citizens to participate in public service design to increase the fit of the service with citizens' needs. The COCKPIT project researches a model-based service design methodology. In it, multiple models are used to describe certain aspects of the service. A generic model for public services, for example, captures information like the service's goals, requirements towards it, or the resources it involves [DHJ09]. Process models describe the service delivery using the Business Model and Notation (BPMN) [BPM10], or costs are described in models following an activity-based cost approach [CA10]. In addition to these models, the methodology includes several approaches to automatically create parts of the models or to utilize them. For example, policy and law retrieval methods crawl public databases for relevant information regarding the service, an opinion mining component reveals opinions stated in Web 2.0 sources about the service in design or similar services, or a simulation engine visualizes and analyzes service designs based on the process models.

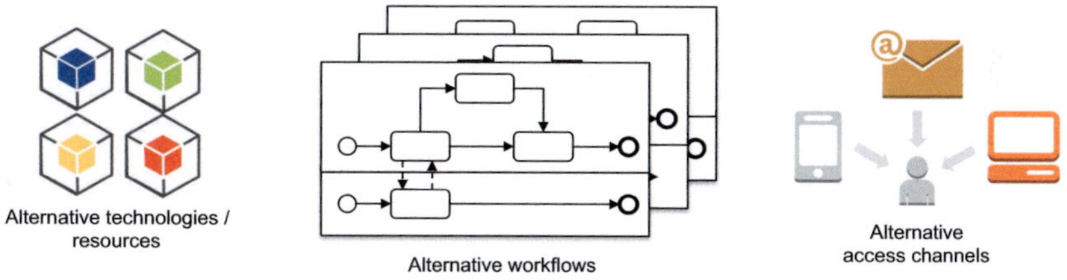

Figure 1.1.: Typical sources of variants when designing public services in the COCKPIT project

Within the project, public administrations designed or re-designed actual public services they offer using the outlined methodology. In this process, experts from the participating administrations concerned with the public service design identified multiple design variants. Typical sources driving these variants are illustrated in figure 1.1.

In a first scenario, the Greek ministry of interior designed the "access extracts of insurance records in social security organization" service. It allows citizens to access their insurance records, which is required if they want to check the payment status of their health insurance or if they apply for a loan or for a new job. The service engineers identified possible design variants of this service, for example, with regard to triggering the process either via Website, telephone, or by visiting a social security office. The retrieval of the requested record can be performed manually by designated clerks, resulting in a delivery of the record via post. Alternatively, the retrieval can be performed using a database system and the delivery can be performed using email. These variants impact the service's properties like the delivery cost, the required execution time, or the validity of the delivered record - for example, some situations may demand for physical, signed copies of a record.

In a second scenario, the City of Venice redesigned the "Internet reporting information system" service. It is implemented as a Web application and accessible to all citizens of Venice. The service allows citizens to report civic issues, for example, occurrences of vandalism, decay, or unreasonable regulations, and track how the city addresses them. In this scenario, engineers concerned with the design identified variants with regard to, for example, designing interfaces to report issues from different devices, for example, personal computers or mobile phones, whether to open the service to other cities or not, or whether to notify tracking reports via short messages or not. These variants impact the service's properties like costs for the public administration or the frequency of in which tracking reports are made available.

The consideration of design variants has been proposed in multiple service design methodologies as means to conceptualize and assess different ways to develop a service [PVDH06, DHJ09, MNDF+10, TÖD11]. While these works motivate dealing with variants during service design, they do not present specific approaches on how to pursue it. In COCKPIT, variants result from variable concerns scattered across models describing processes, resources, or costs. No means exist to explicitly represent these variants and use them to improve the service design. This challenge is further complicated due to the multiple stakeholders involved in public service design, including the participation of citizens. Approaches to represent and assess variants need to enable the participation of these stakeholders.

Overall, ideally, engineers designing public services would have an approach at hand to model service design variants, which integrates with other modeling approaches and limits additional efforts. Based on the resulting models, different stakeholders would be supported in stating their preferences and requirements to select the variants to further develop. Section 5.3 provides details on how we address these issues with this work's contributions.

1.1.2. Financial Web Service Consumption

Financial data services offer consumers a variety of financial data to use in their applications. Common types of data include stock quotes or company financial data, which provides an overview over the financial performance of companies, including information on balance sheets, cash flows, or income statements. Providers like Xignite [Xig] or QuoteMedia [Quo] offer such data via Web APIs.

Web APIs are application programming interfaces that provide consumers data or services via endpoints accessible in the Web.

Web APIs denote variants regarding, for example, data formats, the interface implementation, or authentication mechanisms [DBM13]. Common data formats provided by Web APIs include XML and JSON. The interfaces of Web APIs are typically implemented either using SOAP or in a RESTful way. Further variants exist with regard to the data provided by the Web API. The provided data depends on the endpoint that consumers invoke and on the parameters provided in a request to that endpoint. Data can be historical, here describing past financial situations, or real-time, giving insights into latest developments.

Figure 1.2 illustrates variants to select by consumers of the Xignite's Get Companies Financial service. The corresponding API can be invoked by providing different types of identifiers for the company whose financial data a consumer is interested in, being for example the company's symbol or the Central Index Key (CIK). Provided financial reports can be of different type, for example, quarterly or annual, and cover a definable time period. In addition, data can be provided in different data formats like XML, JSON, or CVS.

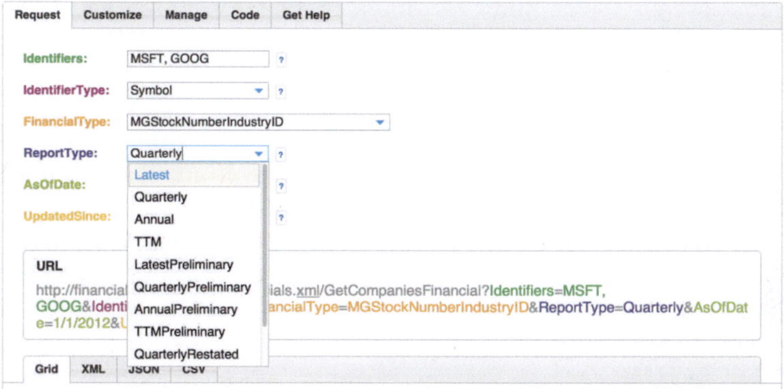

Figure 1.2.: Screenshot showing variants of Xignite's financial data service, source: `http://www.xignite.com/product/company-financials/api/GetCompaniesFinancial/`, accessed: 4th March 2014

Current descriptions of Web APIs, as illustrated for the case of financial Web APIs in figure 1.2, are heterogeneous and dispersed in nature [PCP+12]. Variants are implicitly included in the descriptions, but not stated in a structured, analyzable way. In consequence, (potential) consumers have to manually gather and structure this information. One scenario where structured data is required is the selection among variants, considering for example trade-offs between currentness of data and cost for invoking an API. As it is the case in the example about consuming IaaS (cf. section 1.1.3), selection of variants of Web APIs providing financial data ideally spans across comparable services offered by different providers.

Overall, potential consumers would ideally have a structured representation about the variants offered by financial Web APIs at hand. Using this representation, the consumers would be supported in selecting a suitable variant among multiple, competing services based on their requirements and preferences. We use this scenario throughout the thesis to illustrate how this work's contributions can practically be applied.

1.1.3. IaaS Consumption

The consumption of *Infrastructure as a Service (IaaS)* presents consumers with the challenge to select suitable IaaS variants. IaaS provides virtualized hardware to consumers. Consider, for example, a developer who wants to use a Couchbase[3] NoSQL datastore on top of IaaS. By doing so, the developer, acting as an IaaS consumer, does not have to physically own infrastructure but can rent it on-demand.

In this scenario, the IaaS consumer is presented with variants. There are multiple IaaS services from different providers to choose from, for example Amazon EC2 [Ama] or Rackspace [Rac]. While being independent services, the consumer would like to treat their offers as variants to another as long as they provide the desired capabilities. If the selection of the provider is not predetermined, for example, because the consumer already uses one provider in other contexts, the consumer wants to compare the providers' offers against each other. Looking at an individual IaaS, it denotes further variants because it allows consumers to specify a *configuration*. Here, a configuration is a set of information, for example, configuration parameters, that determines a service variant within a pre-defined scope [SZG+08][4]. A configurable service is capable of taking a configuration as input and providing a corresponding service variant[5].

[3] `http://www.couchbase.com/`

[4] Note: The field of software configuration management considers a configuration, divergently, as a set of components, that can themselves be configurations or configuration items, which are the smallest units of individual change [Tic03]. The term configuration is thus overloaded and needs to be considered in dependence of the context, cf. section 3.2.1.

[5] Note: Service variants can also be realized with alternative methods, for example, through dedicated implementations (also referred to as customization) or through adaptation, cf. section 2.3.5.

Instance Family	Instance Type	Processor Arch	vCPU	ECU	Memory (GiB)	Instance Storage (GB)
General purpose	m3.medium	64-bit	1	3	3.75	1 x 4 SSD[*6]
General purpose	m3.large	64-bit	2	6.5	7.5	1 x 32 SSD[*6]
General purpose	m3.xlarge	64-bit	4	13	15	2 x 40 SSD[*6]
General purpose	m3.2xlarge	64-bit	8	26	30	2 x 80 SSD[*6]
General purpose	m1.small	32-bit or 64-bit	1[*1]	1	1.7	1 x 160

Figure 1.3.: Screenshot depicting different virtual machine types offered by Amazon EC2, `https://aws.amazon.com/ec2/instance-types/`, accessed: 25th February 2014

In the case of IaaS, one source of configuration options is the selection of the type of *virtual machine (VM)* to consume. A virtual machine maps arbitrary, software-defined interfaces and resources on the interface and resources of a physical machine. Offered types of VMs typically differ with regard to the amount of CPU cores, memory, disk space and price [Bar13]. Consumers chose VM types based on the requirements of the software components or applications to deploy on the VM. In this case, for example, the NoSQL datastore can profit from large memory to increase the available cache and therefore avoid random, slow disk I/O. Figure 1.3 illustrates properties of some of the VM types offered by Amazon EC2.

The number of variants further increases from the choice of *images* to load onto the rented VM. Images contain fundamental software to use a VM, including the operating system. Additionally, images may contain pre-packed software, for example, there are images that already contain the Couchbase NoSQL datastore. Pre-packed software enables out-of-the box functionality and releases the consumer of having to manually install software. Images vary further with regard to terms and conditions. Some images, for example, do not allow commercial use or they induce additional cost. Figure 1.4 illustrates some of the images offered by Amazon EC2 that have the Couchbase NoSQL datastore pre-pakced.

Finally, the number of variants to consume further increases as consumers may install additional software on top of an image hosted by a VM. Additional software may include monitoring tools, the network time protocol (NTP), or configuration management tools.

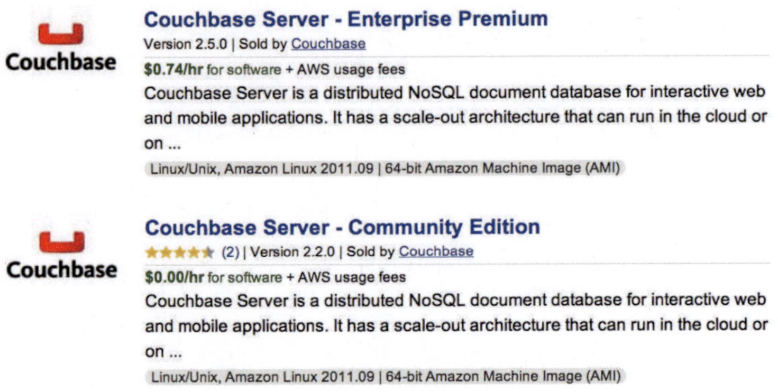

Figure 1.4.: Screenshot depicting different Couchbase images offered by Amazon EC2, `https://aws.amazon.com/marketplace/seller-profile/ref=dtl_pcp_sold_by?id=1a064a14-5ac2-4980-9167-15746aabde72`, accessed: 25th February 2014

Currently, IaaS providers communicate the outlined variants only in an unstructured way in form of HTML descriptions. Correspondingly, consumers select variants based on intuition or experience. Such approaches, however, fall short when the consumer desires a more structured, reproducible way to select variants. In the current way of consuming IaaS, the consumer does not explicitly state his requirements and preferences and can thus not document or iteratively revise them. Automations regarding the selection of variants are currently not supported, thus prohibiting unexpected or repeated selections. For example, a consumer may also wish support in re-evaluating his variant selection in reaction to changing offers, which currently requires repeated manual effort. Finally, while consumption of IaaS can be performed automatically with automation tools like Chef[6], these methods are not integrated with means for structured IaaS variant selection.

Overall, ideally, the consumer would state his requirements and preferences regarding the consumption of Couchbase on IaaS, would be supported in selecting the most suitable variant, and its consumption would automatically be initiated. Section 5.4 provides details on how we address these issues with this work's contributions.

[6] `http://www.getchef.com/chef/`

1.2. Motivations for Software Service Variants

The three examples presented in section 1.1 motivate dealing with software service variants. We differentiate motivations broadly into whether service variants are considered for the development (cf. example 1.1.1) or for the delivery of software services (cf. examples 1.1.3 and 1.1.2).

In service development, variants are defined by the service provider during specification and design activities. The purpose of defining variants during development, as it is motivated in the example about public service design in section 1.1.1 and in related work [DHJ09, PVDH06, MNDF^{+}10], is to assess alternative ways of how to further develop and deliver a service. The variant definition process needs to capture the requirements of the provider and consumer stakeholders involved with the service. Empirical studies from software engineering show that insufficient consideration of stakeholder requirements is the single biggest cause for software projects to fail [HL01]. Following the basic systems engineering process process [Lev00], design variants can be assessed regarding objectives and criteria to chose which variant to implement. Variants can thus be used to perform thorough business case analysis and provide basis for decisions on the service design. In this sense, the definition and later selection of variants corresponds to *design space* approaches [Sha12]. Design spaces encompass a set of decisions to choose an artifact, in this case a service design variant, that best satisfies consumer needs. Not assessing variants tempts developers to stick with the first variant that comes to mind, it avoids building up knowledge about families of designs, and it impedes identifying suitable and innovative designs [Sha12]. In addition, neglecting the assessment of variants increases the risk of having to costly reverse design decisions [Bos13].

Challenges for such approaches result from the negative impacts that considering variants during development induces. Variants need to be defined and managed, which creates efforts and increase complexities in design and implementation activities. Artifacts to support these tasks require creation and maintenance. Furthermore, corresponding methods need to be learned, applied, and possibly be supported by dedicated systems.

In service delivery, the provision of variants allows providers to deal with diverse requirements and preferences of consumers [MMLP09, NCTH11]. Providers offer multiple variants of their service and consumers select those variants that best meet their individual needs. These needs can address the functionalities or qualities of a service [MMLP09]. In the IaaS example from section 1.1.3, different consumers will have different requirements regarding the computational performance of VMs, depending on CPU cores and memory, or the software provided by images. Neglecting the consideration of these requirements to select variants can cause (costly) over-delivery [LNSJ12] or it risks service delivery to deviate from needs [RA11]. In addressing individual consumer needs, the delivery of service variants is a means for customization. Multiple positive effects of service customization have been identified, including increased customer satisfaction [WWMQ10] and perceived quality [PS00]. These, in consequence, positively impact consumers' willingness to pay and recommend the service, and increase consumer loyalty to the service and its provider [RC06, HKH05, AFR97].

Another motivation for delivering service variants is to react to changes in *context*. Context, generically, is "[...] any information that can be used to characterize the situation of an entity" [Dey01, page 5]. With regard to services, common context changes concern requirements, preferences, or environmental conditions, for example, changed competition, technologies, or legal regulations [DNGM+08]. Service variants allow for reaction to such changes, if consumers are enabled to switch to variants that are more suitable in light of the changed context while ensuring continuous service provision. Switching variants, for the consumer, avoids efforts for adapting systems or even exchanging services. The provider, in this scenario, can continue provisioning the service to consumers even in the face of contextual change.

As it is the case in development, delivering service variants also induces negative impacts. Multiple variants need to be deployed in parallel or the adaptation of a single service is required. Again, variants need to be managed, requiring corresponding artifacts, methods, and systems. In the case of delivery, these effects not only concern the service provider, but also the consumer who needs to select the variant to consume.

Overall, both in development and delivery, whether and to what extend considering variants is beneficial depends on the comparison of the outlined advantages with the outlined disadvantages.

1.3. Problem Statement

As already outlined in the motivation in section 1.2, dealing with variants also causes problems, which we discuss in detail in this section. We consider problems to fall into three major categories, for each of which extensive related work exists in the context of software engineering: 1) the definition of variants, using modeling methods [SD07], 2) the management and selection of variants [CABA09], and 3) the realization of variants [SVGB05]. The main contributions of this thesis focus on the first two problems. Thus, the problems addressed in this thesis are how to model and select software service variants. In the following subsections, we outline these problems in more detail and identify concrete challenges not jet addressed by related work.

1.3.1. Problems Regarding Modeling Service Variants

The first problem concerns the definition of service variants using modeling approaches. The description of IaaS variants is provided unstructured in HTML (cf. images 1.3 and 1.4). Similar, the descriptions of Web API variants (cf. image 1.2) are typically heterogeneous and dispersed [PCP+12]. In the example about public service design, variants result from information contained in different artifacts like process or resource descriptions. In all examples, no explicit representation of variants exists, thus impeding efforts to systematically reason about them. Modeling variants results in a structured representation, which enables automatic analysis and usage [BSRC10]. Defining each service variant independently from another causes redundancies, resulting in maintenance efforts and fostering inconsistencies. For example, concerns that are common to multiple variants would be modeled repeatedly and changes to them would require dealing with in multiple instances. In consequence, dedicated languages and modeling methods are required to efficiently represent service variants. To be efficient, these languages and methods need to differentiate between variable and common concerns of service variants.

The so-far outlined problems, while relevant, are rather generic in nature and are not novel to software services - they have been addressed in software engineering (SE): *variability modeling* is a well-researched [SD07] and practically applied [BRN+13] technique used in SE. It is "[...] the discipline of explicitly representing variability in dedicated models that describe the common and variable characteristics of products in a software product line" [BRN+13, page 1]. Variability modeling approaches have already been used for specific types of software services. For example, the variability of Web services has been represented with feature models [NC10, NCH14, GA13]. Or, variability modeling approaches have been applied to support customization of cloud services [MMLP09, BB13]. However, the outlined approaches do not address all challenges regarding modeling software service variants that result from the three examples in section 1.1. Specifically, we identify the following challenges, which we aim to address in this thesis:

Challenge 1. *Representation of characteristics of variants*

All three examples motivate the representation of characteristics of variants. Characteristics result for consumers or providers from developing or delivering a variant. They are typically measurable, meaning that a number can be assigned to them, or boolean in nature, meaning that they can either be true or false. When representing IaaS variants, for example, characteristics denote the number of CPU cores or the disc space of virtual machines. Public service design variants denote different cost for delivering the service or different execution times.

Or, financial Web APIs have different cost depending on the requested information. The representation of characteristics aims to document and communicate the capabilities of variants, for example with regards to *Quality of Service (QoS)* [GL09]. Representing this information allows to use it for the selection of software service variants, as it is already common in approaches to select software services without the consideration of variants, cf. [ARDN09, ZZZ09][7]. In related work, variability modeling approaches like feature modeling already address the representation of characteristics [BTRC05]. In these approaches, however, characteristics are only used to describe individual model elements, for example features. To obtain insights into the characteristics of complete variants, aggregation of individual values is required and currently not addressed. The challenge is thus to introduce means to variability modeling that enable to represent characteristics of variants. While motivated in this context, such means are not only relevant for software services, but also with regard to software systems in general.

Challenge 2. *Including dynamic or complex characteristics*

While the representation of characteristics of variants is important, statically provided characteristics do not suffice to describe service variants. Software services underly an open-world assumption, in which context is constantly changing [DNGM+08]. For example, the performance of virtual machines provided by IaaS is found in related work to considerably change over time [LMLT11, IYE11]. Or, the availability of data-providing APIs is also a function of time and the current availability status might be of interest to consumers. Many characteristics undergo constant change, impeding their static definition during modeling activities. Other characteristics are complex in nature, again impeding their static definition. For example, the cost of IaaS in many cases depend on how it is consumed - next to the bare fees for renting VMs, additional cost result depending on the amount of data transferred from or to the VM or the number of input/output operations [Ama]. In existing variability modeling approaches, service quality attributes are modeled statically, which does not suffice to describe their dynamic or complex nature [LK13]. Thus, the challenge arises to include dynamic or complex characteristics when representing software service variants. Again, while being motivated in the context of services, this challenge is also relevant in the context of software systems in general.

Challenge 3. *Support for expert collaboration in defining variants*

In the design of public service variants as described in the example in section 1.1.1, we were confronted with the challenge to enable expert collaboration

[7]Note: This challenge solely addresses the representation of characteristics. Their selection, definition, metrics, or the means to perform measurements are outside of the scope of this work.

in defining variants. In service development, this need is especially relevant due to the involvement of stakeholders from multiple disciplines [SMBG07]. Collaboration in this context includes the definition and communication of variable concerns and the definition of dependencies between them. In defining variants, experts involved in developing software or a service delimit the solution space of the design and express their individual concerns in terms of concern-specific variants [WSKT12]. These concerns, for example technical, business-related, or legal ones, may be dependent on another. In the end, variants of the overall software or service are derived that consider the specified dependencies. The resulting challenge for variability modeling approaches is to provide methods that enable collaboration by coordinating the (concurrent) creation or revision of models without conflicts. In related work, we find no approaches that address the collaborative definition of service variants. Some variability modeling approaches address fundamentals for supporting collaboration. For example, feature models defined by various stakeholders can be composed [ACLF10] or stakeholder-specific views on them can be realized [HAT+13]. However, these approaches have so far neither, to our best knowledge, addressed a conflict-free collaborative modeling process nor have they been applied to the development of software services specifically. The challenge is thus to enable expert collaboration in the definition of software service variants. Here, again, we see beneficial applications also for variability modeling of software in general.

1.3.2. Problems Regarding Selecting Service Variants

The second problem addressed in this thesis concerns the selection of service variants in development and delivery. In the examples about IaaS and Web API consumptions, consumers need to select their desired variant before consumption or if they desire to switch to another variant during consumption. In the example about variant selection during public service design, providers select the variant to further develop, i.e., design, implement, or deploy. The fundamental requirement towards selection methods is to take as input the needs or preferences of decision-makers as well as possible variants and to output a recommendation of the variant(s) to select. If such methods are not available, decision-makers who select variants for development or delivery are bound to their intuitions and experiences only in their manual efforts to find the variant meeting their requirements and preferences. Disadvantages of such approaches are missing documentations of the decisions made and impeded repeatability. When understanding and having modeled variants to result from variability in individual concerns, the number of variants grows exponentially whenever new variable concerns are added. This introduces the need for selection support methods that are capable of comparing, filtering and ranking large numbers of variants.

As in the case of modeling variants, related work also exists with regard to selecting them. Variability modeling encompasses approaches for selecting variants [CABA09, BSRC10]. Again, existing approaches do not address all challenges regarding selecting software service variants that result from the three examples in section 1.1. We identify the following challenges, which we aim to address in this thesis:

Challenge 4. *Selection process*

For selecting software service variants based on representations fulfilling the above outlined challenges, a selection process is needed. In the context of services, where selection can be used to decide among variants for delivery as in the IaaS example in section 1.1.3, the selection process should be able to perform automatically. Automation in selection enables consumers to switch between service variants on a request basis[8]. Similar approaches are proposed in the context of Web services as dynamic or late binding [AP07]. Even if selection is not performed for every request, other triggers to re-perform software service variant selection exist, like periodic assessments or promoted changes in the offered service variants. To base selection on meaningful information, requirements and preferences of relevant stakeholders need to be considered in this process. Their explicit representation allows to revise or document them and is another important factor in enabling automation in performing the selection process. In related work, approaches focus either on requirements-based feature selection, for example in staged configuration [CHE04], or on preference-based selection, for example in the stratified analytical hierarchy process [BAGS10]. These approaches rely on manual efforts and thus impede automation. In contrast, we see the challenge in providing a comprehensive, automatically performable selection process, considering both requirements and preferences.

Challenge 5. *Comparability of variants from different services*

When consumers select variants of a service to consume, they might not only be interested in the variants offered by a single provider. If services are comparable, a common problem is to select among these services. Related approaches address, for example, the selection among functionally equivalent Web services based on quality of service characteristics [ARDN09] or the selection of comparable cloud services [RHH13]. Incorporating the concept of variants into this task, consumers are presented with the challenge of selecting among variants offered by multiple services. Consider, for example, the consumption of IaaS. A consumer may be agnostic to the provider from which to consume IaaS but only

[8] The applicability of this approach depends on whether switching a service variant can be performed without excessive effort, which depends, for example, on required data migration or integration.

focus on certain requirements and preferences that can be fulfilled by multiple services of offered by different providers. Or, when consuming financial Web services to obtain stock quotes, consumers need to select among different services offered, for example, by Xignite or QuoteMedia that provide the same data but have different interface implementations, data formats, or prices. A necessary precondition to realize such selections is to ensure comparability between service variants offered by different providers. For representations of variants to act as basis in such approaches, they need to address the same variable aspects of a service and be described regarding the same characteristics. Variant selection, then, methodically is performed as in the case of a single variable service, but considers the superset of all comparable services' variants. To our best knowledge, comparability between variability models or the variants represented in them has not yet been addressed in related work. The challenge is thus to ensure comparability of variants offered by different providers and represented in different variability models.

Challenge 6. *User participation in variant selection*

During development of software services, design variants can be assessed by consumers, allowing for participatory service design [WZ11b], which is a positively considered method when developing services [HJR^{+}10]. Empirical studies within the last 30 years report positive impacts of user involvement in software development on system success [BZ13]. Advantages from user involvement in the design of new services are original solution approaches with higher value for the consumers [Mag03]. Using variability models for participatory design is promising given their suitability as a communication medium. For example, feature models have a level of abstraction that is understandable both by technicians and customers [LKL02]. A challenge for participation methods is to present participants with meaningful and relevant information about software or service variants but also abstract from technical, deterrent details. Variability modeling needs to be combined with other abstractions and interaction methods that allow otherwise not involved and potentially non-technical stakeholders, for example users, to engage in variant selection. We do not find approaches supporting participation of consumers in software service development that are based upon variability modeling. This gap is especially evident given that variability modeling's main elements, i.e. features, are commonly defined to be characteristics visible to end-users [ABKS13], rendering such approaches suitable for end-user integration.

In sum, in this thesis, we address all the outlined challenges regarding modeling and selecting software service variants, the ones specific to software service engineering and the ones also applicable to software engineering in general. The examples in section 1.1 create even further challenges, concerning for example the mapping of representation of variants to other service-related artifacts or the automatic realization of selected variants. This work illustrates how we addressed some of these challenges, presenting for example a mapping of service variant representations with other models for public service design in section 5.3 or showing how IaaS variants can automatically be consumed in section 5.4. Because these approaches are bound to specific use cases and not necessarily generalizable, however, we do not explicitly mark their underlying challenges to be addressed in this work.

1.4. Research Design and Contributions

In this work, we apply variability modeling to model service variants and select among them during development and delivery. We focus on the following activities that make use of variability modeling:

1. The (collaborative) definition of service variants by providers and consumers during design activities of development.
2. The selection of service variants for development - selected variants are further considered in design, implementation, deployment, and operation activities - by providers under participation of consumers.
3. The (repeated) selection of service variants by consumers for service delivery.

To address the above-mentioned activities, we introduce *service feature modeling*. Service feature modeling is about the representation of service variants in a *Service Feature Model (SFM)* and the usage of SFMs to select service variants. Correspondingly, the hypothesis underlying this thesis is:

Hypothesis 1. *Service feature modeling (a) provides an expressive and usable language to represent service variants, (b) enables experts to collaborate in specifying service variants, (c) provides useful methods to (participatorily) select service variants.*

To satisfy this hypothesis, we conceptualize a modeling language and selection methods utilizing models based on this language. The conceptualization was initially driven by requirements from public service providers within the research project about public service design presented in section 1.1.1. Early within our work, we started developing proof-of-concept tools, implementing service feature modeling. The concepts and tools were iteratively refined based on the public service providers' feedback and our findings. The research project provided a use case that we used to evaluate the modeling language and parts of the selection methods. Subsequently, we applied service feature modeling in other contexts. We performed a second use case, covering again the modeling language and a more complete set of selection methods, addressing the representation and selection of IaaS variants as motivated in section 1.1.3. The second use case furthermore provided the possibility to assess the realization of service variants based on models described in our language. Overall, through this thesis' contributions, we define a novel approach to model and select service variants. The approach is rooted in and builds upon software engineering, using for example classical feature modeling, while considering the characteristics and challenges of services. We outline the contributions in more detail in the following.

1.4.1. Concepts and Methodology

An initial contribution of this thesis is a specification of concepts related to services and service variants. Definitions for services and their perceptions are manifold [Alt08] so that the understanding underlying this thesis needs to be defined. We focus on and present common types of software services, which we differentiate from generic services. We then discuss service variability, which we define to be the ability of a service to a) be delivered in one of multiple preplanned ways or b) adapt in a preplanned manner. We address fundamental questions related to service variability: who is affected by, controls, benefits or is worse off by service variability? When does it appear? How can it be realized?

We furthermore present a software service life-cycle model that is used throughout this thesis to denote the occurrence and involved stakeholders of service feature modeling activities. Building upon the so far introduced concepts, we present service feature modeling's methodology. It uses a modeling language to represent service variants and combines corresponding methods to model and select service variants.

1.4.2. Modeling Language

A central contribution of this work is the definition of the service feature modeling language. It is based upon classical feature modeling from software engineering [KCH+90]. The models created with this language, SFMs, represent multiple variants of a service in a single model. SFMs can represent diverse variable concerns of a service, including, for example, technical, business-related, or legal ones. Their inclusion in a single representation allows modelers to interrelate these concerns, for example, to state dependencies between legal regulations and technical properties. We design the service feature modeling language to suffice multiple quality properties, which we evaluate within this thesis.

First, we design the modeling language to be expressive. Expressiveness refers to the capability of SFMs to capture relevant variable concerns and define dependencies between them. To achieve expressiveness, we introduce *attribute types*, containing information common to multiple attributes of the same type. Attribute types provide the basis for determining characteristics of variants as it is motivated by challenge 1. Another extension introduced by the service feature modeling language are *feature types* to clearly define the semantics of features. Feature types further provide the basis to define domain models, which enable comparability of variants defined in different SFMs as motivated by challenge 5.

Furthermore, we assess the usability of the service feature modeling language. Usability refers to how easy it is to learn and use the service feature modeling language. We assess how service engineers assess the usability of the service feature modeling language in an empirical evaluation based upon one of the performed use cases.

Finally, we also address the applicability of service feature modeling in this thesis. Applicability refers to the ability of our approach to be used in realistic scenarios. Given the possibly large amount of scenarios in which service feature modeling can be used, we cannot assess applicability in absolute terms. However, we illustrate applicability exemplarily by applying the language to model software variants of financial Web APIs throughout this thesis and by applying it to the two use cases addressing the scenarios outlined in sections 1.1.3 and 1.1.1.

1.4.3. Methods

We present a set of methods to create SFMs and use them to select service variants. A first method concerns the modeling of SFMs - that is, the process of defining service variants. To ensure that the combination of different concerns modeled in an SFM remains useful, their abstractions must be meaningful and compatible. To this end, we exemplarily integrate service feature modeling into larger service engineering methodologies in two use cases. We define mappings between service features and artifacts from other methodologies. Examples are work flow elements and cloud service configuration options. Where possible, based on the mappings, automatic creation of model parts or reuse of existing parts is used to decrease modeling efforts.

Another method addresses challenge 3 about supporting collaboration of stakeholders, i.e., experts, in modeling. Methods to realize collaboration include composition of SFMs from services and corresponding coordination for composition to be efficient and conflict-free. Our approach renders SFMs to act as central, structure-providing artifacts that compose diverse concerns, which can be provided by human or software services. Through composition, service feature modeling further allows modelers to integrate dynamic or complex attributes on-demand, as motivated by challenge 2.

Another set of methods concerns the usage of SFMs for selecting service variants. We provide a selection process as motivated by challenge 4 that flexibly combines methods allowing service providers and consumers to determine service variants that match requirements and preferences. *Configuration set determination*, which extends existing approaches with attribute aggregation, produces all service variants represented by a given SFM. A novel *requirements filtering* approach is used to exclude variants from further consideration that do not meet minimal needs. *Preference-based ranking* applies a well-known multi-criteria decision making approach [Saa90] to rank remaining variants based on stakeholders' individual preferences regarding modeled attributes. Before preference-based ranking, *skyline filtering*, adapted from database systems [BKS01], can be used to dismiss variants that are dominated by others. SFMs represent concerns of, among other stakeholders, a service's consumers and can thus support participation in development activities: service feature modeling's usage methods allow consumers to participate in development by selecting service variants to further design, implement, and deploy, thus addressing challenge 6.

The usage methods aim to be useful, which we evaluate in this thesis from the users' perspective. Usefulness depends on whether users perceive the selection of variants modeled in an SFMs to be relevant and its outcomes beneficial. Usefulness needs to be assessed in light of utilizing service feature modeling in addition to other service engineering approaches and as opposed to other selection methods.

1.4.4. Tools

The final contribution provided by this thesis are tools implementing service feature modeling's modeling language and methods. These tools are available as open source[9]. The primary intention behind the tools is to act as a proof-of-concept for the realizability of service feature modeling. In addition, the tools allow for assessment of the application of service feature modeling to real world use cases.

The *SFM designer* is an Eclipse-based editor that allows modelers to model SFMs. The SFM designer furthermore provides capabilities to select service variants specified in an SFM using the methods for requirements and skyline

[9] `https://github.com/ErikWittern/sfm-toolsuite`

filtering and preference-based ranking. To enable collaborative service feature modeling, the SFM designer interacts with the *collaboration server*. This sever stores models that multiple stakeholders work on, composes these models on demand, and coordinates stakeholders' activities to edit them. A *valuation server* exposes the preference-based ranking method to select variants of an SFM. It transfers given SFMs to evaluations which are made accessible to diverse stakeholders on a *interaction platform*. The interaction platform provides a graphical interface where stakeholders state their preferences regarding service variants using the evaluations. In combination with the valuation server, a stakeholder's preferred service variant can thus be determined.

The tools are combinable to form concrete systems, which can be utilized in specific application scenarios. For that purpose, the tools denote service interfaces to enable their flexible composition. The result is a modular architecture where parts can be used independently. Additionally, the architecture can be extended to fulfill so-far unforeseen needs.

1.5. Structure of this Dissertation

Chapter 2 introduces terms and concepts relevant throughout this thesis, including a service concept and life-cycle model, and concepts related to variants and variability. The chapter also provides an overview of the service feature modeling methodology. The first chapter thus acts as a basis for the remainder of this dissertation.

Chapter 3 describes this work's contributions with regard to modeling software service variants. It introduces feature modeling, upon which our approach builds, and the extensions denoting the service feature modeling language. Its modeling elements refer back to the variability concepts introduced in chapter 2. The modeling chapter further discusses the process for creating service feature models, both for individuals as well as through composing SFMs from services. At the end, the chapter presents related work on modeling software service variants before concluding with a discussion.

Chapter 4 presents methods to use SFMs to select software service variants. Initially, an overview of the usage process, combining the multiple usage methods introduced by this work, is presented. The methods are discussed individually in the following sections, including the configuration set determination, the requirements filter, the preference-based ranking and skyline filter. As in the previous chapter, at the end, related work on selecting software service variants is presented, followed by a discussion.

Chapter 5 presents the evaluation of service feature modeling, consisting of multiple parts. Initially, the proof-of-concept implementation is described, which shows the realizability of all methods presented in this dissertation and acts as a basis for further evaluations. Based on the proof-of-concept implementation, a performance evaluation presents the applicability of the usage methods to differently sized SFMs. Two use cases are presented, showing how service feature modeling was applied to realistic scenarios. Finally, an empirical evaluation based on one of the use cases is presented.

Chapter 6 completes this thesis by summing up and discussing the previous chapters. The chapter further provides an outlook to future work extending service feature modeling.

The reader should start with the fundamentals chapter 2, which provides a basis for understanding the subsequent chapters. Chapter 3 about modeling and chapter 4 about using SFMs can theoretically be read independently from another or in reverse order. Some usage methods presented in chapter 4, though, are enabled only by modeling elements presented as part of the service feature modeling language in chapter 3. For the convenience of readers who skipped chapter 3, corresponding cross-references are provided. The evaluation in chapter 5 and the conclusion in chapter 6 build upon the previous chapters and should thus only be read subsequently.

2. Concepts and Methodology

In this chapter, we present the concepts fundamental to this thesis and the methodology underlying service feature modeling. This thesis' service concept differentiates between generic services and software services as discussed in section 2.1. An important part of service feature modeling's methodology is the service life-cycle model, building upon the priorly defined service concept, presented in section 2.2. It enables to define when, how, and by whom service feature modeling is utilized. The model is applied to describe the development and delivery of software services with variants and used throughout this thesis to describe and classify presented methods in a coherent way. In section 2.3, we present concepts and a discussion of service variants. In section 2.4, we outline the general purpose of modeling approaches in software and service engineering and present the generic modeling process. Building upon this generic version, we introduce service feature modeling's methodology in section 2.5.

2.1. Service Concept

Within this section we define in detail our understanding of *service* and related concepts, which builds upon our previous work [WF13]. This section thus provides the fundamental understanding and vocabulary used throughout this thesis. The term service has gained a lot of attention in the last years. Because of its generality and broad adoption, the understanding of the term depends on the point of view and context. To depict which services are targeted by service feature modeling, we discuss relevant service characteristics in this section.

2.1.1. Generic Services

Various generic service definitions have been proposed. For example, the World Wide Web consortium (W3C) defines a service, generically, as "[...] an abstract resource that represents a capability of performing tasks that form a coherent functionality from the point of view of providers entities and requesters entities. To be used, a service must be realized by a concrete provider agent." [W3C04]. Or, from a business perspective, services denote "[...] activities provided by a service provider to a service consumer to create value for a service consumer" [CVW09, page 17]. The field of *service science*, which sets out to reconsider nowadays economic activities under the umbrella of services, defines a service as "[...] the application of competences for the benefit of another, meaning that service is a kind of action, performance, or promise that's exchanged for value between provider and client." [SMBG07, page 72]. In their generic nature, these definitions aim to incorporate the diverse views upon services. The range of disciplines involved in generic services is very broad, including for example computer science, operations research, economics and law, industrial engineering, or even urban planning [Spo08]. The attempt to accommodate all these fields rises the risk of service definitions to become meaningless. They do neither clearly delimit what services are, nor do they capture all characteristics of the diverse types of existing services. In consequence, we will not attempt to provide a concise service definition. Rather, in this section we will present those characteristics common to different kinds of services that influenced the creation of service feature modeling.

The range of definitions from different disciplines illustrates the *multidisciplinary* nature of service engineering for generic services. We perceive *service engineering* to be the systematic application of methods and tools for the development and delivery of a service. The diversity of involved stakeholders creates the need for methods and tools that foster these stakeholders' collaboration in service engineering.

The above definitions emphasize a universal characteristic of a service, namely the involved *roles*. Services involve the *service provider* and the *service consumer*. Generically, the service provider performs activities for the sake of the service consumer. In return, the service consumer compensates the service provider, for example in form of payments. Some authors identify additional roles, like *service creator* in cloud computing [IBM11] or the *service broker* in Web services [BD06]. However, because these roles might only be sensible in certain service contexts, we concentrate on the two fundamental roles of provider (who is also assumed to have developed the service) and consumer.

Considering services as *activities* reveals their procedural nature. Services take an input, often provided by the consumer in the form of information or physical goods and transform it. Correspondingly, procedural methods and tools, for example work flow models based on the *Business Process Model and Notation (BMPN)* [BPM10], can be used in designing and operating services.

Services enable consumption *on-demand*. Service consumers can invoke a service (only) when they actually need them. This service characteristic induces flexibility. If the need for a service does not occur, no consumption occurs, and correspondingly no efforts and cost arise.

Services also denote a *pay per use model*. The amount that the consumer has to reimburse to the provider depends on the number and type of service invocations. This characteristic creates potential for cost savings. The consumer can adapt his consumption in reaction to changing requirements. If the demand for an activity is high, consumption can be increased (given sufficient services are provided). If the demand for an activity is low, consumption can be decreased, avoiding under-utilization of related resources. The advantage of this characteristic becomes especially clear when a service is used in compensation of otherwise required self-fulfillment. For example, in cloud computing, consumers use resources as they need them instead of having to acquire them upfront (i.e., in form of physical hardware) and risking to over- or under-utilize them. Here, the pay-per-use model creates cost savings 1) by avoiding initial acquisition cost (please note: the service consumption, however, likely induces set-up costs) and 2) by avoiding opportunity costs in case of under-utilization and loss in case of over-utilization, which leads eventually to the breakdown of operation.

2.1.2. Software Services

Having presented fundamental characteristics of generic services in section 2.1.1, we here focus on *software services*. Software services denote an increasing importance in nowadays service delivery (cf. chapter 1). The development and delivery of software services involves the utilization of software engineering techniques, from which service feature modeling stems. Software services are thus an ideal context for the utilization of service feature modeling. We define software services in the following way:

Definition 1. *A software service is a deployed capability that is realized by software and consumed / provided on-demand over networks.*

This conceptual view of software services is illustrated in figure 2.1. *Software* depicts the implementation of a capability to be provided as a service. This software artifact contains the implementation or specification of interfaces. The interfaces are, however, not accessible before the software is deployed as a service. The provided capability may be an application, a platform or even infrastructure. Required is only that these capabilities are realized by software. Our definition does thus not correspond to definitions that consider software services to be equal to the concept of Software as a Service (SaaS) solely. To our understanding, SaaS covers only software on the application level, which is provided to end-users [LKN+09].

Through *deployment*, the capability is made accessible to consumers, transforming software into a software service. Technically, through deployment the software is packed (for example, within a Java ARchive (JAR) or an image) and

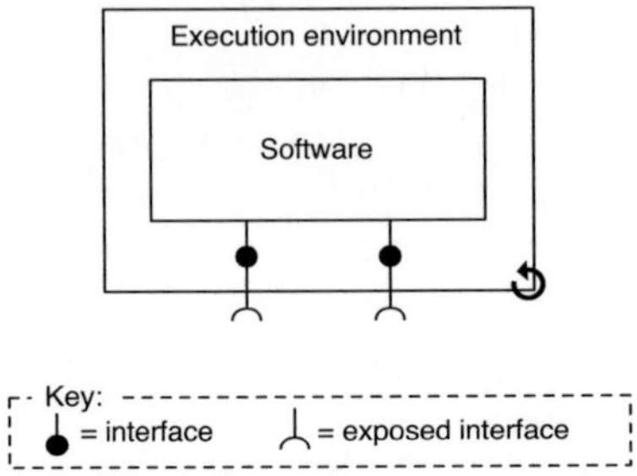

Figure 2.1.: Software service concept, based on [WF13]

loaded into an execution environment. An execution environment is software that enables the execution of, in this case, services [UML11]. Exemplary execution environments are an operating system, a Web server, or a virtual machine. The interfaces defined as part of the software are exposed and thus made accessible to consumers by the execution environment. Furthermore, deployment can be recursive, as indicated in figure 2.1 by the round arrow. For example, a Web service can be packed as a JAR and deployed to a Web server, for example a Tomcat server. The Web server, again, can then be packed in an image and deployed to a virtual machine. The necessity of software services to be deployed is important to differentiate them from classical software *products*. The latter are typically sold using a license-model, whereas deployment by the provider implies service characteristics like consumption on-demand and pay-per-use billing (cf. section 2.1.1). The provision over networks is a logical consequence of software services being deployed by the provider.

Given our definition, software services denote a set of characteristics that do not necessarily hold for generic services. Due to the provisioning over networks in combination with the ubiquitous Web, software services can (theoretically) be accessed globally. Constraints to this capability are legal frameworks or technical limitations (for example, regarding high latencies for distantly deployed services). In contrast to traditional software products, software service updates can much easier be rolled out because the service provider (who we assume to be also the service developer) controls the deployment and can thus simultaneously update the service for all consumers.

Various types of software services exist that we want to introduce in the following. These types are neither mutually exclusive nor do they collectively exhaustive cover software services. Rather, they address different service aspects, for example, their deployment environment or their interfaces. Thus, the following definitions cannot be used for clear classification of software services, but exemplify the changing paradigms and concerns in services computing.

The field of service-oriented computing deals with *Web services*. Web services denote software that provides interoperable machine-to-machine interaction over a network [W3C04]. We denote Web services to be a more specific type of software services in that the network they are provided over is the Internet. *Atomar* Web services provide a single functionality, whereas *composite* services make use of Web service's interoperability by composing them. Web service compositions are commonly captured in business process notations, such as the *Business Process Execution Language (BPEL)* [BPE07] or the *Business Process Model and Notation (BPMN)* [BPM10]. Composite Web services can, again, be offered as a service, making composition a recursive operation [CKM+03]. While its definition is rather broad (it includes, for example, cloud services as described below), the term Web services is nowadays closely related with the usage of technologies from the Web services stack [Wee08]. For example, we term software services as Web services if they are made available using SOAP / WSDL.

Another type of of software services are *cloud services*. Cloud computing is about on-demand provisioning of scalable, abstracted IT infrastructures, platforms and applications with a pay-per-use model [BKNT11]. Within Cloud computing, different service classes can be distinguished [LKN+09]: *Infrastructure as a Service (IaaS)* provides virtualized hardware to consumers (cf. section 1.1.3). Typical examples of IaaS include compute or storage services. Infrastructure as a Service can thus be used to deploy other services on, for example Web services as described above. *Platform as a Service (PaaS)* provides integrated development environments on top of virtualized hardware. For example, Google's App Engine runs various runtime environments and libraries on top of their infrastructure whose APIs developers can use for building applications [Goo]. *Software as a Service* provides applications to end users (instead of to developers). Other, less commonly used, classes of Cloud services include, for example, *Human as a Service (HuaaS)* [LKN+09], or *Database as a Service (DBaaS)* [PC12].

2.2. Software Service Life-Cycle Model

Service life-cycle models typically define phases that a service goes through from its earliest conceptualization to its shutdown. The goal of such models is to provide an overview and order of the relevant activities for developing and delivering a service. Within this thesis, a software service life-cycle model is used to discuss when service feature modeling can be applied, by whom, and for what purpose. The life-cycle focuses on engineering activities only. Other activities, concerning for example customer relationship management, marketing, or sales, are left out of the model to keep it focused. The presented life-cycle model builds upon and extends the one presented in our previous work [WF13].

2.2.1. Software Life-Cycle Models

Software life-cycle models (also known as *software process models*) have been guiding the practice in the software engineering domain for decades. Software life-cycle models define related activities that lead to the production of a software product [Som11]. These models typically split a life-cycle into phases like *specification, design and implementation, validation*, and *evolution*. Sequential, non-iterative descriptions of software development processes, often referred to as *waterfall models*, were first formally described in the 1970ies [Roy70]. Rather than recommending how software development processes should look like, sequential approaches presented observed (mal-) practice. On the other hand, recommending approaches commonly depict iterative structures. They foresee that life-cycle phases are repeatedly entered to refine software or continuously improve and adapt it. For example, the correspondingly named *spiral model* [Boe88] is cyclic in nature. The *rational unified process (RUP)* includes three perspectives on software development [Kru04]. The dynamic perspective defines four distinct phases. Each phase as well as the overall process can be iterated. The static perspective defines the activities performed during the development process, denoted in RUP as *work flows*. By separating phases from work flows, it is compliant with the RUP to perform work flows during any phase, making the model very flexible and capturing the realities of modern development methods, for example agile development [DD09]. Finally, the RUP's practice perspective describes six recommended software engineering practices.

While software life-cycle models indicate phases relevant also for services (especially software services), they do not embrace service characteristics (cf. section 2.1) sufficiently to be seamlessly reused in that context. Software life-cycle models are used by developers and focus on the development of software products. In services, the consumer's activities should also be considered. Moreover, in services the provider does not only have to develop, but also to deploy and operate the service. Life-cycle models suited for services need to consider these activities.

2.2.2. Service Life-Cycle Models

While the presented software life-cycle models focus on engineering tasks, service life-cycle models are more diverse in nature as they address different types of services and have a different scope. Life-cycle models in the context of *IT governance* of *service-oriented architectures (SOA)* include the introduction and enforcement of company-wide policies for adopting and operating SOA [JNS11]. Thus, they denote a holistic view upon services and related activities. For example, the *SOA service life-cycle management approach* presented by IBM includes people, processes, and technology [McB]. In the context of *IT service management*, the service life-cycle defined in the *Information Technology Infrastructure Library (ITIL)* encompasses the phases service design, transition, and operation as well as a variety of related processes [ITI07]. Other models focus more clearly on software service engineering. For example, the *Web service development life cycle* denotes a methodology to foster analysis, change, and evolution of Web services [PVDH06]. It's phases includes planning, analysis and design, construction and testing, provisioning, deployment, and execution and monitoring. Or, the integrated life-cycle for IT services in a cloud environment covers the five phases requirements, discovery, negotiation, orchestration, and consumption and monitoring [JFY09]. These phases are performed iteratively and imply sub-phases with activities for both providers and consumers.

Evaluating the presented approaches, we notice some drawbacks:

Mixing of different concerns: The plethora of models from IT governance and management (e.g., [ITI07, McB, OBB$^+$09]) provide a very holistic view that encompasses also organizational aspects. In contrast, we aim to provide a model that focuses on engineering-related aspects of providing and consuming services.

Rigid order of activities: Service life-cycle models are based on ordered phases, which imply corresponding activities to be performed in this order as well (e.g. [JFY09]). In the case of sequential phases, corresponding activities can also only be performed sequentially. This neglects the concurrent and dynamic order of activities in real life service engineering. For example, design and implementation activities are inseparable in agile development and evolve iteratively [DD09], which we aim to be able to express with our life-cycle model.

Coupling activities with service status: Life-cycle phases imply a (single) status in which a subject, in this case the service, is in at any given time. Correspondingly, in service life-cycle model that couple status to activities (e.g., [McB]), only activities related to this status can be performed. This capability has advantages when it comes to prescribing activities. On the other hand, this coupling delimits flexibility to describe that many activities can be performed independent of the service's status. For example, while a service's status is deployed, providers and consumers may perform design activities to evolve the service or, respectively, plan its consumption.

We aim to describe the usage of service feature modeling with our life-cycle model and thus avoid coupling of activities with the service status.

Implied longevity of service phases: The term "phase" used in many life-cycle models (e.g., [Som11, Boe88, ITI07]) implies that a service remains in a corresponding status for long time. However, what is described as a phase in service life-cycle models may in reality only be short-lived. For example, deploying a software service on Cloud infrastructure in many cases only takes a few seconds (i.e., it is a matter of a single command).

To avoid these pitfalls and provide a precise wording, we define our own service life-cycle model in the following.

2.2.3. Our Software Service Life-Cycle

The software service life-cycle used in this thesis is influenced by approaches from software engineering, especially the rational unified process, and (Web) service engineering. It assumes an engineering-centric view on software services, leaving out aspects concerning, for example, organizational operation, strategy, marketing, or controlling. In our model we differentiate 1) two *status*, 2) five *activities* performed by providers and consumers, and 3) the two *roles* involved in services. Corresponding with the characteristic roles in services (cf. section 2.1.1), we differentiate *providers* and *consumers*. In the following, we offer a more detailed description of the status and activities in consideration of the two roles.

Status

The two status a service can be in are *offline* and *deployed*. While a service is offline, it is not yet deployed and can therefore not be consumed. For example, a service might still be in development before being initially deployed. Both status can be further divided into sub-status. For example, while offline, a service may be in development or testing, it can be deployed for testing or production, it can be temporarily unavailable due to maintenance, or even discontinued. However, because a further differentiation does not add to the fundamental propositions of our life-cycle model, we only focus on the two presented status. The two status are mutually exclusive, i.e. a service may only be in one of them at a given time. The consideration of a service's status is relevant in software service engineering because it has impact on how activities are performed. For example, changing a deployed service requires deployment activities to be performed to ensure continuous service availability. A service's status is global in that it affects both provider and consumer activities.

Activities

We further differentiate five types of activities, namely *specification*, *design*, *implementation*, *deployment*, and *operation*. Figure 2.2 illustrates how the dimensions status and activities relate to the software service concept introduced in section 2.1.2. The gray arrows indicate activities on the service. While the ser-

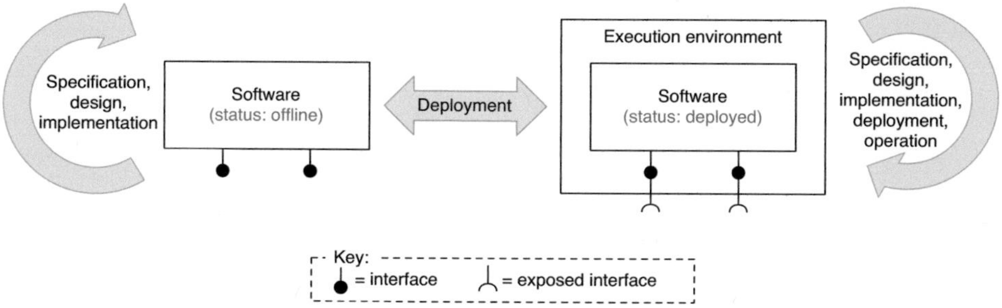

Figure 2.2.: Relation of status and activities to the software service concept, based on [WF13]

vice is offline, specification, design, implementation activities can be performed. Deployment activities lead to a transition to the deployed status. While the service is in deployed status, any activities can be performed. Thus, except from operation activities, which are not possible while the service is offline, any activity can be performed at either service status. Performing undeployment transfers the software service back into the offline status. We perceive *undeployment* to be one of the deployment activities (compare figure 2.3), which explains the double arrow.

It is important to note that activities are generally not determined by the service's status. This characteristic of our model allows it, for example, to depict that a consumer performs design time activities while a service is deployed, which is only unintuitively possible in existing life-cycle models. Furthermore, while there is a typical sequence of the type of activities, their timely occurrence can be switched or can overlap. For example, considering agile software development methods, design and implementation activities can be concurrent. When activities occur and whether they overlap depends on the methods used in them and on the type of service. For example, when applying participatory design methods, providers and consumers perform design activities. It has to be noted that not all activities must be pursued when developing or delivering a service. Their individual utilization depends on the type of service and on the context.

An overview of the types of activities and their typical sequence is provided in figure 2.3. In the following, we will describe the activities in detail.

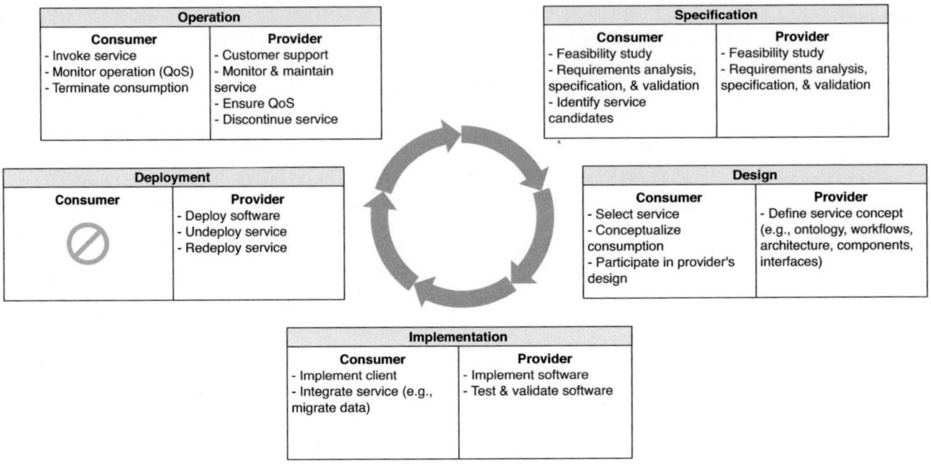

Figure 2.3.: Overview of providers' and consumers' activities throughout service life-cycle and their typical sequence [WF13]

Similar to software engineering [Som11, page 36], **specification activities** for services aim to define requirements and constraints on the service provision or consumption. Both, providers and consumers check the technical and business-related feasibility of offering / consuming the service and perform requirements analysis, specification, and validation. In these activities, providers will focus on the realizability of a service, while consumers will, for example, analyze whether to consume a service vs. in-house realization. Consumers also perform a service candidate identification in cohesion with the feasibility and requirements activities. The service candidate identification allows them to assess the general applicability of service consumption to fulfill the required functionalities.

Using **design activities**, service providers conceptualize the service and how it will be provided. For software services, design activities match largely those performed in software design. They include the description of the service's architecture, components, data models, interfaces, or algorithms [Som11, page 38]. In contrast to software design, software service design further includes design of service interfaces, deployment, and operation methods and tools (for example, how to monitor or maintain the service). Consumers' design activities aim to plan and conceptualize service consumption. Based on requirements, preferences, and/or optimizable goals (for example, cost) and the identified service candidates, service selection is performed. The consumers' design activities also include the conceptualization of how the service will be used. Required changes to existing systems that will interact with the service need to be determined. New interfaces or even systems to work with the service are conceptualized. A special case is participatory service design, where consumers participate in the design activities usually fulfilled solely by providers. In an exemplary use case from the public services domain, opinions of citizens (i.e., public service consumers) expressed in Web 2.0 media and their explicit statements regarding the service design are considered [KKP+12].

Implementation activities of the service providers aim to realize the service based on the priorly defined design. In the case of software services, implementation includes the development of the software artifact, its testing and validation. Depending on the utilized implementation methodology, the activities' order may differ. For example, test-driven development starts with defining tests before actually implementing. From the consumers' point of view, the envisioned service consumption must be realized. Contracting must be performed with the provider, specifying for example the service's price or service level agreements (SLAs). In the case of software services, the consumers' implementation activities also include the creation of client components. Integration efforts may be required to utilize a new service with existing services or systems. When utilizing services to host systems or data, for example cloud infrastructure services, their migration is required [MR12].

Deployment activities aim to transfer the service implementation to a deployed status. Exemplary deployment activities include the packaging of software artifacts and loading them to execution environments. We differentiate deployment activities from implementation activities because they do not necessarily co-occur. For example, recurring deployment of once implemented cloud services is a common approach to realize horizontal scalability [BKNT11, page 2]. Prevalent deployment approaches are manual, script-based, language-based, or model-based ones [TMW+05]. The deployment of services is performed by service providers alone. For this statement to hold, the service that the life-cycle model describes and the role of stakeholders regarding that service are fundamental. For example, if the life-cycle model is applied to an IaaS offer, deployment activities concern the provider's setting up of the IaaS, including the installation and configuration of hardware and hypervisors for virtual machines to run on. When an IaaS consumer rents a virtual machine from the IaaS and loads an image on top of it, this is an operation activity (=invoke service) regarding the IaaS itself. The IaaS might be used by the consumer to host another service - when applying the life-cycle service to this other service, the renting of a VM and loading an image on top of it may be deployment activities. In this case, however, the IaaS consumer acts as the provider of the other service. In consequence, in our model, deployment activities are only performed by providers.

Operation activities of providers aim to ensure ongoing service provision considering targeted quality of service (QoS) properties. Providers maintain the service, reacting for example to errors, changing numbers of requests and resulting performance impacts, or adaptation needs. A typical approach to detect the need for such interventions is *monitoring*. For example, based on the monitored development of demand, scaling might be required to cope with rising numbers of requests or, reversely, to remove sparse resources when the number of requests declines. Additionally, customer support needs to be provided. When the provider decides to discontinue the service provision, corresponding activities, for example data retrieval or consumer notification, may be required. Consumers' operation activities include, foremost, the actual invocation of the service. Consumers may additionally perform activities to ensure smooth consumption, for example by monitoring the service. When terminating consumption, consumers may have to retrieve their data or actively dissolute running contracts.

Example

Figure 2.4 shows the service's status and activities performed by a provider and consumer in dependence of time for an exemplary service.

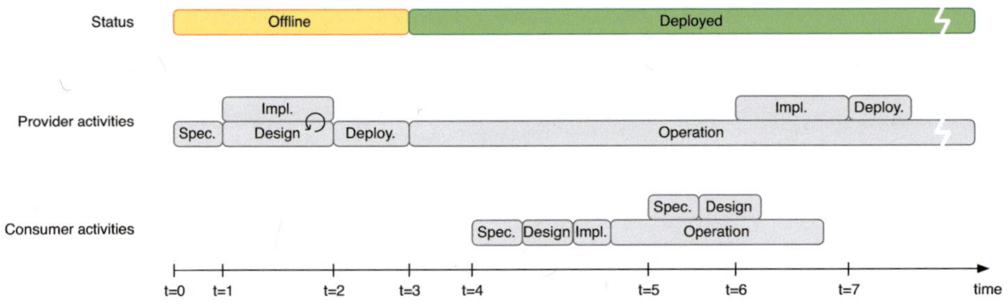

Figure 2.4.: Example of our service life-cycle model

At t=0, the service provider starts with specification activities. Subsequently, at t=1, embracing agile development techniques, the provider simultaneously performs design and implementation activities. Using the implementation, in t=2 deployment activities are initiated which result in t=3 in an operating service, thus the service status changes to deployed. The provider, from now on, performs operation activities. At t=4, the consumer initializes his consumption process with specification activities, followed by design and implementation activities and eventually the service operation activities. At t=5, the consumer again performs specification and design activities, leading for example to an adaptation of the service consumption. At t=6, the provider also begins new design and implementation activities, resulting finally in a (re-) deployment of the service in t=7. In this example, the service never leaves the deployed status, while diverse activities are repeatedly performed, some of them concurrently and not necessarily in a predetermined order.

Derived Service Concept Definitions

Based on our service life-cycle model, we define further terms associated with services. First, we define *service development* in the following way:

Definition 2. *Service development encompasses a service provider's specification, design, and implementation activities.*

Next, we define *service provision* in the following way:

Definition 3. *Service provision encompasses a service provider's 1) deployment and operation activities of a service in general, and 2) operation activities in reaction to a service request.*

Service provision thus depends on a priorly created service as the subject for deployment and operation. This definition allows us to explicit reveal the differentiation between software services and software components: the latter are provisioned by their user (i.e., the consumer).

Similar to provision, we define *service consumption* in the following way:

Definition 4. *Service consumption encompasses a service consumer's 1) activities of all kind throughout the service life-cycle, and 2) operation activities concerned with a service request.*

Finally, we define *service delivery* in the following way:

Definition 5. *Service delivery encompasses a service provider's and consumer's operation activities concerned with a service request.*

This notion corresponds to the idea that value in service delivery depends on co-creation, thus including providers and consumers [VMA08]. Note that the provider's part in service delivery can also be denoted as service provision and the consumer's part in service delivery can be denoted as service consumption based on definitions 3 and 4.

2.3. Service Variants and Variability

In this section we aim to define our understanding of *service variant* and *service variability*. Again, the terms introduced here will provide the foundation for subsequent chapters. Furthermore, this section will allow us to classify this work within and delimit it from related work.

We define service variability in the following way, based on the definitions given in [BC05, MHGA13] and making use of our definitions of service development and delivery in section 2.2.3:

Definition 6. *Service variability is the ability of a service for a specific context to be developed or delivered in one of multiple preplanned ways.*

We consider service variability to affect both service status, namely offline and deployed. In contrast to our definition, the definitions found in [BC05, MHGA13] focus solely on the adaptation of services. They neglect service variability that is dealt with in development activities while the service is offline.

Having defined the concept of service variability, we denote the subject it is applied to, a *variable service*, in the following way:

Definition 7. *A variable service is a service that denotes service variability.*

Thus, a variable service can, for a specific context, be consumed or provided in one of multiple preplanned ways or it can be adapted in a pre-planned manner.

Finally, we define *service variant* within this thesis in the following way:

Definition 8. *Service variants are alternative instances of a variable service's design, implementation, deployment, or operation.*

Variants should not be confused with *versions* (also referred to as *revisions* [CSFP04]). Variants exist in parallel, while versions are ordered variants over time [ABKS13]. Thus, versions refer to different states in the evolution of software, so that version management is sometimes subsumed as part of change management [Som11]. Following our definition, service variants may result from different development activities and can thus also be referred to as versions, which is also proposed in related work [CW98]. In contrast, however, a service that exists in multiple versions does not denote variants if these versions are not made accessible in parallel. In version management, the concept of branches exist, which are copies of the same artifact that are maintained separately from another [CSFP04]. In the case that branches exist in parallel, it is feasible to denote them as variants [ABKS13]. Consequently, version control for software that denotes variability and the related field of software configuration management (SCM) is a topic of research, addressing questions like if it is necessary to introduce new versions of every variant if their common variation point changes [BLP04]. Research on the relationship between versions and variants and their evolution, however, is out of scope of this thesis. Summarizing, versions may be denoted as variants and variants may be denoted as versions - the important question to ask is whether they are created to exist in parallel or not.

Another important differentiation concerns variability and *agile development* methods. Agile development methods were developed in response to traditional engineering methods, which incorporate extensive planning, especially with regards to defining requirements before implementing software. Such traditional approaches are infeasible in many scenarios because requirements only become clear while using software and underly constant change [Som11, page 57]. In consequence, agile methods aim for an adaptive, flexible, and responsive development approach [DD09]. They apply an iterative development process, in which requirements engineering and the design and implementation of software are concurrent [Som11, page 63]. As a result, agile methods like extreme programming allow developers to rapidly adapt software to changing requirements, leading to the frequent release of new versions. The differentiation between agile development methods and variability is relevant, because they both address the reaction to changes in context (cf. section 1.2). However, agile methods address this but fostering a fast iteration of versions, while variability is about the co-existence of variants. Thus, agile development methods do not address scenarios where multiple consumer groups co-exist with different needs. Overall, agile methods and variability are not opposites of another but orthogonal to another - agile methods may well be used when developing variable software services. The exploration of such synergies, however, lies outside of the scope of this thesis.

Variability of software services is a widely researched problem, also with regard to our focus on intentionally implemented variability. The understanding of variability and how it is addressed, however, differs. While the given definition of service variability contributes to our understanding of the term, it is not suitable to sufficiently classify service feature modeling or delimit it from other service variability approaches. To obtain a clear understanding of the nature of service variability and corresponding approaches, we address their individual characteristics in the following subsections.

2.3.1. Origins of Service Variability

A fundamental differentiator of different types of service variability is the question *why* it appears. In its general meaning, variability can occur *on purpose* or *by chance.* These two kinds of service variability and the approaches addressing them differ significantly.

Variability by chance is often considered an undesirable characteristic of a service. For example, variability by chance denotes that the response time of a Web service varies over time. Approaches addressing variability by chance aim to measure or eliminate it to ensure a uniform service experience or to be compliant with service level agreements. For example, existing related work in this area aims to measure the volatility of cloud service performance [IYE11]. Virtual machine provisioning policies are designed to reduce the variability of cloud service performance [BSCB13]. Or, various approaches are researched that aim to diminish the variability of large-scale Web services' latency [DB13].

On the contrary, variability on purpose may be a desirable service characteristic, as we already discussed in section 1.2. Summarizing, in development, it allows for decision-making on alternative designs, fosters reuse of artifacts, and can drive collaboration and participation. In delivery, it enables consumption of requirements- and preferences-matching variants and to react to changes in context. Many approaches aim to implement variability on purpose in a service. For example, cloud services may offer customization to their consumers [MMLP09] or Web services are provided in variants [NCH14].

In this thesis, we associate the term service variability with variability on purpose. The occurrence of uncontrollable service variants, for example due to changing response times, availability, or generally volatile QoS properties, is excluded from our understanding of service variability.

2.3.2. Variability Subject

Variability can concern different *variability subjects* or parts of subjects. A variability subject is "[...] a variable item of the real world or a variable property of such an item" [PuFvdL05, page 60]. For each variability subject, multiple *variability objects* exist. A variability object is "[...] a particular instance of a variability subject" [PuFvdL05, page 60].

Variability that denotes a single service or property of a single service can be denoted as *intra-service variability.* In composite services, which compose multiple (atomic) services (cf. section 2.1.2), the variability subject may also be the composition itself. In this case, the variability object can be a specific work flow instance. Such variability, affecting the interactions of multiple services, can be denoted as *inter-service variability.* Inter-service variability also encompasses the selection of a service among multiple candidates from the consumer point of view.

Based on the here made definitions, we outline in detail the variability subject represented by service feature models in section 3.2.1.

2.3.3. Affected Service Roles

As outlined in section 2.1.1, services include the roles of provider and consumer. Service providers have to define and implement service variability and manage it. On the other hand, consumers resolve service variability by choosing which service variant should be implemented or which variant to consume. Consumers define the context in which a service is utilized. This context influences which service variant is consumed, affecting, for example, requirements for the quality of service properties like security mechanisms or availability rates.

A more detailed breakdown of the providers' and consumers' activities with regard to service variability results from the distinction of the different times when it occurs.

2.3.4. Time of Occurrence

Software services undergo a life-cycle and induce diverse activities as presented in section 2.2. Depending on the service status and the activities pursued, service variability creates new challenges and corresponding activities, extending the ones stated in section 2.2. Figure 2.5 illustrates typical service variability-related activities for providers and consumers mapped to our life-cycle model.

During specification activities, providers identify the need for service variability, for example during the requirements analysis. Reasons may include diverse consumer groups or the need to provide multiple access channels. Simultaneously, the consumer may consider offered service variability in the service candidate identification.

During design activities, service providers conceptualize which service variants to provide. They define a set of variants and iteratively expand it or narrow it down. When using participatory design methods, consumers can be involved in these activities [HJR+10]. Consumers, during their design activities, resolve service variability by determining which variant to consume. This process requires matchmaking of requirements and preferences with the service variants' capabilities.

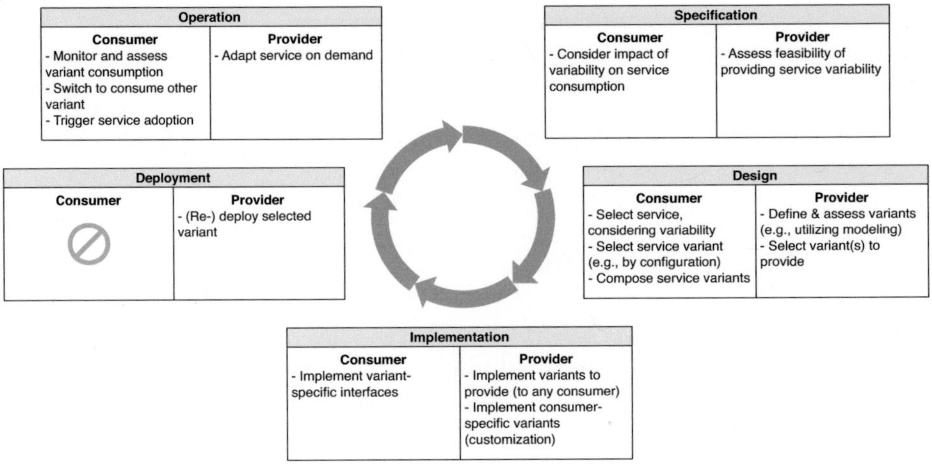

Figure 2.5.: Service variability-related provider and consumer activities throughout the service life-cycle [WF13]

Service providers develop service variants during the implementation activities. Either, the designed service variants are implemented as individual services, or mechanisms are implemented allowing to transition between variants based on deployment or operation activities (cf. section 2.3.5). Simultaneously, consumers perform implementation activities to consume individual variants or trigger the transition between variants. For example, consumers implement an interface to consume a specific service variant or a monitoring device that dynamically triggers the consumption of a variant through re-deployment.

The deployment activities regarding service variability are performed by providers and aim to deploy a (set of) service variant(s). The variant(s) to deploy can either result from prior implementation activities or can be determined by consumers. Deployment activities regarding service variability can also include the re-deployment of services or variants, again, potentially on consumer request.

Operation activities regarding service variability concern both providers and consumers. For providers, they include the transition between service variants utilizing priorly implemented mechanisms. Also, the providers' generic operation activities are affected by service variability: support, monitoring, and maintenance must address the provided variant(s). For consumers, operation activities include the monitoring of the consumption. Eventually, consumers initiate the consumption of a different variant or trigger adaptation if possible.

Summarizing, variants induce various new activities to be performed - for example, providers need to implement, deploy and operate variants and consumers need to select among them or switch them during operation. Other activities (cf. figure 2.3) need adaptation or extension when considering variants. For example, the providers' assessment of feasibility of providing a service needs to consider multiple variants instead of a single service. Variants overall introduce new or adapt existing activities, thus emphasizing the need for methods and tools to efficiently support these activities.

2.3.5. Realization of Variability

A plethora of approaches exists to realize service variability, sometimes referred to as *variability mechanisms* [SD07]. In this section, we cannot conclusively present all realization approaches. Rather, we aim to present an overview of and discuss typical approaches. Consolidated characteristics of these approaches are presented in table 2.1.

Multiple approaches *model* service variability. Modeling service variability is a design activity. Service variability models aim to define and communicate service variability. They are used by providers as a basis for implementation or deployment activities or by consumers to select variants in specification, design, or operation activities. Thus, modeling is integral part of multiple other service variability realization approaches and is consequently considered here. Exemplary approaches capture variability in work flow models. For example, the "Provop" approach allows users to specify options on a basic process model [HBR10]. These options allow modelers to alter the work flow model to derive a process variant by deletion, insertion, moving, or modification operations on process elements. Or, variability modeling approaches from software engineering are commonly used to represent variability. For example, feature models can be used to represent variability of Web services with regard to their composition and their intra-service variability [NCH11]. Feature models are also used to represent the configuration options that cloud services offer [SMML12].

Customization aims to provide a service that matches requirements and preferences of an individual consumer or a subset of consumers. Customization can include all activities defined in our life-cycle model. For example, a service that meets consumer requirements can be designed, implemented, deployed, and operated. Customization involves both service providers and consumers (who accompany the service provisioning, stating for example requirements or assessing implementations). An advantage of customization is a high degree of flexibility because providers and consumers can closely work together to deliver a tailored software service. However, customization also induces the risk for the providers to deal with redundant implementations, which complicates testing and maintenance and easily causes inconsistencies.

Realization approach	Involved life-cycle activities	Involved roles	Goals
Modeling service variants	Design	Provider, consumer	Capture, assess, select, communicate variants, provide input for implementation, deployment, and operation
Customization	Specification, design, implementation, deployment, operation	Provider, consumer	Develop and provide a service variant that meets individual consumer's requirements and preferences
Configuration	Deployment, operation	Provider, consumer	Determine a service variant through the provision of information
Deployment	Deployment	Provider	Provide requested service variant
Adaptation	Operation	Provider	Transition between variants during delivery
Service selection	Design	Consumer	Determine service that best fulfills consumer needs
Composition	Operation	Consumer	Determine how a set of services collectively best fulfills consumer needs

Table 2.1.: Overview of service variability realization approaches

Configuration aims to determine a service variant through "[...] setting pre-defined parameters, or leveraging tools to change application functions within pre-defined scope" [SZG+08]. In contrast to customization, configuration does not require to change the service's implementation [SZG+08]. The actual realization of a configuration by a variant can be based on adaptation or re-deployment mechanisms. Providers perform configuration in deployment or operation activities to define how their service will be provided, for example by stating deployment parameters. Providers also pass on configuration options to their consumers. Consumers provide configuration information, triggering, for example, the re-deployment of a service. For example, cloud infrastructure services typically allow consumers in a design activity to configure firewall settings or the preferred pricing scheme [Ama] (cf. section 1.1.3). Or, in Software-as-a-Service (SaaS), *multi-tenancy* allows multiple consumers to be served by configured variants of the same service without conflicts or mutual insights in their data [BKNT11, MMLP09]. A configurable service is capable of taking a configuration, i.e. the set of information about pre-determined parameters, as input and providing a corresponding service variant.

Deployment activities realize variability by deploying multiple service variants in parallel. A major disadvantage of this approach is that operation activities, for example maintenance, monitoring, or scaling, must be performed for multiple variants instead of a single service. Alternatively, redeployment can realize service variability. For example, VMs hosted by IaaS can be redeployed in differently located data centers in reaction to monitored performance changes [KZZL11]. Re-deployment is a viable approach to realize variability in reaction to changes in a service's configuration.

Adaptation is an operation activity provided by the service provider to transition between service variants during service delivery. Adaptation mechanisms need to be implemented and deployed to enable transitions. Three common classes of adaptation approaches can be distinguished in software services, namely 1) *dynamic aspect-oriented programming* or *delegation models*, 2) *fractal components*, and 3) *implementation replacement* [IFMW08]. The advantage of utilizing adaptation mechanisms instead of, for example, deploying multiple service variants in parallel is that only a single service must be operated while realizing variability. For example, while a service is in operation, the combination of model-driven engineering and aspect-oriented development allows users to transition between service variants that were defined in design activities [MBJ+09]. Adaptation is often automatically triggered based on contextual change. For self-adaptive systems, for example, control loops are commonly used to collect information about the system and its context and trigger adaptation if needed [DNGM+08].

Consumers perform *service selection* as a design activity performed by consumers to chose a service that best fulfills their needs. To do so, consumers identify service candidates and evaluate them, for example using matchmaking of requirements with the candidates' capabilities. Selecting a service is an inter-service variability approach rather than a distinct consumption, if, from the consumer's point of view, the service candidates are functionally equal. For example, Web services, due to their standardized interface abstractions, can dynamically be selected for every service request to optimize quality of service [ASR10]. Even though this selection is performed while the candidate services are in operation, we consider it a design activity because it is performed (immediately) before service consumption.

Consumers perform *composition* as a design activity to determine how a set of services collectively best fulfills their needs. The result of compositions are *composite services* that fulfill complex functionalities. Variability in composition results from service selection approaches that bind multiple Web services in a composition dynamically based on changing quality of service attributes, for example, response time or availability [ASR10]. Also, variability in compositions results from changing the underlying business processes, using for example composition languages that are extended with variability elements [KaSSA09].

As seen, there are diverse software service variability realization approaches. Many of these approaches involve different activities throughout the service lifecycle. Typically, variability is specified in design activities, corresponding mechanisms are implemented, and the variability is resolved during consumer design or operation activities. This observation underpins the importance of methods and tools to represent service variants and select among them.

2.4. Fundamentals of Modeling

Modeling is at the core of service feature modeling. We thus outline characteristics of modeling and present the generic modeling process. Based on this discussion, we derive service feature modeling's methodology in section 2.5.

2.4.1. Characteristics of Modeling

There is no, and cannot be, a generally approved definition of the term "model" due to their omnipresence throughout human history and their resulting appearance in the most diverse contexts [Lud03]. In this section, we focus on models from the software and service engineering perspective. Even in this specific context various definitions of the term model exist [MFBC10], but an absolute or agreed on definition does not. In the following, we focus on relevant characteristics of models.

An agreed upon characteristic of models is that they *abstract* from reality. They present a less detailed view upon a real world entity (for example, a system), making it thus possible to deal with its complexity [Sel03]. The same real entity can be represented by different models focusing on different aspects. For example, system modeling languages rely heavily on the *Unified Modeling Language (UML)* [Obj]. Its various sub languages address the structure, behavior, and architecture of systems, as well as business processes and data structures. In software engineering, correspondingly, different models present different views on a system [Som11, page 119]. A quality addressing the abstracting nature of models is their *accuracy*. Useful models must "[...] provide a true-to-life representation of the modeled system's features of interest" [Sel03, page 22].

Another agreed upon characteristic of models is that they denote a *purpose*. Their creation is driven having a goal in mind. Two generic classes of purpose can be differentiated, namely models being *descriptive* or *prescriptive* [Lud03]. Models that change between these two purposes during their life-cycle are denoted as *transient*. In software engineering, transient models are common [Hes06]. For example, a class diagram is initially used to design a software and later is reused for documentation.

Descriptive models do not intend to influence the real world entity they represent. A typical usage of descriptive models is the *documentation* of systems [Som11, page 120]. Due to their abstractive nature, models allow users to focus on relevant aspects of a system. An important quality of descriptive models is their *understandability*. This characteristic is especially important when documenting software because of the difficult to parse textual, syntactically complex programming statements they are described in [Sel03]. Descriptive models in consequence rely on graphical notations that ease their interpretation.

Prescriptive models intend to influence the real world entity they represent. In software engineering, prescriptive models are typically used in requirements engineering and design activities [Som11] (cf. section 2.2). Basing design activities on models is useful because it allows modelers to "[...] better understand both a complex problem and its potential solution before undertaking the expense end effort of a full implementation" [Sel03, page 21]. For this argument to hold, prescriptive models require to be *inexpensive*. Inexpensiveness is impacted on the one hand by the complexity of the used modeling language and how its modeling process is designed and on the other hand by the tools supporting modeling.

2.4.2. Generic Modeling Process

The generic modeling process is depicted in figure 2.6. It consists of three activities, namely *modeling*, *usage*, and *realization*.

The basis for any modeling activities are either a real world system or the idea of such a system. The modeling activity is the process of creating an abstract representation of this system [Som11, page 119]. Depending on the modeler's goals, modeling will concentrate on certain aspects of the system, for example on requirements, components, interfaces, or work flows. The aspects in focus will influence which stakeholders are involved in the modeling process. For example, modeling of requirements likely includes (input of) the intended users of the system. Or, the definition of a system's architecture includes the developer, while business analysts might be concerned with specifying work flows. Modeling in itself can play an important role in the design of a system because it requires and ideally guides modelers to externalize their ideas about the system.

The created model is used corresponding to its purpose (cf. section 2.4.1). For example, it provides basis to communicate and discuss aspects of a system or

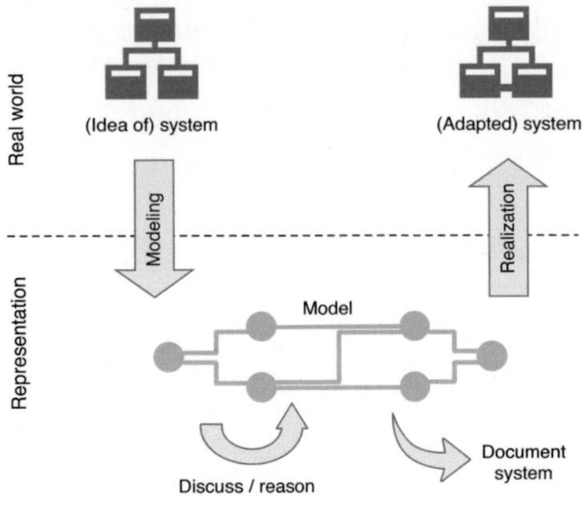

Figure 2.6.: Generic process of modeling

to reason about them. The model can also be used to document an existing system. A study finds that practitioners consider the four modeling purposes 1) *database design and management*, 2) *business process documentation*, 3) *improvement of internal business processes*, and 4) *software development* to be the most important ones in software engineering [DGR+06].

Prescriptive models provide input for the realization or adaption of the system. Models act as plans or blueprints for the system or provide input for (automatic) realization methods. An exemplary method is *model-driven engineering*, where artifacts (for example, software components) are synthesized from models using transformation engines and generators [Sch06]. An advantage of this approach is to ensure "[...] consistency between application implementations and analysis information associated with functional and QoS requirements captured by models." [Sch06].

2.5. Methodology of Service Feature Modeling

Based on the fundamental characteristics of modeling and the generic modeling process presented in section 2.4 we here provide an overview of service feature modeling's goals and methodology. The outlined service feature modeling methodology closely relates to the basic systems engineering process [Lev00]. In it, after defining objectives and criteria for assessment, alternative system designs are created. These designs are evaluated against the objectives and criteria and one (or a subset) of alternatives is chosen for implementation.

Service feature modeling is designed to address challenges related to service variability and to foster its advantages (cf. chapter 1). SFMs capture the variants of a service, or, consequently, service variability. The nature of SFMs is prescriptive (see section 2.4.1) in that they aim to induce change in the service they represent. Figure 2.7 provides a high-level view on the service feature modeling methodology to indicate the approach's different purposes. This view corresponds with the generic process of modeling depicted in figure 2.6. We aim to enable the utilization of SFMs during different activities of the software service life cycle defined in section 2.2.

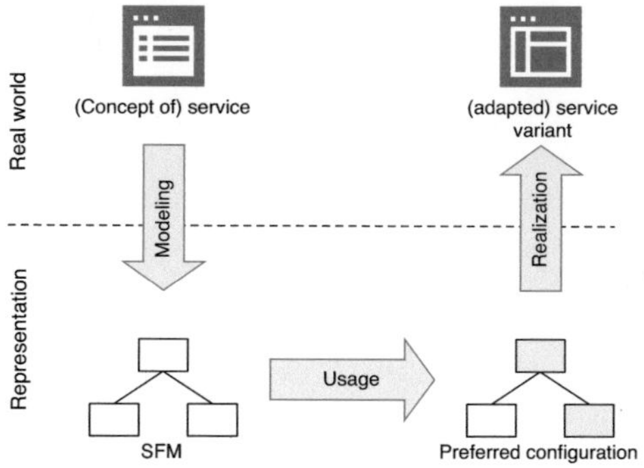

Figure 2.7.: Generic process of service feature modeling

Modeling aims to create an SFM that represents a service's variants. The process and intention of modeling depends upon whether the service is already designed or not. If the service is not jet designed, service feature modeling supports the conceptualization of the service's variants. It supports the modeler in keeping hold of and sorting out ideas about the variants. Alternatively, if the service is already designed, service feature modeling is used to document variants. In both cases, the fundamental reason for modeling SFMs is to use them to select among service variants. Modeling is performed as a design activity (see section 2.2.3). It is performed primarily by the service provider stakeholders (cf. section 3.3.1). These stakeholders can have diverse backgrounds and correspondingly address diverse concerns in modeling. For example, technicians denote the interface variants a service offers while business analysis are concerned with work flow variants. Modeling can either be performed by a single stakeholder or collaboratively by multiple stakeholders. We present service feature modeling's language and the (collaborative) modeling process in chapter 3.

Created SFMs are used to communicate, evaluate, and resolve service variability, that is, to select service configurations, reflecting variants in the real world system[1]. Selection of variants has two purposes depending on the scenario it is performed in:

- **Usage for service development** Service providers use SFMs in design activities to determine a (set of) service variants to further design, implement, deploy and operate. To support the determination of variants, provider stakeholders state their requirements or preferences with regard to the service variants to create. Service feature modeling's usage methods delimit inappropriate service variants and suggest feasible and preferred ones. Participatory methods allow future consumers to take part in the provider's design activities. Here, SFMs communicate service variants feasible from the providers' point of view. Consumers state their requirements and preferences regarding these variants and thus help providers to decide which variant(s) develop.
- **Usage for service delivery** Service providers and consumers together use SFMs to customize the delivery of a service. Service providers, having priorly modeled the service's variants in an SFM, provide this model to consumers. Consumers, in design activities regarding the service consumption, use the SFM to determine the service variant best matching their requirements and preferences. The determined variant is communicated to the provider and delivery of the variant is initiated. The providers' communication of variants and receiving of the consumers' preferred variants are operation activities.

We present details on service feature modeling's methods for variant selection in chapter 4.

Given a (set of) service variant(s) has been selected using service feature modeling, either for development or delivery, these variants need to be realized. Realization in the case of using SFMs for development encompasses design, implementation, and/or deployment activities. Realization in the case of using SFMs for delivery encompasses deployment and/or operation activities. Realization for development is performed by providers, whereas realization for delivery includes both, providers and consumers. Realization of service variants is not in focus in this thesis. We presented possible realization approaches in section 2.3.5. We further illustrate exemplary realization of service variants during development in section 5.3.4 and for delivery in section 5.4.4.

[1]For simplicity, we speak of selection of service variants in the following.

3. Modeling Service Variants

In this chapter we present the service feature modeling language and modeling process. In section 3.1 we introduce standard feature modeling from the software engineering domain, which is the basis for service feature modeling. In this chapter's main part, in section 3.2, we present the service feature modeling language's elements and their relations. We then present the processes for creating service feature models in section 3.3. We present a special case of this process in section 3.4, which addresses the composition of SFMs from services, allowing for collaborative service feature modeling. In section 3.5, we discuss related work on modeling service variants. Finally, we sum up and discuss service feature modeling's language and process in section 3.6

3.1. Standard Feature Modeling

Before presenting service feature modeling's language, we here introduce standard feature modeling, which is the basis of our approach. Standard feature modeling stems from the software engineering domain. Feature models were originally used to capture the commonalities and differences of a domain [KCH+90], which is understood to be a set of related software systems, or system variants. Typical feature model processes encompass two phases [SD07]: *domain engineering* concerns the creation and maintenance of reusable artifacts, denoting a product family, represented as a feature model. *Application engineering* concerns the selection and reuse of the reusable artifacts to create a product, commonly started by configuring a feature model. Nowadays, feature models are used in various contexts like software development, including model-driven development [TBD07], feature-oriented programming, software factories, or generative programming [BSRC10]. Furthermore, feature models are increasingly used in non-implementation activities. They are used in requirements dependency analysis [ZMZ06], they denote configuration options for virtual machine image provisioning [LNSJ12], or they support Web service customization [NC10].

3.1.1. Appeal of Feature Modeling

Different characteristics of feature modeling cause its broad uptake. First, feature modeling's appeal stems from its applicability to different problem domains. Industrial practitioners value feature modeling primarily for its application to the management of existing variability, product configuration, requirements specification, derivation of products, and design / architecture [BRN+13].

Another major appeal of feature models is the capability to perform *automatic analysis operations* on them. Automatic analysis operations are understood as computer-aided extraction of information from feature-models [BSRC10]. They are important to deal with large productive feature models that can denote hundreds or thousands of features. Further, automatic analysis operations help in dealing with the numerous and eventually complex feature relations [KOD10]. Consistency of (especially large) feature models can be ensured using automatic analysis operations, a process which is error-prone and tedious if performed manually [BSRC10]. Various analysis operations have been introduced [BSRC10]. They include, for example, checking the *validity* of a feature model by ensuring that no contradictory constraints are specified. Or, they allow to determine the complete set of system variants captured by a feature model.

Features are an effective communication medium [LKL02]. The term "feature" is used both by customers as well as engineers. As they are meaningful to different stakeholders, features bear potential for use in participatory approaches [WZ11a].

We use feature models as a basis for our approach due to a combination of factors: feature models are designed to represent system variants, which goes in line with the intention behind service feature modeling. The potential of feature modeling to communicate variants renders it suitable as a basis for participatory approaches. Feature models are widely known and applied in practice [BRN+13], increasing the chances that service or software engineers have some basic familiarity with the approach before using service feature modeling. Feature models have successfully applied to different domains [BRN+13], indicating their potential to be applied to services as well. The extensive research existing on feature models [BSRC10] has produced various methods and tools that can be used with service feature modeling as well.

3.2. Service Feature Modeling Language

The service feature modeling language comprises the elements that depict a *service feature model (SFM)* and the relationships between them. Service feature modeling's language builds upon and extends that of standard feature modeling in the following aspects:

1. It extends the notion of features through *feature types*
2. It introduces *attribute types*

A *language* consists of a syntactic notation (the syntax) and the relation of the syntax to a semantic domain (the semantics) [HR04]. The syntactic notation consists of syntactic elements. Service feature modeling is a diagrammatic language (or visual formalism, in contrast to being a textual language) because its syntactic elements are, next to the models (SFMs) themselves, different boxes and lines or arrows relating them. The definition of service feature modeling's syntax is provided in the English language and mathematical expressions in the following and, for computers to be able to process it, in a meta model in section 5.1.2. The semantic domain serves as an "[...] abstraction of reality, capturing decisions about the kinds of things the language should express" [HR04, page 67]. Service feature modeling's semantic domain is described in English language in the discussions of service variability, variable service, service variant, variability subject and object in chapter 2. The following subsections furthermore provide a semantic mapping between the semantic domain and syntactic elements. Especially, section 3.2.3 explicitly presents the mapping between service feature modeling's feature types and configurations to elements of the semantic domain presented in chapter 2.

3.2.1. Basics of the Service Feature Modeling Language

In this section, we present the basics of service feature modeling's language. They correspond to the language of standard feature modeling as outlined in section 3.1. We also present a formalization of this language's syntax (cf. [Kuh11, WKM12]), which we will extend for service feature modeling in subsequent sections. The here presented language is based upon the *extended feature model* language [BTRC05].

Service feature model

Service feature models (SFMs) are the modeling artifact created in service feature modeling. Service feature modeling is a variability modeling language, thus representing variability subjects and variability objects. The variability subject represented by an SFM is a variable service (cf. definition 7) and the variability object is a particular instance of that service, which we denote as service variant (cf. definition 8). Each SFM addresses the intra-service variability of a variable service (cf. section 2.3.2). Using dedicated methods, service feature modeling can also be applied to inter-service variability, allowing for example to select among service candidates (cf. section 4.5).

An important question is what denotes service variants in contrast to being separate services. To answer this question, in software product line engineering, domain engineering is concerned with defining the limits of a domain for which related software products exist. Defining the scope of a domain involves a trade-off: "The broader the domain of a product line is the larger is the number of possible stakeholders' requirements that can be covered in the form of individually tailored products. However, the broader the domain, the smaller is the set of similarities among products." [ABKS13, page 20]. Ultimately, there is not (and cannot) be a predefined answer to the question of how broad to define the domain. Service providers need to define for themselves what they consider a service variant and what not. Doing so does not only depend on technical arguments, but is also driven by business-related (for example, marketing) or economic considerations [Cap13], product portfolio considerations, competition, organizational, or legal constraints.

As variable services evolve over time, so do the SFMs describing their variants. Modelers need to adapt or refactor SFMs to keep them in line with the service. Given SFMs are persisted in textual data formats like XML, their versions can be managed using systems like Subversion [CSFP04] or Git [Git]. As with versions in general [ABKS13], SFM versions supersede each other and reflect the evolution of the SFM. Version control for software that denotes variability and the related field of software configuration management (SCM) (cf. [BLP04]) as well as version management for SFMs specifically are outside of the scope of this work, as already stated in section 2.3.

Another consideration is how to deal with variants of SFMs themselves. Changing the variability of a service, typically, requires the SFM describing its variants to be adapted, leading eventually to a new SFM version (see above). There are, however, situations where variants of an SFM may occur: consider an SFM that does not describe variants based on alternative deployments of a variable service. If this service is deployed in multiple instances and the variability of these instances evolves differently, variants of the SFM may result. In such cases, these SFMs can either be merged to denote the superset of variants [SBRCT08]. Alternatively, the SFMs can be kept separate and their commonalities and differences can be managed using, again, variability modeling approaches like service feature modeling, marking it a recursive operation. Approaches to manage variability of models with feature modeling have already been presented in related work [AGGR07]. Given the very context-specific nature of this situation, we do not further consider it within the scope of this work.

Feature diagram

Feature diagrams are graphical representations of an SFM. An SFM's feature diagram SFM^{diag} is a directed graph $G = (V, E)$ with the set of vertices V representing features and attributes and the set of edges E representing relationships between features as well as attributes and features [Kuh11]. In a feature diagram, higher level features denote a higher level of abstraction.

Features

Features are the main artifacts to capture multiple system variants in a single model. In their first appearance in software engineering, in the *feature-oriented domain analysis (FODA)*, features were defined to represent "[...] a prominent or distinctive user-visible aspect, quality or characteristic of a software system or systems" [KCH+90]. Since this introduction, the meaning of features has been redefined frequently. A proposed classification of the definitions considers whether features address a system's problem space (requirements, goals etc.), its solution space (functionalities, implementations etc.), or a combination of both [CHS08]. An example for an entirely problem-oriented definition of features states that a feature represents "[...] a product characteristics from user or customer views, which essentially consists of a cohesive set of individual requirements" [CZZM05]. On the other hand, a solution-oriented definition states that a feature represents an "[...] increment in product functionality" [Bat05, BSRC10]. As pointed out in studies about different meanings of the term feature, there is not one correct definition - rather, they make each sense in their specific context [CHS08].

One of service feature modeling's contributions is a typology of features, which we present in section 3.2.2. The meaning of features in service feature modeling, correspondingly, depends on their type. Before going into details about these meanings in section 3.2.2, we here just note that the meaning of features in service feature modeling is solution-oriented. Features can thus, for example, represent a service's work flow activity, a software component used in the service, or a utilized resource.

We denote the set of features as $F \subseteq V$. A feature model contains a single root feature $f^{root} \in F$ which contains all further features.

Configurations

Configurations denote valid selections of features from an SFM. Each configuration represents a variant of the service represented by an SFM. The set of all valid configurations of an SFM is denoted as the *configuration set* C, which thus denotes the set of all variants of the represented service. A configuration $c \in C$ denotes a subset of features $F^c \in F$ so that all relationships R (cf. next section) of the SFM are fulfilled. It has to be noted that in feature modeling the term configuration also refers to the process of determining a variant through feature selection [CHE04]. The term configuration thus has a different meaning depending on the context: with regard to feature modeling, (1) it denotes a set of features and (2) it denotes the process of selecting features. Additionally, with regard to realizing a service variant, it (3) denotes the determination of a service variant through provision of predetermined information (cf. 2.3.5). In the context of software configuration management, it (4) denotes a set of components, that can themselves be configurations or configuration items, which are the smallest units of individual change [Tic03].

Relationships

Relationships express constraints between features. These constraints delimit valid combinations of features from a feature diagram as part of the configuration process [MC10]. The set of relationships R is part of a feature diagram's edges:

$$R \subseteq E \tag{3.1}$$

A relationship $r \in R$ is described by the initial vertex $init(r) \in F$ and the terminal vertex $ter(r) \in F$:

$$r = \{init(r)\ ,\ ter(r)\} \tag{3.2}$$

We distinguish between two types of relationships [KOD10].

In *decomposition relationships* $R^{de} \subseteq R$ we denote the initial vertex $init(r)$ as a *parent feature* and the terminal vertex $ter(r)$ as *child feature*. We differentiate four types of decomposition relationships ($R^{man}, R^{opt}, R^{XOR}, R^{OR} \subseteq R^{de}$):

- *Mandatory* decomposition relationships $R^{man}(i,j) \mid i,j \in F, i \neq j$ state that the relationship's child feature j needs to be selected if the relationship's parent feature i is selected.
- *Optional* decomposition relationships $R^{opt}(i,j) \mid i,j \in F, i \neq j$ state that the relationship's parent feature i needs to be selected if the relationship's child feature j is selected.
- *Alternative* decomposition relationships (also referred to as XOR-decompositions) $R^{XOR} \mid i \in F, J \subset F, i \notin J$ state that a parent feature i must be selected if any of the child features of the relationship $j \in J$ is selected. Furthermore, only one child feature $j \in J$ can be selected. Because it involves a set of

child features, we classify the alternative decomposition relationship as a *group relationship.*

- *OR* decomposition relationships $R^{OR} \mid i \in F, J \subset F, i \notin J$ state that a parent feature i must be selected if a child feature of the relationship $j \in J$ is selected. Furthermore, at least one (but potentially multiple) child features $j \in J$ needs to be selected. Because it involves a set of child features, we classify the OR decomposition relationship as a *group relationship.*

Cardinality-based feature models enrich decomposition relationships between features with cardinalities, thus increasing feature model's conceptual completeness [CHE04]. While service feature modeling can be extended to incorporate cardinalities, we focus on standard decomposition relationships for sake of easiness in the following. Having introduced decomposition relationships, we can now define that a feature model's root feature does not have a parent feature:

$$f^{root} \in F : \nexists R^{de} \subseteq R \mid init(f) \wedge term(f^{root}) \; ; \; \forall f \in F \tag{3.3}$$

In *cross-tree relationships* $R^{cr} \subseteq R$, the initial vertex $init(r)$ and the terminal vertex $ter(r)$ do not need to be in a parent-child relationship. Rather, they can be arbitrary features in the feature diagram. We differentiate two types of cross-tree relationships $(R^{requires}(i,j), R^{excludes} \subseteq E^{cr})$:

- *Requires* cross-tree relationships $R^{requires}(i,j) \mid i, j \; inF, i \neq j$ state that if i is selected, j needs also to be selected.
- *Excludes* cross-tree relationships $R^{excludes}(i,j) \mid i, j \; inF, i \neq j$ state that is i is selected, j cannot also be selected.

Attributes

Attributes are elements of *extended feature models* [BTRC05]. We define attributes in the following way based on existing definitions [BTRC05]:

Definition 9. *Attributes represent characteristics of a feature or configuration.*

Attributes can be of different nature: on the one hand, they can express measurable, quantitative characteristics of features and configurations, for example cost, availability, or response time. On the other hand, they can express qualitative characteristics of features and configurations, for example accessibility, usability, security. Concrete instances of qualitative characteristics, for example "home delivery", "touch input", or "encryption", are either true or not – they are boolean in nature. The features denoting these characteristics can, for example, represent a work flow activity “send documents home”, a source code library to enable touch input, or an encryption algorithm. While features are mappable to entities of the service, attributes describe characteristics induced by these entities.

Despite the lack of a formalization of attributes and their exact semantics [Kuh11], common building blocks can be identified [BSRC10]: attributes have a *name* that is used to describe, identify, and reference them [Kuh11]. Further, attributes denote a *domain*. It states the space of possible values where attributes take their values [BTRC05]. Thus, domains restrict the set of valid values. Further, they provide additional semantics on the attributes. An exemplary domain might state that the value of an attribute must be a positive integer. Finally, the *value* denotes the specific characteristic denoted by an attribute. An exemplary value of an attribute named “cost” might be “5 €”.

We define $A \subset V$ to be the set of vertices representing attributes. Attributes cannot solely define the set of vertices in a feature diagram because they are bound to features. Every attribute $a \in A$ denotes a belongs-to relationship $ar(n, m) \in AR$ to the feature or configuration it describes:

$$\forall a \in A : \exists ar(n, m) \mid n = a; m \in (F \vee C) \tag{3.4}$$

We denote the set of belongs-to relationships as AR. An additional constraint for attributes is that they cannot belong to multiple features:

$$\forall ar_{a,f} : \nexists ar(n, m) \mid f = n, a \neq m\ ;\ i, m \in F; f, n \in AT \tag{3.5}$$

A novelty in service feature modeling is that attributes cannot only describe features, but also configurations. The motivation for this capability lies in the methods to select configurations (and thus service variants) which rely on configurations being comparable based on attributes (cf. chapter 4). A resulting challenge, which we address with the notion of attribute types in section 3.2.4, is how to derive overall values for attributes describing configurations from the values of attributes describing features (cf. challenge 1 motivated in section 1.3.1).

Formalization of sets

Having introduced the elements of feature diagrams, we can now more clearly define their building blocks. In a graph $G = (V, E)$, representing a service feature model's feature diagram SFM^{diag}, the set of vertices V encompasses the set of features and attributes, where a single vertice can only represent one of those:

$$V = \{F \cup AT\} \mid F \cap AT = \emptyset \tag{3.6}$$

Similarly, we can now define the elements of the edges set more clearly to contain relationships between features and relationships between attributes and features:

$$E = \{R \cup AR\} \mid R \cap AR = \emptyset \tag{3.7}$$

Simple example

A simple example of an SFM utilizing the so far introduced concepts is represented in figure 3.1. The shown model builds upon the example about variants in financial data Web APIs motivated in section 1.1.2. The example is used throughout chapter 3 and 4 to illustrate the applicability of service feature modeling. The SFM in figure 3.1 models variants for delivering a "stock quotes

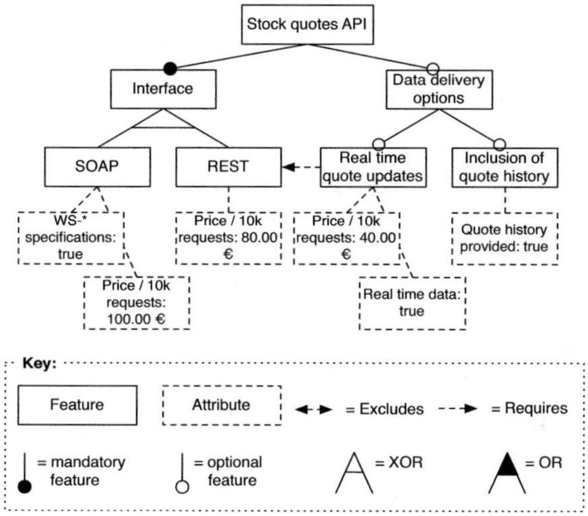

Figure 3.1.: Simple example of an SFM

API", like the ones offered by Xignite [Xig] or QuoteMedia [Quo]. Using such services accessible via Web APIs, consumers obtain the current or historic stock quotes of specified companies. The variants that consumers have to deal with in such services are manifold, including data formats or types of identifiers for the companies of interest (cf. section 1.1.2). We concentrate on a subset of variable aspects here for illustration purposes. The stock quotes API has variants regarding its "interface", which is implemented either using "SOAP" or following the "REST" architectural style. Attributes express characteristics of these variants. The "SOAP" interface allows consumers to use "WS-* specifications" in conjunction with the API. They include, for example, WS-Security, addressing integrity and confidentiality of SOAP messages, or WS-ReliableMessaging, addressing the reliable delivery of messages. The "SOAP" interface further induces a price for every 10,000 requests of 100.00 €. On the other hand, the "REST" interface induces a smaller price for every 100,000 requests of 80.00 €. Variants of the service result furthermore from "data delivery options". On the one hand, "real time quote updates" can optionally be selected. They induce a price of 40.00 €for every 10,000 requests but also set the attribute "real time data" to true. A cross-tree relationship models that "real time quote updates" can only be delivered via the "REST" interface. Another optional selection concerns the "inclusion of quote history". An attribute "history provided" with the value true models the inclusion of historic data on the stock quote.

3.2.2. Feature Types in Service Feature Modeling

The main goal of service feature modeling's language is to represent service variants. Therefore, SFMs need to represent a service's variability subjects and corresponding variability objects (see section 2.3.2). Both, variability subjects and objects, can concern the design, implementation, deployment, or operation of the service. Variability subjects may appear at different abstraction levels of a service. Thus, service feature modeling must equally support their representation on different levels. Additionally, parts of the service that are not subject to variability must be captured in an SFM. These parts can also be denoted to be *common* to all, or a set of, service variants. Despite SFM's purpose to capture service variants, the representation of common concerns is nonetheless required because common service parts can denote relations to variability objects. For example, variants can imply other concerns, which are common to a group of service variants.

The main elements of an SFM, namely *features*, address the outlined requirements regarding the representation of variability. In service feature modeling, features act in different roles: they represent both variability subjects and variability objects. Features have thus a solution-oriented semantic (cf. 3.2.1), they represent variable concerns of the service's design, implementation, deployment, or operation. Additionally, features are used to structure an SFM's feature diagram. Consider, for example, the root feature "stock quotes API" in figure 3.1. For service feature modeling, we aim to more clearly differentiate these diverse semantics. Thus, as has been proposed comparably in related work [CHE04], we differentiate three feature types: *grouping features*, *abstract features*, and *instance features* [WKM12]. The semantics of features becomes clearer through differentiation. These additional semantics do not impact the applicability of automated analysis operations on SFMs as compared to standard feature models [CHE05]. For example, a standard feature model analyzer to determine all configurations of an SFM will produce the same result whether feature types are considered or not. The reasoner will only consider the relationships between features and ignore the typing. We argue that a clearer semantic increases unambiguous understandability of SFMs. Additionally, through additional rules on the three feature types, we delimit the number of valid modeling choices, thus guiding the modeling process. Furthermore, we perceive potentials for better automated processing of SFMs that denote feature types. For example, deriving the superset of instantiable features only requires selecting all instance features in an SFM. Or, the superset of abstract features denotes the variability points a represented service possesses. Another reason for the feature typology is enabling comparability of SFMs. Multiple SFMs that possess the same structure with regard to their grouping and abstract features, though having diverse instance features, can be compared to one another. We make use of this capability to model SFMs with similar structure (cf. section 3.3.3) and use them for requirements filtering and preference-based ranking across multiple SFMs (cf. section 4.5). In the following, we outline each feature type in detail.

Grouping features $F^G \subseteq F$ contain further features, which all address the same concern. We define grouping features in the following way:

Definition 10. *A grouping feature represents a category of related variability points and their variants.*

Their purpose is to organize and structure an SFM. Because grouping features contain further features addressing a similar concern, they provide a comprehensive view for different stakeholders. For example, a grouping feature can be used to contain all other features concerning the technical implementation of security. The root feature of an SFM is a grouping feature, which represents the service in focus. The contained features, thus, all concern this service. The parent features of a grouping feature can be other grouping features or instance features. The child features of a grouping feature are either other grouping features, abstract features, or instance features. Because their purpose is solely to provide structure, grouping features are always mandatory. Correspondingly, grouping features do not increase the number of configurations represented by an SFM.

Abstract features $F^A \subseteq F$ denote variation points. A variation point is "[...] a representation of a variability subject within domain artefacts [...]" [PuFvdL05, page 62]. Correspondingly, we define abstract features in the following way:

Definition 11. *An abstract feature represents a variation point with regard to (parts of) the design, implementation, deployment, or operation of a service.*

An abstract feature can, for example, represent an abstract activity of a work flow, a type of security mechanism like encryption, a type of service to invoke, or an interface to implement. The parent features of abstract features are grouping features or instance features. The variation point represented by an abstract feature can be fulfilled by one of potentially multiple ways. Thus, in the course of a configuration process, abstract features must be instantiated by selecting a child *instance feature.*

Instance features $F^I \subseteq F$ denote concrete instantiations of a variation point - they represent variants. Here, a variant is "[...] a representation of a variability object within domain artefacts" [PuFvdL05, page 62]. Correspondingly, we define instance features in the following way:

Definition 12. *An instance feature represents a variant regarding (parts of) the design, implementation, deployment, or operation of a service.*

In software services, instance features can, for example, represent source code like a module or an aspect, (a set of) configuration parameters, protocols, or data. In generic services, instance features can, for example, represent resources (human or physical), work flow elements, activities, a software component, or a human resource. Instance features do not need to be directly mappable to a single artifact of the service's design, implementation, deployment or operation. An instance feature can also be realized in the service through combination of artifacts or by parts of them. For example, an instance feature representing a service's security mechanism may depend on source code in different service components and the existence of policies. Thus, feature diagrams should not be confused with part-of hierarchies or the decomposition of software modules [CHE04].

	Parent feature types	**Child feature types**	**Parent-decompositions**	**Child-decompositions**
Grouping feature	none (for root feature), grouping, instance	grouping, abstract, instance	mandatory	mandatory, optional
Abstract feature	grouping, instance	instance	mandatory, optional	mandatory, optional, XOR, OR
Instance feature	grouping, abstract	grouping, abstract	mandatory, optional, XOR, Or	mandatory

Table 3.1.: Constraints on service feature modeling's three feature types

By including deployment and operational aspects into the definition of abstract and instance features, they can also concern the service environment. For example, features can represent legal restrictions for using the service, the geographic location a service runs in, or technical properties of the execution environment.

Collectively, the three types of features denote all features in an SFM:

$$F = \{F^G \cup F^A \cup F^I\} \mid F^G \cap F^A \cap F^I = \emptyset \tag{3.8}$$

Table 3.1 presents an overview of the constraints on the three feature types.

Figure 3.2 extends the simple example from figure 3.1 with feature types. We introduce different outline styles and text styles to graphically differentiate the feature types. The root feature "stock quotes API" is a grouping feature whose purpose is solely to unite all further features addressing the service. "Interface" is an abstract feature, that can be instantiated by one of the two instance features "SOAP" or "REST". Similarly, "data delivery options" is an abstract features, which can be instantiated either by "real time quote updates" or "inclusion of quote history" or both.

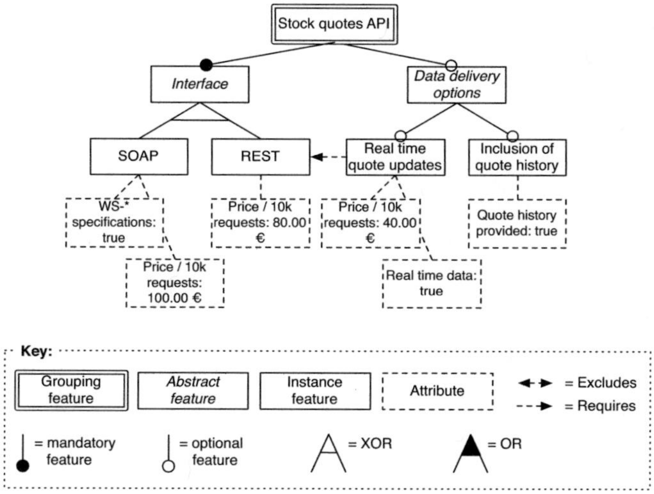

Figure 3.2.: Simple example of an SFM with feature types

3.2.3. Representation of Service Variability with Feature Types

We have now introduced concepts of service variability (see section 2.3) and the representation of service variability generically and using service feature modeling in section 3.2.2. The relations between these concepts are illustrated in figure 3.3. These relations thus correspond to the semantic mapping between the semantic domain (variable services etc.) and syntactic elements in an SFM.

With regard to real-world artifacts, service variability implies the existence of variable services. Such services denote at least one but potentially many variability subjects, that can be instantiated by one of multiple variability objects. A service variant of a variable service denotes a specific combination of variability objects.

On a generic representational level, the variable service is represented by a variability model. In the context of software, such models are, for example, feature models or orthogonal variability models [PuFvdL05]. Variability subjects and variability objects are represented by variation points or variants. The relationships between these representational elements reflect those of their real world counterparts.

Service feature modeling is a concrete instance of a variability modeling approach. Here, the variability model is denoted as a service feature model. Its abstract features relate to variation points and its instance features to variants. The real world concept of a service variant is reflected by a configuration that relates to a selection of instance features.

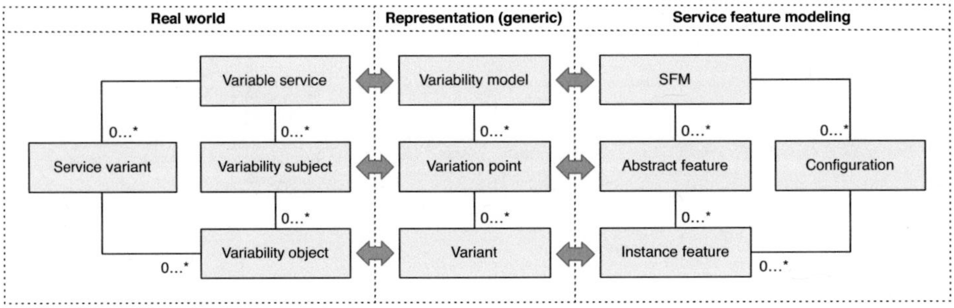

Figure 3.3.: Concepts of service variability and their representation, generically and in service feature modeling

3.2.4. Attribute Types in Service Feature Modeling

To enhance the usage of attributes in service feature modeling we introduce *attribute types*. Attribute types model properties that are common to all associated attributes. By defining an aggregation rule (see below), attribute types provide the basis to express characteristics in SFMs not only with regard to features, but also with regard to configurations representing service variants as motivated by challenge 1 in section 1.3.1. Another motivation for attribute types is to store recurring information centrally, for example, the name of all attributes of a type. Storing information centrally reduces modeling effort when adding attributes of the same type: they are associated with an existing attribute type without having to enter the information again. Additionally, changing information for multiple attributes only has to be performed once for the attribute type. Doing so avoids potential inconsistencies because changes do not manually have to be executed in multiple places.

The following information is stored in attribute types in service feature modeling:

- The **name** of the attributes related to this type. Denoting multiple attributes' names centrally secures their consistency throughout an SFM, enabling, for example, their comparison. In contrast, storing names per attribute might, through typos or miscommunication between multiple modelers, lead to semantically equivalent but differently named attributes. Such errors impact and eventually distort automatic operations on feature models.
- An attribute type further denotes the **domain** of all attributes relating to it. The domain defines, as in standard feature modeling, the range of values an attribute can take. *Continuous* domains are used, for example, for the attributes "cost" or "performance". *Integer* domains are used, for example, for the attributes "'number of users" or "storage". *Boolean* domains are used, for example, for attributes that denote functional capabilities such as "home access" or "personal assistance".
- An attribute type denotes the **measurement unit** for the attribute values. For example, an attribute type "cost" defines the measurement unit as "Euro". The measurement unit supports interpretability of attribute values for both, human actors and computers. The latter can, for example, perform conversions as part of automatic operations based on the measurement unit provided.
- A **description** is also stored in the attribute type. It is used to capture human-understandable explanations about the attributes. Capturing such information is especially relevant for SFMs, whose methods include collaborative modeling (cf. section 3.4). When multiple stakeholders work on the same model, unambiguous understanding of the semantics of attributes is relevant to ensure their correct utilization. An attribute type's description fulfills this purpose.
- Attribute types also capture the **aggregation rule** for attributes. In standard feature modeling, attributes only concern individual features. In service feature modeling, however, we also use attributes to describe configurations (cf. section 3.2.1). The resulting configuration attributes play

an important role in the selection among configurations and respectively service variants (cf. chapter 4). Difficulties of achieving this goal with standard feature modeling's language become clear when looking back at the way attributes are represented in figure 3.1: "price / 10k requests" is defined in multiple features. However, it is not defined how to combine or interpret these values in configurations where multiple attributes "price / 10k requests" are present. One solution would be to define within each attribute how its value impacts a configuration's overall value. However, this solution bears potential for contradictory statements among similar attributes. Thus, we define an aggregation rule centrally within an attribute type. The aggregation rule specifies how to aggregate individual values in cases where configurations contain multiple attributes of the same type. The resulting value can be associated with the configuration. Possible aggregation rules are *sum*, *product*, *minimum*, *maximum* and *at least once*. For example, the attribute type "cost" has an aggregation rule *sum* given that the cost of multiple features are additive. Aggregation based on the aggregation rule *at least once* results in *true* if at least one considered attribute has a value of *true*. This aggregation rule is designed to aggregate qualitative attributes. For the aggregation rules *minimum* and *maximum*, the overall value equals the lowest or highest observed value. We discuss the aggregation of attributes and the aggregation rules in detail in section 4.2.2.

The so far introduced information is relevant for attributes irrespective of the intended usage of SFMs. For the sake of completeness, we here introduce additional information stored in attribute types that is relevant for the preference-based ranking approaches presented in section 4.4.

- The **scale order** defines how to interpret the values of associated attributes in the ranking process. *Higher is better* denotes that higher values are considered to be better. *Lower is better* denotes that lower values are considered to be better. For example, for attributes denoting "cost" a lower value is generally considered positive. Finally, *existence is better* denotes that a value of *true* is considered to be better in cases where the attribute type's domain is boolean.

- The boolean property **to be evaluated** denotes whether an attribute type should be considered in the ranking process.

- The **custom attribute type priority** denotes how much better features / configurations are to be interpreted in the ranking process if they have an attribute with boolean domain whose value is *true* compared to if it is *false*.

Capturing the stated information, including name and domain, in attribute types rather than attributes themselves, attributes consequently only denote a value. We denote this value in service feature modeling as **instantiation value**. An attribute's instantiation value depends on the feature or configuration that the attribute relates to. Thus, values cannot be centrally stored but must remain with a single attribute. We define the instantiation value as $iv(m, at)$, $m \in (F \vee C), a \in A$.

We define the set of a feature model's attribute types as AT. Each attribute $a \in A$ is associated with one attribute type at with an attribute type relationship $atr(a, at)$:

$$\forall a \in A \ : \ \exists \ atr(a, at) \mid a \in A, at \in AT \tag{3.9}$$

Consequently, we can access the type of an attribute with $type(a) = at$.

Figure 3.4 extends figure 3.2 with attribute types[1]. The four attribute types

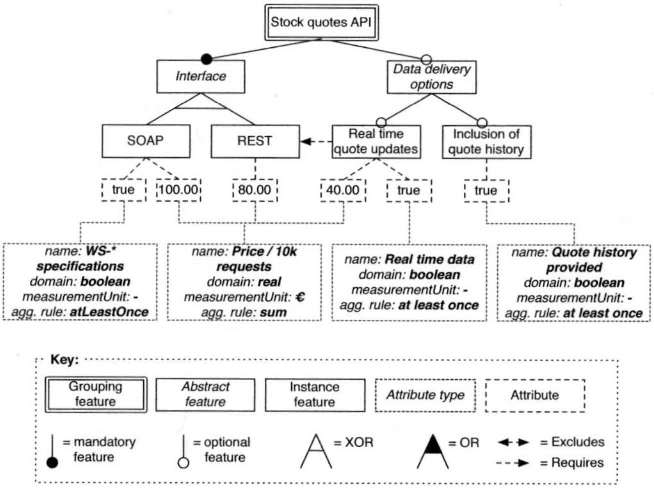

Figure 3.4.: Simple example of an SFM with feature types and attribute types

contain a richer set of information compared to the information stored in the attributes in figure 3.2. Attribute type "price / 10k requests" additionally avoids redundant modeling of this information because multiple attributes are related to that type.

[1]Note that for better readability, we do not show all information stored in an attribute type in the figure.

3.3. Service Feature Modeling Process

In this section, we describe how service feature modeling's language is used to model service variants. We discuss involved stakeholders (cf. section 3.3.1) as well as how to perform service feature modeling (cf. section 3.3.2). We also present an approach of using domain models to ensure comparability between multiple SFMs (cf. section 3.3.3).

3.3.1. Involved Stakeholders

The stakeholders involved in the creation of SFMs must fulfill requirements. They must obtain knowledge about the the service's variability subjects and objects. This knowledge concerns either the whole service or addresses only certain service aspects, for example technical properties or access channels. Stakeholders concerned with modeling furthermore require modeling experience. The degree to which modeling knowledge is necessary is impacted, at least partly, by the support provided by the utilized modeling tools (cf. section 5.1).

The stakeholders involved in service feature modeling can be diverse, provided they fulfill the stated requirements. They can thus, for example, include technicians, decision-makers, legal experts, managers, or marketers. Given that the variability subject represented by SFMs is a variable service, a *service engineer* is an obvious stakeholder involved in service feature modeling. The role of service engineers, however, is only vaguely defined in related work (cf., for example the definition of generic skills required by service engineers [LG10]). Service engineers can thus be understood to be characterized by their involvement in the service development or delivery process, rather than by their background and qualification or specific tasks they fulfill.

A more concrete group of stakeholders likely to be involved in service feature modeling are *software engineers*. Due to the distribution of standard feature modeling in software engineering, they are likely to be familiar with service feature modeling's concepts as well. In service feature modeling, software engineers typically act both as *domain* and *application engineers* [SVGB05] in that they define service variants but are also involved in their selection.

In the following, we refer to the creator of a service feature model as *modeler*. The modeler can be any of the above-mentioned stakeholders.

3.3.2. Modeling Procedure

Creating SFMs can be performed manually. Given the tree-structure of an SFM, modeling is performed top-down. The modeler identifies and represents with corresponding abstract and instance features the variability subjects and related variability objects of the service. Iteratively, the modeler also specifies grouping features to structure the feature diagram. If service feature modeling is performed as part of conceptualizing a new service, the outlined steps are likely to be repeated, revised, or even reversed. Thus, an SFM is continuously refactored during modeling.

Service feature modeling, similar to standard feature modeling, comprises various challenges for the modeler: the domain, that is the scope in which variants are considered to belong to the same service, must be defined (cf. section 3.2.1). Features need to be identified, named and organized. To ease these tasks, concepts and guidelines have been proposed in related work on standard feature modeling [LKL02, TÖ13]. These concepts are applicable to manual service feature modeling as well.

Next to manual service feature modeling, automatic methods ease or complement modeling. Automatic methods synthesize SFMs based on provided input artifacts. For example, existing work flow definitions can be used to derive an SFM representing work flow variants [WZ14]. We provide an example for the automatic modeling of SFMs based on previously defined work flow variants in section 5.3.2. Automatic modeling methods depend on the service being already (partly) conceptualized. Thus, the modeling of SFMs in this case does not assist in the initial definition of service variability, but results in the *explicit* representation of variability. In the artifact from which SFMs are derived, in contrast, variability might only be an afterthought. For example, multiple approaches exist to define work flow variants in a single work flow model [RvdA07, GVDAJVLR08]. In these approaches, however, the representation of variability is mixed with the primarily targeted representation of work flows. Separating these representations by automatically deriving SFMs that focus on variability result in increased separation of concerns. Furthermore, within SFMs, cross-tree relationships can be used to constrain variability, which might not be possible in mixed representations. Automatic modeling reduces modeling effort and can be used to obtain desired and predictable model structures.

Overall, the exact nature of how modeling SFMs is conducted depends on its integration into broader service design methodologies. We present two use cases in which SFMs were modeled in sections 5.3 and 5.4.

3.3.3. Modeling SFMs with Similar Structure

In many applications, a desirable characteristic is that SFMs follow a common structure. Similarly structured SFMs enable modelers to more easily familiarize themselves with new models. If a structure is provided to the modeler, he can use it as input for the modeling process, thus reducing efforts. Additionally, (automatic) comparisons between similarly structured models and their configurations are possible, as motivated in challenge 5 in section 1.3.1. We present methods to select service variants using different SFMs that are based on the same structure in section 4.5. A similar structure is achievable for services of types where the same variability subjects and objects appear. For example, a study of the configuration options of IaaS reveals configuration options that are common to different providers, allowing for derivation of a shared SFM structure [Bar13, page 31 ff.]. On the other hand, specific contexts might impede the opportunity to create similarly structured SFMs, for example because a modeled service is unique in its variants.

One way to achieve similar structures are automatic modeling capabilities (cf. section 3.3.2). For a well-formated input, they synthesize SFMs with a predictable structure. Another approach to create multiple SFMs with similar structure is to use a *blueprint* or *domain model* [WKM12]. The domain model's goal is to provide a common structure for other models. It defines the scope of what to express in other models derived from the domain model and structures of features in all of these models' feature diagrams. The domain model thus pre-defines which concerns and variability subjects to consider in the modeling process. For example, a specific selection of technical, business-related, legal, or organizational concerns are captured in the domain model. For this purpose, the feature diagram of a domain model $G_D = (V_D, E_D)$ has a reduced set of vertices and edges. It consists of grouping and abstract features only, it does not include any instance features or attributes:

$$V_D = V \setminus F^I \cup A = F^G \cup F^A \tag{3.10}$$

A domain model does further not contain cross-tree relationships and does not contain relations between features and attributes (it only contains decomposition relationships):

$$E_D = E \setminus R^{cr} \cup AR = R^{de} \tag{3.11}$$

The domain model does further define attribute types for all models derived from it.

The feature diagram of an SFM based on the domain model, $G_{SFM(D)} = (V_{SFM(D)}, E_{SFM(D)})$, contains the same structure and exhibit attributes of the attribute types defined in the domain model. It captures service variants with regard to the concerns defined in the domain model. For this purpose, the SFM contains the same abstract and grouping features as the domain model:

$$F^G_{SFM(D)} \subseteq F^G_D \wedge F^A_{SFM(D)} \subseteq F^A_D \tag{3.12}$$

An SFM based on the domain model further contains the same attribute types:

$$AT_{SFM(D)} \subseteq AT_D \tag{3.13}$$

Additional grouping, abstract, or instance features as well as attribute types can be defined in the SFM. Thus, the comparability between different SFMs based on the same domain model is only guaranteed for the structure defined in the domain model. In addition to the domain model, an SFM based on it contains instance features and attributes, thus denoting the same elements as any other SFM.

An example of a domain model and two SFMs derived from it is illustrated in figure 3.5. The domain model defines a grouping feature "Financial API" as the root feature. It also defines the concerns "interface" and "data delivery options" to be relevant variability points using abstract features. Three attribute types, "WS-* specifications", "price / 10k requests", and "quote history provided" are defined. The two SFMs derived from this domain model, representing services "Stock quotes API" and "REST Quotes Service", denote the same structure. They have, however, specific instance features and attributes extending the common structure. For example, while "Stock quotes API" offers two interfaces "SOAP" and "REST", service "REST Quotes Service" has "REST" as its mandatory interface. In consequence, service "REST Quotes Service"'s SFM has no attribute of the type "WS-* specifications". Due to this attribute type's aggregation rule of "at least once", no configuration of service "REST Quotes Service" offers this characteristic.

Noteworthy is that even though the derived SFMs follow the same structure, their comparison based on features is impeded by different naming conventions (consider the feature named "inclusion of quotes history" in contrast to "include history"). This obstacle to comparability could be addressed by agreeing on a shared name space across SFMs. Approaches to address this shortcoming include the definition of namespaces or the utilization of semantic technologies like ontologies, which lie outside of the scope of this work. We believe, however, that these problem primarily highlights the necessity to provide usage methods

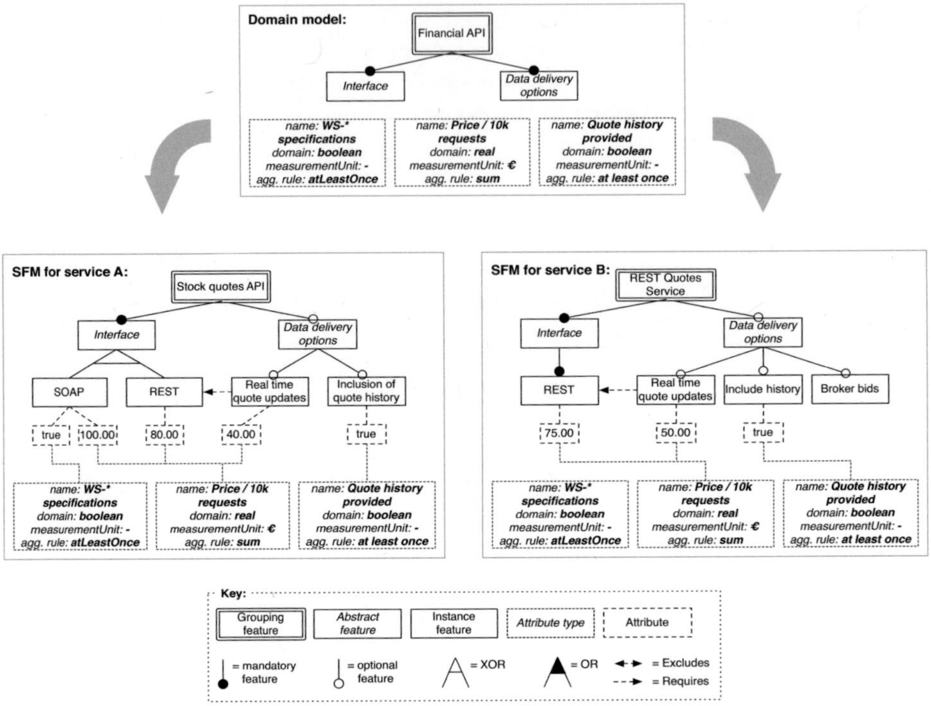

Figure 3.5.: Example domain model for cloud data storage and two SFMs based on it

in service feature modeling that rely on comparable characteristics represented by attributes for variant selection (cf. section 4).

Modeling SFMs with similar structure underpins the important role that feature types play in service feature modeling: they allow modelers to clearly differentiate the scope of domain models.

3.4. Coordinated Composition of Service Feature Models

The modeling process outlined in section 3.3 is similar to that used for standard feature modeling. For service feature modeling, however, we propose an extended modeling procedure: the multidisciplinary nature of services (cf. section 2.1.1) requires multiple, diverse stakeholders to take part in service design activities. Here, SFMs are an ideal artifact to interrelate design concerns because features can represent various variability subjects of a service (see section 3.2.2). Thus, service feature modeling should allow multiple stakeholders to create a single SFM collaboratively as motivated in challenge 3 in section 1.3.1. Each stakeholder can contribute relevant concerns, which can be interrelated using relationships in the SFM. We refer to the resulting process, in which multiple stakeholders as well as software services participate in the creation of an SFM, as *collaborative service feature modeling.*

Furthermore, the purpose of SFMs is to select service variants for further development or delivery. Decision-relevant information needs to be incorporated into an SFM during modeling. Such information often changes over time or results from complex calculations. For example, attributes denoting the cost or the performance of a service request vary over time. When using SFMs for variant selection delayed in time from modeling the SFM, such information is likely to be outdated, thus impeding the correctness of the made decision. Thus, we aim to incorporate changing, complex information into SFMs on demand as motivated in challenge 2 in section 1.3.1.

To realize these requirements, we propose to *compose SFMs from services* so that the overall SFM is a combination of model parts, which are contributed by human or software services. For example, a legal expert provides a SFM branch representing the alternative options with regard to realizing encryption for a service. Or, a Web service provides the latest benchmark results denoting the performance of a cloud infrastructure service. The solution approach presented here has been published in previous work [WSKT12].

An example of composing SFMs from services is illustrated in figure 3.6[2]. A software engineer starts modeling the stock quotes API service. He defines a feature “data delivery options”. Because the software engineer is not responsible for data delivery options in his organization, he requests a data engineer to provide input. The data engineer defines the service’s options for data delivery to be “real time quote updates” and “include history”. The software engineer further defines the two “interface” variants “SOAP” and “REST”, each denoted by an attribute of type “price / 10k requests”. To retrieve up-to-date pricing information, he includes a “pricing service” that provides the required information on demand. The overall SFM will eventually be a result of the software engineer, the data engineer, and the pricing service each providing model parts.

Composing SFMs from services introduces challenges. The contribution of SFM parts must be *coordinated* to detect and resolve potential inconsistencies between

[2]For readability of the image, we do not display attribute types.

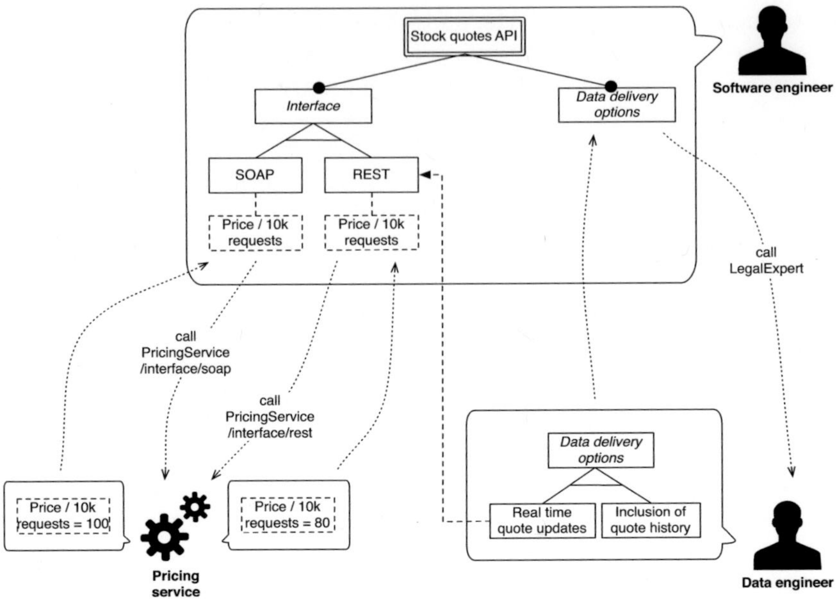

Figure 3.6.: Example of composing SFMs from services, based on [WSKT12]

model parts. Consider the example illustrated in figure 3.6. The data engineer defines a requires cross-tree relationship between the features "real time quote updates" and "REST". However, when the software engineer, who is responsible for the root part of the SFM, later changes or even deletes the required feature, inconsistencies or errors may arise. Thus, coordination of the composition is required. To ensure coordinated composition of SFMs, we introduce a *composition model* which defines what constitutes a composed SFM. We define *roles* involved in the creation of composed SFMs. Finally, we define *coordination rules* that ensure coordinated composition.

3.4.1. Composition Model

The composition model defines the elements involved in composing SFMs from services. These elements and their structure are illustrated in figure 3.7.

Services represent human or software services. Services interact through machine-understandable interfaces. In the case of software services, these interfaces can be invoked through corresponding clients. In the case of human services, invocation of corresponding software interfaces triggers human interac-

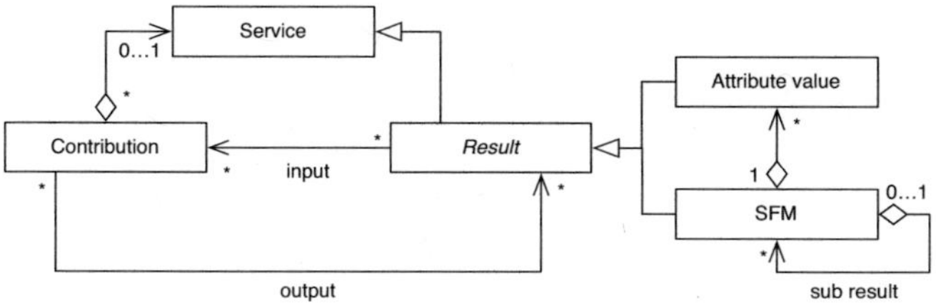

Figure 3.7.: Service composition model [WSKT12]

tion. For example, notification mechanisms like e-mails can be invoked through software, which again notify the corresponding human about the invocation.

Individual parts of an SFM composed from services relate to *results*. Results can be instantiated by *SFMs* themselves. Thus, a feature structure decomposed according to the definitions in section 3.2 can be a result. The *sub result* association ensures that results of type SFM can be nested. In the example in figure 3.6, one SFM result is created by the software engineer, containing the root feature "stock quotes API", features for the "interface" and the feature for "data delivery options". The second SFM result contains the features representing the service's variability with regard to "data delivery options" and is created by the data engineer. Alternatively, results can be instantiated as *attribute values*. These results are used to store individual attribute values, denoting, for example, a service's up to date performance or cost information. Attribute value results themselves must be contained by an SFM result. For example, in figure 3.6, two attribute value results for "price / 10k requests" are created by the pricing service. They both are contained in the software engineer's SFM result. Provision of attribute values is either motivated by the need to include complexly derived values into a SFM (cf. challenge 2), which cannot solely be calculated with service feature modeling's aggregation rules (see section 3.2.4). For example, values for "cost" frequently derive from a complex calculation scheme, which considers the total consumption of a service. Alternatively, provision of attribute types is motivated by the need to include dynamic, temporal values. For example, benchmarking results or usage counts change over time (cf. section 1.1.3). Results themselves inherit from service elements in the composition model, allowing them to be offered as a service.

Finally, *contributions* relate services and results with one another. Contributions denote activities by a service that produce a result, denoted by the *output* relationship. Contributions themselves can rely on existing results provided as input. For example, the data engineer's contribution in figure 3.6, which outputs the "data delivery options" SFM result, depends on the "stock quotes API" result as input as to define the requires relationship between the features "real time quote updates" and "REST". A contribution is associated to a service responsible for its completion.

3.4.2. Roles

When composing SFMs from services, participants act in different roles. Each role is defined by a set of related activities. Every participant can engage in one or multiple roles at the same time or change roles over time.

- **Modelers** are concerned with hierarchically decomposing a design concern into features. Modelers define features, parent-child and cross-tree relationships between them, and their attributes and corresponding attribute types. The activities performed by modelers thus are similar to the modeling activities of standard feature modeling (cf. section 3.3.2). Correspondingly, either human actors or software components can perform the role of a modeler. The result of modelers' activities are SFMs, which are contributed to the collaborative modeling process.

- **Attribute value providers**, as their name suggests, provide attribute values to SFMs. As in the case of modelers, this role can either be fulfilled by human actors or software components. Depending on the required frequency of delivering (updated) attribute values, software components are more suited to fulfill this role.

- **Coordinators** perform two activities. First, they identify contributions whose results should be provided by modelers other than themselves and assign modeling tasks for both SFMs and attribute values to them. This activity requires coordinators to have a basic understanding of the modeling process in order to correctly interpret an SFM. Second, coordinators assign suited services to the identified contributions. This activity requires coordinators to possess knowledge about the stakeholders involved with designing the service to be aware of potential contributors and how to reach them. Services can be assigned either in the role of modelers or attribute value providers, depending on the nature of the required contribution. Coordinators can further also delegate coordination activities with respect to a single result. This allows the assigned participant to further split up and delegate a contribution, depending on his (possibly concern-specific) knowledge. For example, the participant concerned with "data delivery options" aspects may be best suited to knowing which participant to involve with regard to specific sub-concerns regarding data delivery. Additionally, the capability to assign coordination activities marks composition of SFMs from services a recursive and thus flexible process.

3.4.3. Coordination Rules

Coordination rules aim to ensure error- and conflict-free composition of SFMs from services. They are created, updated, and deleted automatically during the composition to denote all constraints necessary for a specific SFM at a specific modeling stage. Alternatively, they can be instantiated manually to ensure the adherence of the composition process to specific requirements. Coordination rules follow the event-condition-action (ECA) pattern, which originally stems from the area of active database management systems [MD89]. Coordination rules specify an event upon whose occurrence a condition is checked. Depending on the outcome of this check, an action specified in the coordination rule is performed. Coordination rules are expressed in a computer-understandable way. This allows software components to detect the occurrence of an event, to check the condition, and to trigger an (automated) action.

Coordinating changes to cross-tree relationships

A first set of coordination rules is concerned with handling inconsistencies resulting from cross-tree relationships. As defined in section 3.2.1, cross-tree relationships define dependencies between any features in an SFM, irrespective of their position in the feature diagram. Thus, they can be defined between features belonging to different results (of types SFM) when composing SFMs from services. This capability renders cross-tree relationships as potential sources for inconsistencies or conflicts: consider a cross-tree relationship $r \in R^{cr}$ defined in SFM A to target a feature $i = tar(r)$ defined in SFM B. The modeler of B may not be aware of feature i being part of a cross-tree relationship and might change or delete it without intention of harm. The validity of r, however, might be impeded by such actions. For example, as the semantics of feature i are changed, the cross-tree relationship might be obsolete.

To deal with such inconsistencies, upon creation of a cross-tree relationship in SFM A with $tar(r) \notin F^A$, a rule is established that triggers a corrective action upon edit or deletion of the targeted feature. Having defined events `FeatureUpdated` and `FeatureDeleted`, the modeler of the cross-tree relationship can be notified about a potential inconsistency:

```
EVERY FeatureUpdated(tar(r)) OR FeatureDeleted(tar(r))
DO notify(modeler(r));
```

Coordinating changes to attribute types

As in the case of cross-tree relationships, composing SFMs from services can result in conflicts when it comes to attributes and attribute types. Attribute types can be defined in any result of type SFM. Consider attribute type $at \in AT$ being defined in SFM A. Embracing their role to avoid redundant modeling, however, attributes associated to at can be defined in another SFM. For example, attribute $a \in A$, defined in SFM B, is associated to at so that $atr(a, at)$. If the modeler of A decides to change or even delete at, the association $atr(a, at)$ might be wrong or obsolete.

To deal with such inconsistencies, upon creation of an attribute in SFM A with $atr(a, at) : at \notin F^A$, a rule is established that triggers a corrective action upon edit or deletion of the attribute type. Having defined events `AttributeTypeUpdated` and `AttributeTypeDeleted`, the modeler of the attribute can be notified about a potential inconsistency:

```
EVERY AttributeTypeUpdated(at) OR AttributeTypeDeleted(at)
DO notify(modeler(a));
```

3.4.4. Service Binding

To allow services to contribute results to SFMs, they need to be bound. Figure 3.8 illustrates the service binding protocol used for this purpose, which is derived from previous work [SZS11, WSKT12]. Initially, the state of the binding is *open*. When a coordinator assigns a contribution to a service, the state changes to *asked for binding*. This request corresponds to asking the service to commit to contribute a result. Either if this process is aborted by the coordinator or if the service declines the request, the binding is again open. On the other hand, if the service accepts the binding, its state is set to *accepted*. Software services are expected to accept requests for binding automatically. In this case, the correct selection of services to contribute results relies on the coordinator. Human services need to assess their capabilities to deliver the requested result and respond respectively. Once a service is bound it can deliver results related to assigned contributions. This can be done repeatedly to update delivered results. While being bound, the service can additionally be contacted by the coordinator, for example to send reminders to contribute results. From the accepted state, the binding can again be transferred to the open state if either the coordinator or the service deletes the binding. The coordinator deletes the binding typically upon approving of the contributed results.

To take part in the described interactions, a service must implement the service binding protocol. As mentioned, software services will implement the protocol

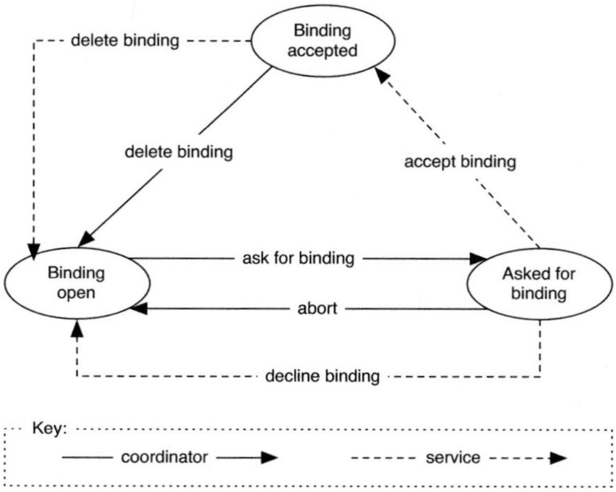

Figure 3.8.: Service binding protocol, based on [SZS11]

in a way so that binding requests are automatically accepted (or declined based on pre-defined conditions). The interface of the protocol for services will likely consist of endpoints to invoke by the coordinator. For human services, the protocol will rely on a user interface that allows the human actor to review requests for binding and accept or decline them. Details on the implementation of *service adapters* that realize this protocol are presented in section 5.1.4.

3.5. Related Work on Modeling Service Variants

Within this section, we present related work on modeling service variants. We outline work on variability modeling languages in general in section 3.5.1. In section 3.5.2, we focus on the utilization of feature modeling for services, which denotes the bulk of related approaches. We specifically address common use cases in related work dealing with feature-based modeling of the variability of Web and cloud services. For each approach, we present a short discussion as compared to service feature modeling. We furthermore present other approaches apart from feature modeling to represent service variability in section 3.5.3. In section 3.5.4, we present related work with regards to composing SFM from services, which is a means for collaborative modeling (cf. section 3.4).

3.5.1. Variability Modeling Languages

A set of related work addresses variability modeling approaches in general and their application in different contexts (not necessarily services).

Selected variability modeling approaches for software product line engineering have been classified [SD07]. Different types of variability modeling are identified, focusing either on features, use cases, or (for the rest) other aspects. Six exemplary approaches are selected and classified regarding the categories modeling (considering the language and its abstraction) and tools (considering tool-support provided with regard to domain and application engineering).

A systematic review of variability management approaches, comprising modeling and reasoning facilities, in software engineering has been conducted [CABA09]. This study provides a chronological overview of how variability management approaches have been developed, starting from the earliest approach of feature-oriented design-analysis [KCH+90]. The authors state the life-cycle phases that the approaches support and what variability models they utilize. Here, the omnipresent role of feature modeling is reflected and its utilization by various management approaches throughout the software life-cycle is illustrated.

Another study addresses the utilization of variability modeling approaches in industrial practice [BRN+13]. The authors present the results of an empirical study sent to 42 industrial practitioners. The questions asked address typical application scenarios for variability modeling, its perceived benefits and challenges, used notations and tools, and the scale of industrial models. The authors find that feature modeling is by far the most utilized variability modeling notation, being used by nearly three quarters of respondents. Variability modeling approaches are used in a wide field of applications, including management of existing variability, product configuration, requirements specification, or design / architecture.

The presented works underpin our choice to utilize feature modeling to represent service variability: feature modeling is a highly researched and in practice utilized variability modeling approach. Thus, a strong basis of experience and approaches exists that can beneficially be utilized. Further, feature modeling's dissemination in industrial practice lowers entry barriers for using this technology. Given their broad utilization across application domains, feature modeling-based approaches seem an suitable starting-point for utilizing variability modeling for service development and delivery, as we propose in this work.

3.5.2. Feature-based Modeling of Service Variability

Feature modeling approaches, given their broad utilization across domains (cf. section 3.5.1), have previously been utilized to model service variability. The majority of these approaches addresses either modeling variability of Web services or of cloud services. We thus present related work for modeling variants of these types of services in the following.

Modeling Web Service Variability

The use of feature modeling to represent Web service variability has been motivated with fast and automatic creation of consumer-specific variants [RF03]. In this approach, exemplary feature models are presented that address variability of utilized communication technologies, the Web service itself, or the consumer. However, the complete scope of the models is not exhaustively discussed, their utilization is only motivated, and more elaborate modeling elements like attributes are not used.

Feature modeling has been utilized to represent functional characteristics and Quality of Service (QoS) attributes of Web services in electronic contracts [FdSGdT07]. A main motivation behind the approach is to foster structure and reuse of contractual clauses across multiple contracts. However, Quality of Service characteristics are only represented coarsely using features that represent QoS levels. No quantitative values, using for example attributes, are considered, thus limiting the approach's expressiveness.

Runtime customization of Web services with explicit modeling of the variability has also been addressed [NC10]. The authors propose to extend WSDL documents to depict interfaces of service variants. Variability points and corresponding variants, denoting for example the inclusion of further services to fulfill subtasks of the service delivery, are explicitly modeled in a feature model. In further work, the same authors focus on explicitly modeling variability of Web service compositions [NCH14]. They consider dependencies between variability in the composition and within the services used in the composition. Again, feature modeling is used to express variability. Additionally, a methodology for developing corresponding processes is presented. It uses an extended version of the Business Process and Model Notation 2.0. However, feature modeling's capabilities to model characteristics of features with attributes are not used.

Other approaches focus solely on variability resulting from selecting different services in a service orchestration [KSB+10]. Here, no variability is considered within individual services or with regard to the order of abstract tasks in the orchestration, but only with regard to selecting services to fulfill these abstract tasks. Thus, this approach is comparable to service feature modeling only in cases where features are used to represent services that collectively denote the overall modeled service.

Some authors motivate the need for handling variability in Web services primarily by their utilization in dynamic contexts, where variability is a precondition for reusing services [GA13]. The authors enumerate Web service specifics, which make dedicated variability handling necessary, including a dynamic execution environment, organizational issues, or the relevance of QoS. Different variability subjects in Web services are identified and shortly discussed. The outlined specifics of Web services correspond to those we identified for software services in general in section 2.1.2. The authors outline the handling of Web service variability with (feature-based) variability modeling approaches and extensions of typical Web service artifacts (WSDL or BPEL documents) with variation points and variants. However, no specifications on how to represent the identified variability subjects with feature models are made.

The application of feature modeling to model Web service variability has not yet made use of feature modeling's full potential. Some approaches focus solely on features and neglect attributes ([RF03, FdSGdT07]). Others lack specification of what the feature models should look like ([NC10, NCH14]). In contrast, service feature modeling makes use of recent advances in feature modeling like attributes and even extends its language with feature and attribute types, reflecting the important role quality attributes play for services [LK13]. We also propose concrete blueprints that indicate what service feature models for specific domains like IaaS should look like (cf. section 5.4.2) or integrate the approach to automatically derive feature structures (cf. section 5.3.2).

Modeling Cloud Service Variability

The utilization of variability modeling approaches for cloud services is motivated by the need to configure them. Software-as-a-Service (SaaS) frequently utilizes multi-tenancy so that tenant-specific configurations need to defined. Infrastructure-as-a-Service (IaaS) offers various configuration options when it comes to consuming virtual machines, for example with regard to geographical placement, machine size, or pricing [Bar13]. Variability modeling approaches can be used to represent the configuration options and provide the basis for configuration processes by the consumer.

Some authors assume a common reference architecture underlying Software as a Service (SaaS) applications [TÖ13]. The authors propose to capture design decisions regarding applications based on this architecture in a feature model. The structure of this model is correspondingly described. On a high level, features represent the layers of the SaaS reference architecture. Within each layer, features represent (alternative) components, for example "load balancer" or "firewall" in the "distribution layer". Each component can be decomposed into further features, representing sub-components, functionalities, or utilized methods.

Similarly, a collection of cloud service reference architectures represented as feature models has been published [GJNS13]. Considered reference architectures include those of public organizations (for example, the National Institute of Technology (NIST)), industry (for example, Amazon, Microsoft or IBM), and research. In the resulting models, features represent various concepts, including layers, functionalities and non-functionalities, technical properties, or software components. While this flexibility is in line with what features in service feature modeling can represent, a structure underlying the various models is missing. As a result, the models are not comparable to another and express different levels ob abstraction.

In the so far presented approaches, cloud architectures can be derived from the reference architectures by configuring the feature model. However, the result architecture is merely a basis for implementing a Cloud solution. In contrast, service feature modeling aims to model the variability of a concrete service, not its underlying architecture.

Other approaches focus on modeling the variability of individual Cloud services. It has been proposed to utilize feature modeling to support the deployment of applications on cloud services [QDH+12]. Feature models represent software components and technologies both of the application to be deployed and of potential cloud services (IaaS or PaaS). Cross-tree constraints between features of these models denote constraints on the selection of cloud service features for given selections of application features. For example, if a certain data-base type is selected for the application, only cloud services that provide this database type can be selected. Attributes are used to express concerns related to the software components or technologies. For example, "SSL" encryption addresses the concern for "security".

Other approaches aim to represent Software as a Service variants using feature models [MTW+12]. Here, SaaS applications are assumed to be composed of services that fulfill certain functionalities. In the feature model, each feature represents one of these services.

The outlined approaches, similar to the modeling subject of service feature modeling, model variability of concrete services. As in the utilization of feature modeling for Web services, attributes are not utilized in the approaches [TÖ13, GJNS13] or their usage is mentioned but not illustrated [QDH+12]. Some approaches do not prescribe how the feature models should be structured at all [QDH+12], while others prescribe incomparable structures with different levels of abstraction [GJNS13].

3.5.3. Other Approaches to Represent Service Variability

While feature-based variability modeling approaches denote the biggest group of related work on modeling service variability, other modeling approaches have also been suggested.

Orthogonal Variability Modeling (OVM) was created to explicitly model variability in software products [PuFvdL05]. The variability defined in orthogonal variability models can be related to any other software development models, such as feature models, use case models, or component models, thus providing an orthogonal view of variability across all software development artifacts. OVM has been applied to model variability of Web services to support their adaptation to different contexts [KD08]. Architectural and behavioral variation points are identified, addressing the service interface, the work flow underlying Web service-based systems, and the service level agreements. The decision to use OVM is not discussed. OVM is also used to model variability of Software as a Service applications to enable customization and deployment for multiple tenants [MMLP09]. The SaaS variability model differentiates between external variability, which is visible to service consumers (for example, the capability to send E-mails, availability) and internal variability, which is visible only to the provider (for example, the used database). Apart from this differentiation, no further constraints exist with regard to the structure of the variability model or how it is derived.

The **Configuration in Industrial Product Families Variability Modeling Framework (COVAMOF)** was developed to explicitly represent variability in software product families [SDNB04]. In contrast to feature modeling, COVAMOF allows for n-to-n dependencies between represented variants and to model relations between dependencies. COVAMOF has been applied to model the variability of Web service-based systems [SRS+10]. The approach uses an UML profile, which is compatible with COVAMOF, to represent architectural variability of Web service-based systems. Architectural variability includes replacing services with the same or with different interfaces, changing service parameters, changing the composition of services, and creating complex dependencies between them. A runtime management method allows for performing these changes while the service is deployed, resulting in adaptation of the service delivery.

Both, OVM and COVAMOF, in contrast to service feature modeling, do not support the notion of attributes, which we consider fundamental for services.

While OVM is motivated by separating variability modeling from other concerns, feature modeling can and is often used equally for the sole purpose of modeling variability [CGR+12]. Furthermore, feature modeling is much more used in practice [BRN+13] and denotes a much richer set of related work [CABA09]. We thus consider the choice to utilize feature modeling as a basis for our approach feasible.

Goal modeling approaches from the field requirements engineering (RE) are typically used in early software development activities [CA09]. They aim to capture relevant goals and support reasoning about goal achievement strategies [LKSL13]. Goal models capture objectives of diverse stakeholders for a system in design. Goals can be either functional (denoted as hard) or non-functional (denoted as soft / fuzzy). Functional goals have different levels of abstractions, allowing for decomposition by defining sub goals. Goal models also capture alternative ways on how to achieve goals, for example by specifying that sub goals are alternatives to one another. In some languages, corresponding variability points are explicitly modeled [YdPLLM08]. Between functional goals and soft goals, contribution links capture the impact of the functional goal on the soft goal. The extent of positive or negative impact on a soft goal can be expressed using values (for example, "++", "+", "-", and "- -"). Typical languages include *i**, which is designed to "[...] model and analyze stakeholder interests and how they might be addressed, or compromised, by various system-and-environment alternatives" [Yu97]. Similar to goal models, SFMs can be used in early service design activities. Attributes with boolean domains, denoting functional characteristics induced by features, are comparable to goals in goal modeling. Decompositions of attributes cannot be expressed as in goal modeling. Dependencies between attributes can be expressed only by defining dependencies between their containing features. Attributes representing non-functionalities are comparable to soft goals in goal modeling. In goal modeling, soft goals are only specified once and distribution links denote the extend of impact functionalities have on them. In contrast, in service feature modeling, multiple attributes of the same type can be defined whose overall value results from aggregation. This approach allows SFMs to express more fine-granularly how service variants perform with regard to soft goals. Another difference between the approaches is that configurations in service feature modeling relate to realizable service variants. Thus, no further integration between goal models that typically capture the problem domain and approaches that capture the solution domain (for example, software product line engineering approaches) is required, which is a common challenge in goal modeling [YdPLLM08, LKSL13].

As part of the WS-* stack, **Web service policies** are used to express conditions on an interaction between two Web service endpoints [Wor07]. Policies denote multiple alternatives, which are (potentially empty) sets of policy assertions. Each assertion represents a requirement, capability, or other property of a service's behavior. The existence of multiple alternatives implies a choice in requirements or capabilities expressed through assertions. Thus, policies denoting multiple alternatives model variability where alternatives correspond to different service variants. In contrast to feature modeling-based approaches, expressibility of WS policies is low. No dependencies between assertions can be expressed above them being contained in the same alternative. If assertions are contained within multiple alternatives, they must repeatedly be specified. Extensions of standardized WS policies have been proposed that focus on customization of Web services [LSZJ06]. Here, providers state customization options for Web services in customization policies. Using these policies, consumers select their desired customization, which leads to the deployment of a corresponding service variant. As in standard WS policies, the expressiveness of this approach is limited. Overall, some policy-related approaches include the notion of variability. However, the expressiveness of these approaches is, again, limited, lacking means to express XOR or OR relationships or more complex dependencies between variants. Each variant of how to use a service is represented by an alternative. With a rising number of variants, this representation mechanism results in increased workloads and is error-prone if changes are required that address multiple variants. Furthermore, variability is not modeled explicitly, but integrated with other modeling subjects. This makes the explicit handling of variability more difficult, for example when checking the validity of variants, which is especially important if the number of variants rises.

A common source of variability in the context of Web services is their **composition**. Composition approaches typically define an abstract process in which multiple Web services are invoked to collectively accomplish a task [ASR10]. The binding of Web services is performed for each invocation of this process, typically in reaction to a service request. The Web services to bind are then selected based on request-specific quality requirements, current availability of functionally matching services, and their recent fulfillment of desired qualities. Many approaches to deal with variability resulting from Web service composition do not model this variability. Rather, they denote algorithms that select Web services from a set of candidates considering Quality of Service goals (cf. [ASR10]). Or, modeling is understood as applying mixed integer linear programming or loops peeling [AP07]. Some approaches introduce variability into the definition of abstract work flows or compositions. It has been proposed to represent alternative compositions using variability modeling approaches [PBP06]. The resulting variability models can be used to communicate composition options to consumers. Selection of the services to fulfill the abstract tasks in the compositions, however, is not supported. The Business Process Execution Language (BPEL) is extended in VxBPEL to incorporate variability [KaSSA09]. VxBPEL allows modelers to specify variation points, variants, and realization relations by extending standard BPEL documents. While dependencies between variants can be expressed, the mix of variability with other concerns in the BPEL diagram delimits means for automatic processing. The utilization of service feature modeling to represent work flow variants (cf. 5.3) is similar to the here presented approaches. In contrast to VxBPEL, service feature modeling explicitly models variability, allowing its users to perform dedicated reasoning on the models and fostering separation of concerns. Service feature modeling can be used to represent work flow variants (cf. section 5.3), however, its main focus lies on representing the variability of a single service. Service feature modeling additionally can be used to represent variable concerns beyond work flows, allowing for a broader application of the approach.

Another method to model variability of Web services proposes to **extend common Web service artifacts** [CK07]. The authors identify four types of variability relevant for Web services, namely work flow variability, composition variability, interface variability, and logic variability. Variability concerning interfaces is represented by extending the Web Service Description Language (WSDL). These extensions enable different work flow variants, compositions, or interfaces to be used while a service is operating based on changing context. Variability is not explicitly modeled separately from other modeling subjects and no dependencies between variable objects in different artifacts can be expressed.

3.5.4. Collaborative Modeling

The creation of SFMs based on their coordinated composition as presented in section 3.4 is a means for expert collaboration in defining service variants. This related work section is an extension of the one presented in previous work [WSKT12].

The need for collaborative approaches for software engineering projects has been attested to their inherent cooperative nature [Whi07]. The authors characterize collaboration in software engineering to be frequently driven by engineering artifacts, for example models. This goes in line with collaboration enabled by composition of SFMs from services, where the SFM is the artifact driving collaboration. Collaboration methods are presented, addressing different activities throughout a service life-cycle. However, no approaches based on feature-modeling are presented even though feature modeling is named as a future area in which collaboration could beneficially be applied.

Regarding collaborative modeling, some approaches discuss the creation of models in the computer aided design (CAD) domain where several experts work together to derive a graphical model of a product. For instance, the authors of [BBB01] present an approach for collaborative editing of a central model maintained on a server, also addressing basic coordination problems, for example concurrency and synchronization. They do not consider a human coordinator or the creation of model parts by services. In contrast, we aim to allow a coordinator to split the model into parts to be delegated to responsible experts. We thus provide a coordination mechanism on an application level.

Several works address how multiple *feature models* can be combined. [ACLF10] proposes to compose feature models that address specific domains, aiming to better deal with rising complexity for large feature models, to foster the models' evolution, and to engage diverse stakeholders in modeling. In [BEGB11], a representation of feature models using description logics and a corresponding configuration method are presented to allow multiple experts to model and configure feature models. Graph transformations, based upon a catalog of merging rules, are utilized to support the automatic merging of feature models [SBRCT08]. However, the implied semantics of the presented merging rules to solve conflicts between two models do not account for special cases presented in our approach, for example continuously updated attribute values. All presented works focus on how to combine multiple models but do not address the coordinated creation of models or the integration of up-to-date values. Methodologies addressing the modeling of modular feature models are named as an intended future work. In contrast, we focus on the coordination of creating modular feature models collaboratively.

In software engineering, an approach to realize collaborative modeling with the unified modeling language (UML) has been presented [DLFST07]. It allows software engineers to decompose UML diagrams into fine-grained design model parts that can be modified by distributed participants. The approach has some similarities to our approach, for example, it hierarchically breaks down models into parts, it uses event-based notifications and coordination mechanisms to manage concurrent access and dependencies between model parts. In [ZKL+09] a model and tool are presented that enable software architects to collaboratively capture architectural decision alternatives and decision outcomes in a specialized Wiki. In the modeling phase, architects can define dependencies between decisions. Alternatives are used to ensure consistent and correct decision-making during the configuration phase. Despite some similarities, both presented approaches do not (yet) support delegation of modeling parts through a coordinator and do not enable the integration of content provided by software services into the models.

Flexible composition of services through end-users has been discussed in the mashups area [YBCD08]. Mashups allow end-users to easily compose and integrate (Web) services into artifacts. In addition, approaches for the integration of human-provided services into collaboration exist [STD08]. However, we are not aware of any approach that allows participants to create models through a mashup mechanism.

Overall, having analyzed related work in various research areas, we believe that our approach uniquely combines coordination and service-composition concepts to support the participation of various experts in defining variability models.

3.6. Discussion

Service feature modeling's language sets out to capture the variants for developing or delivering a service. Various approaches exist that equally aim to represent service variability (cf. section 3.5.3). Many of them, while addressing variability of services, mix statements about variability with other concerns (cf. [LSZJ06, CK07, KaSSA09]). This impedes a clear separation of concerns, making communication of variants and reasoning about them harder. Service feature modeling focuses on representing variability with the purpose of allowing modelers to design, communicate and reason about it. If required, artifacts addressing other concerns can be associated with SFMs (cf. section 5.3 and 5.4).

Given the dissemination of feature modeling, we consider it to be an ideal basis for service feature modeling as well (cf. section 3.5.1). Feature modeling has successfully been applied in various domains and provides a large base of related work. Using feature modeling to represent services, most notably Web and cloud services, has already been proposed (cf. section 3.5.2). However, we find that service feature modeling is different from these approaches in multiple regards.

The utilization of feature modeling approaches for services frequently focuses on specific aspects. For example, feature models are used to represent work flow or composition variants of Web services (cf. [PBP06, KaSSA09]) or architectures of cloud services (cf. [RA11, SMML12, GJNS13]). Narrowing down the variability subject under consideration has advantages: it allows us to define concrete mappings to artifacts of the solutions design, for example other models, source code, or configuration parameters. This enables the automatic creation, update, or validation of feature models based on these artifacts. Further, the realization of service variants profits from relationships between feature modeling elements (features, attributes etc.) and other design artifacts. With service feature modeling, however, we aim to provide more flexibility regarding the variability subject. We illustrate how service feature models can relate to other design elements like work flow variants (cf. section 5.3.3) or deployment configurations (cf. section 5.4.3). Not limiting service feature modeling to one of these contexts allows its broader application. This flexibility has already led classical feature modeling, where it is reflected by the generic definition of what a feature is, to be beneficially utilized in various contexts (cf. [BRN+13]). Service feature modeling should similarly be applied to represent variability of diverse subjects in the context of services, and add mappings to specific artifacts where needed.

In contrast to many of the presented approaches [RF03, FdSGdT07, NC10, NCH14, TÖ13, MTW+12], service feature modeling makes use of the notion of attributes from feature modeling. They allow to specify functional or non-functional characteristics that result from the inclusion of features in a service variant. Attributes play an important role for selection among service variants (cf. section 4) and should thus be considered. Different from all other feature modeling approaches, we introduce attribute types. Typing of attributes has been proposed in previous work, but only concerned the data type of an attribute's value [CHE05]. In contrast, attribute types in service feature modeling contain much richer information, including descriptions, scale orders, or measurement units. Attribute types reduce efforts in specifying similar attributes. They further specify aggregation rules. They allow to determine instantiation values for attributes describing configurations by aggregating the instantiation values of the attributes describing features in a configuration as motivated in challenge 1 in section 1.3.1. This novel approach enables the annotation of configurations with attributes, thus supporting the comparison between configurations in service feature modeling's usage methods (cf. chapter 4).

Service feature modeling further introduces feature types. In related work, a comparable typing of features has been proposed [CHE04]. Here, features are typed as concrete (being realized by individual components), aspectual (being realized by a number of components or modularized using aspect technologies), *abstract* (representing requirements mapped to component and or aspects), and *grouping* (representing variation points or having a pure organizational purpose). We find the semantics of this typing unclear, especially with regard to the double role played by grouping features. In contrast, we aim to make clear how service feature modeling's feature types relate to variability concepts like variability subject and variability object (cf. section 3.2.3). We also clearly separate solution-oriented semantics of features from problem-oriented attributes. Our introduction of feature types aims to increase the understandability of SFMs and the modeling process, guiding modelers on how to define features. Furthermore, feature types in service feature modeling support unambiguous (automatic) interpretation of SFMs, enabling for example requirements filtering for multiple SFMs (cf. section 4.5).

Our approach for composing SFMs from services (cf. section 3.4) is novel and unique. Enabling expert collaboration in service feature modeling, as motivated in challenge 3 in section 1.3.1, through composing SFMs from services is directly derived from the identified need for such mechanisms in service development (cf. section 1.2). Existing approaches addressing collaborative variability modeling outline how to combine, for example, feature models [ACLF10, BEGB11, SBRCT08]. The required methods for performing collaborative modeling, however, are either neglected or mentioned as future work. Other approaches address the methods for collaborative modeling, but focus on different types of models [BBB01, DLFST07, ZKL+09].

Another advantage of composing SFMs from services is the possibility to include attribute values provided by services as motivated in challenge 2 in section 1.3.1. A limitation of any feature modeling-based approach is how to deal with dynamic or complexly derived values. Here, composition from services enhances service feature modeling's capabilities to consider such values compared to standard feature modeling approaches.

4. Using Service Feature Models

In this chapter, we describe the intended usage of service feature models within software service engineering. We assume an SFMs as input that depict the variants of a service, either deployed or not. Within this chapter, to illustrate the usage methods, we rely on the SFM illustrated in figure 3.4, representing a financial data service motivated in section 1.1.2 and used throughout chapter 3. First, we outline the goals of using service feature modeling and the proposed usage process in section 4.1. Next, we discuss in detail the individual methods denoting the usage process: we start with the automatic determination of service variants from an SFM in section 4.2. We then discuss means for requirements filtering to reduce the set of variants to ones adhering to minimal consumer needs in section 4.3. We discuss our approach to rank remaining variants based on preferences in section 4.4. We show how the presented methods can be applied to select service variants from multiple SFMs in section 4.5. We discuss related approaches for variant selection in section 4.6. Finally, we summarize and discuss service feature modeling's usage in section 4.7.

4.1. Usage Process

In this section, we present the process of using SFMs. The process directly addresses the corresponding challenge 4 motivated in section 1.3.2. We outline the goals of the usage process in section 4.1.1. Usage methods are applied in two scenarios, either for variant selection during development or for variant selection for delivery. We further present an overview of the usage procedure in section 4.1.2. It encompasses the different usage methods and illustrates their recommended flow. Finally, we discuss the stakeholders involved in the usage process in section 4.1.3.

4.1.1. Goals of Usage

It can be argued that *intention* is a first-class property in the modeling process [MFBC10]. Correspondingly, service feature modeling's appeal and usefulness will only show in the usage of SFMs. The intention and thus goal of using

SFMs is to select one or a subset of the service variants it represents. Selecting service variants can have different purposes depending on the scenario it is performed in:

- **Variant selection for development** Variant selection for development is a design activity performed by the service provider. The goal is to determine a (subset of) service variant(s) from those represented in an SFM that should further be developed. In this sense, usage is similar to approaches in goal modeling that aim to support reasoning about goal achievement strategies [LKSL13]. Another way to look at this use of service feature models is the design-time approach of handling of variability in consumer requirements [NC10]: because requirements differ among consumers, suiting service variants to address a majority of them need to be provisioned. Or, usage in this context is comparable to the dealing with design spaces, which encompass a set of decisions to choose an artifact (service design variant) that best satisfies needs [Sha12]. In this usage scenario, potential for participation of future consumers arises. They can specify their needs and wishes while the provider develops the service. The provider can consider this input to develop (the) variant(s) that best satisfy consumers, leading eventually to higher profits.

- **Variant selection for delivery** On the other hand, variant selection for delivery is performed as a consumer design activity. The goal is to determine a service variant to deliver that best matches consumer needs. The assumption here is that a candidate service to consume denotes variants and that these variants can be realized in delivery. The realization of variants for in delivery can be achieved by providing one single customizable service (e.g., [NC10]) or by deploying individual service variants on-demand (e.g., [LNSJ12]).

The selection of service variants adheres to sub goals. A functional subgoal for the usage process is to provide consider consumer *requirements*. Requirements define what stakeholders like users, customers, suppliers, developers, or businesses want from a system [HJD11], in our case from service variants. If a variant does not fulfill requirements, its consumption is not feasible from the consumer point of view. Thus, requirements in the following denote necessary prerequisites for designing or consuming service variants. The usage process needs to provide means to 1) identify whether variants adhere to consumer requirements or not and 2) exclude variants not fulfilling requirements from further consideration. Another functional subgoal for the usage process is to incorporate consumer *preferences*. Preferences relate to desirable, but not inevitable characteristics of a service variant. The adherence to preferences is thus, in contrast to that of requirements, negotiable. Typically, multiple preferences denote trade-off relationships to another: if the adherence to one preferred characteristics is increased enough, certain dismissal of other preferred characteristics is acceptable in return. Another subgoal of the usage process is to provide the right amount of *structure*. Providing structure reduces the risk of dismissing relevant steps in service variant selection. On the other hand, too narrow structure can restrict benefits or applicability of the usage process. The process should thus offer structure to assist, while not restricting users. Finally, another subgoal for the selection process is automation. Given the required input (i.e., an SFM, requirements and preferences), the selection should be performed automatically and thus be repeatable. Automation increases the applicability of using SFMs for variant selection in scenarios where manual intervention cannot be guaranteed. For example, automation is necessary if selection needs to be performed unexpectedly, like in the case of a disaster. Performing selection again instead of just relying on previous selection results is necessary in light of eventually changed attributes composed into SFMs (cf. section 3.4).

4.1.2. Usage Overview

The usage process in service feature modeling consists of multiple steps, which are illustrated in figure 4.1.

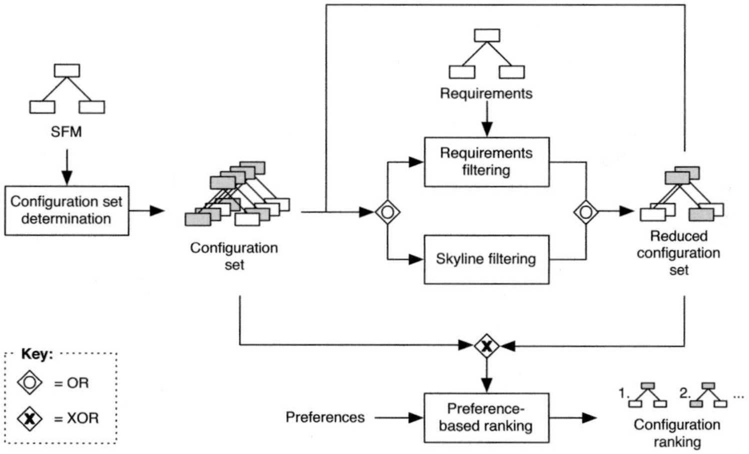

Figure 4.1.: Overview of the usage process of service feature models

Usage starts with an SFM, whose feature structure, cross-tree relationships, attribute types and attributes are defined. The SFM does not need to be completed - the usage process can also be performed on intermediary SFMs. The first step of the usage is the *configuration set determination*. It produces a set of all configurations valid according to the SFM. Depending on the size and structure of the model, this set can contain thousands of configurations. Configuration set determination can be repeated on-demand, for example in reaction to changes in the SFM. Having determined the configuration set, *requirements filtering* and / or *skyline filtering* can be applied. Requirements filtering, based on the notion of requirements as necessities, dismisses configurations that do not fulfill stated requirements from the configuration set. To perform this step, a priorly defined set of configurations and specified requirements are necessary input. Skyline filtering compares configurations based on their attributes and releases the configuration set of ones that are strictly dominated by others. Skyline filtering is especially relevant to reduce the problem size when performing preference-based ranking. Requirements and skyline filtering can be performed in combination or repeatedly, for example, in reaction to changes in requirements. *Preference-based ranking* produces a ranking of configurations based on provided preferences. Thus, as input it requires a set of configurations, either produced by the configuration set determination or a reduced one resulting from the skyline and / or requirements filtering, and stated preferences. Again, preference-based ranking can be performed repeatedly, for example in reaction to changes in preferences. The resulting configuration ranking has to be evaluated in light of the previously performed steps. If requirements filtering was performed, it denotes a ranking of feasible configurations only. Otherwise, it denotes a ranking of any configuration, feasible or not. The ranking can either be assessed manually by human actors, who consider it as a recommendation for the service variants to develop, deploy and operate from a provider's point of view or to consume from a consumer's point of view. Alternatively, the ranking can be automatically processed, selecting for example the highest ranked service variant for development or delivery.

Depending on the utilization in either provider or consumer design activities (cf. section 4.1.1), additional sub steps are required. To enable participation, SFM need to be transformed and transfered to make them available to participants in dedicated abstractions. We discuss the necessary steps as part of the participatory preference-based ranking approach in section 4.4.6. When usage addresses variant selection for delivery, SFMs stating realizable service variants need to be send from the provider to consumers. In reverse, selected variants need to be communicated from the consumer to the provider for realization.

4.1.3. Involved Stakeholders

The stakeholders involved in service feature modeling's usage process depend on the pursued goals (cf. section 4.1.1). When usage addresses variant selection during development, it is likely performed by the same stakeholders who modeled the SFM. Thus, typical users are service or software engineers (cf. section 3.3.1). Next to requiring background in modeling to be able to deal with SFMs, these stakeholders need to be capable and authorized to state requirements and preferences for variant selection, for example as representatives of the institution developing the service. In the case that SFMs are used for participatory development, stakeholders who are typically not involved in software service development also perform usage activities. These stakeholder include, for example, citizens in case of public services [HJR+10] or end users [SC04]. Given they may be non-technicians, dedicated abstractions from technical details are required to enable their involvement in the development process. When usage addresses variant selection for delivery, involved stakeholders are consumers or prospect consumers. If they interact directly with SFMs for variant selection, for example using skyline or requirements filtering, they require knowledge in modeling. Other required skills depend on the concerns modeled in an SFM based upon which variant selection is performed. The SFM may contain technical, business, legal, or other concerns, which require corresponding knowledge and decision-making powers. For example, a consumer's legal department may have to check the compatibility of terms of services represented by features with their own regulations.

In every case, stakeholders apply usage methods to select service variants, in other words, to decide among them. In the following, we thus refer to a stakeholder involved with the usage process as *decision-maker*.

4.2. Automatic Determination of Variants

The automatic determination of variants produces the set of all valid configurations for a given SFM. It consists of two steps: first, it transfers the SFM to a constraint satisfaction problem (CSP) and solves it as described in section 4.2.1. Second, it aggregates the attributes for each configuration, as described in section 4.2.2.

4.2.1. Mapping of SFMs to Constraint Satisfaction Problems

To automatically determine the configurations of an SFM, similar to standard feature models, it needs to be represented in a computer-understandable way. Various *formalization* approaches have been proposed for this purpose [BSRC10]. The most common approaches are to represent feature models as *constraint satisfaction problems (CSP)* [BTRC05], in terms of *propositional logic* [Bat05], or using *description logic* [WLS+05]. While the formalization using propositional logic builds upon binary variables only, the formalization as a CSP includes integer and interval ones [PLP11]. Propositional logic-based formalizations make use of *binary decision diagrams (BDD)* or *satisfiability solvers (SAT)* to perform analysis operations. One differentiator between these approaches is their expressiveness with regard to the supported analysis operations but also with regard to the specific feature model language, for example, cardinality-based, extended [BSRC10]. Another factor for using one approach over the other is the performance of corresponding solvers with regard to computational effort. Extensive studies have been performed to determine each approaches performance in different contexts, i.e., different model sizes, different analysis operations [PLP11]. The authors find that CSP solvers perform especially good for "small" model sizes, defined as having up to 100 configurations, and in scenarios where the solver is called frequently. Based on the good performance with small models and due to their capability to be extended to use integer and interval variables, we choose constraint satisfaction problems (CSP) as the formalization to use for service feature modeling.

SFM element	**CSP constraint**
Mandatory feature	P is a parent feature and C is a child feature in a *mandatory* relationship. Then: $C.sel \Leftrightarrow P.sel$
Optional feature	P is a parent feature and C is a child feature in a *mandatory* relationship. Then: $C.sel \Rightarrow P.sel$
OR constraint	P is a parent feature and $C_1, C_2 ... C_n$ are child features in a *OR* relationship. Then: $C_1.sel \lor C_2.sel \lor ... \lor C_n.sel \Leftrightarrow P.sel$
XOR constraint	P is a parent feature and $C_1, C_2 ... C_n$ are child features in a *XOR* relationship. Then: $(C_1.sel \Leftrightarrow (\neg C_2.sel \land ... \land \neg C_n.sel \land P.sel)) \land ... \land (C_n.sel \Leftrightarrow (\neg C_1.sel \land ... \land \neg C_n - 1.sel \land P.sel))$
Requires relationship	X and Y are features in a requires relationship $R^{requires}(X, Y)$. Then: $X.sel \Rightarrow Y.sel$
Excludes relationship	X and Y are features in an excludes relationship $R^{excludes}(X, Y)$. Then: $\neg(X.sel \land Y.sel)$

Table 4.1.: CSP constraints for SFM elements, based on [KOD10]

The mapping of an SFM to a CSP follows the rules defined in related work [KOD10]. The formalizations for decomposition and cross-tree relationships are outlined in section 3.2.1. Table 4.1 lists the corresponding constraints to be created in the CSP depending on the type of node traversed, based on [KOD10]. The notion *.sel* indicates that a feature is selected.

Our mapping algorithm is described in listing 1. It iterates a given SFM twice. In the first iteration, for every feature $f \in SFM$, a binary variable is created in an object CSP representing the constraint satisfaction problem. In addition, the mapping between every feature and the corresponding binary variable is stored in a map. In the second iteration, for every relationship r, depending on this relationship's type, constraints between the binary variables are created. The constraints adhere to our definitions in table 4.1. To create the constraints, the mapping between features and priorly created binary variables is conducted as to identify the correct variables in the constraint satisfaction problem. In the end, the completely modeled CSP object is returned.

Having mapped a SFM in this way to a CSP, it can be solved. Solving results in any possible (if existent) combination of setting all binary variables to true or false that adheres to all defined constraints. Each combination is a valid solution of the CSP and represents one valid configuration of the SFM. Empirical analyses of the performance of different CSP solvers applied to feature modeling have been presented in related work [PLP11].

Id	Selected instance features	WS-* specifications	Price/10k requests	Real time data	Quote history provided
c_1	SOAP	1	100.00	0	0
c_2	SOAP, inclusion of quote history	1	100.00	0	1
c_3	REST	0	80.00	0	0
c_4	REST, real time quote updates	0	120.00	1	0
c_5	REST, inclusion of quote history	0	80.00	0	1
c_6	REST, real time quote updates, inclusion of quite history	0	120.00	1	1

Table 4.2.: Configurations of example in figure 4.2

Table 4.2 lists all valid configurations from the example presented in image 3.4. Specifically, column two states the selected instance features for each configuration. The root feature "stock quotes API" and abstract feature "interface" are selected in every configuration. Abstract feature "data delivery options" is selected given that either "real time quote updates" or "inclusion of quote history" is also selected.

Algorithm 1 Mapping SFM to CSP

```
procedure MapSFMtoCSP(SFM)
    CSP ← ∅                ▷ variable to hold constraint satisfaction problem
    fv ← { }               ▷ map to store relationship between features and CSP variables
    for all Feature f ∈ SFM do
        x ← new BinaryVariable()
        fv.put(f, x)
        CSP.addVariable(x)
    for all Relationship r ∈ SFM do
        switch type(r) do
            case R^man
                CSP.addConstraint(fv.get(ter(r)).sel ⇔ fv.get(init(r)).sel)
            case R^opt
                CSP.addConstraint(fv.get(ter(r)).sel ⇒ fv.get(init(r)).sel)
            case R^OR
                cf ← ter(r)        ▷ array to store all child features of OR rel.
                CSP.addConstraint(
                    fv.get(cf[0]).sel ∨ ...∨
                    fv.get(cf[n]).sel ⇔ fv.get(init(r)).sel)
            case R^XOR
                cf ← ter(r)        ▷ array to store all child features of XOR rel.
                CSP.addConstraint(
                    (fv.get(cf[0]).sel ⇔
                    (¬fv.get(cf[1]).sel ∧ ...
                        ∧¬fv.get(cf[n]).sel ∧ fv.get(init(r)).sel))
                    ∧...∧
                    (fv.get(cf[n]).sel ⇔
                    (¬fv.get(cf[0]).sel ∧ ...
                        ∧¬fv.get(cf[n − 1]).sel ∧ fv.get(init(r)).sel))
            case R^requires
                CSP.addConstraint(fv.get(init(r)).sel ⇒ fv.get(ter(r)).sel)
            case R^excludes
                CSP.addConstraint(fv.get(init(r)).sel ∧ fv.get(ter(r)).sel)
    return CSP
```

4.2.2. Attribute Aggregation

Having determined an SFM's valid configurations, attributes are aggregated for each one. The service feature modeling language, as described in section 3.2.4, allows multiple attributes in an SFM to be associated with the same attribute type. The attribute type, among other things, defines the aggregation rule $AR(at)$ for attributes of that type at. Table 4.3 provides an overview of the available aggregation rules.

Name	Aggregation rule
Sum	If the aggregation rule $AR(at)$ of attribute type at equals `sum`, the overall aggregated attribute's instantiation value $iv(c,a)$ for configuration $c \in C$ is calculated as follows: $iv(c,a) = \sum i(a_k), \quad \forall a_k \in A$ such that $\exists ar_{a_k,f}, f \in c$
Product	If the aggregation rule $AR(at)$ of attribute type at equals `product`, the overall aggregated attribute's instantiation value $iv(c,a)$ for configuration $c \in C$ is calculated as follow: $iv(c,a) = \prod i(a_k), \quad \forall a_k \in A$ such that $\exists ar_{a_k,f}, f \in c$
Minimum	If the aggregation rule $AR(at)$ of attribute type at equals `minimum`, the overall aggregated attribute's instantiation value $iv(c,a)$ for configuration $c \in C$ is calculated as follows: $iv(c,a) = min(i(a_k)), \quad \forall a_k \in A$ such that $\exists ar_{a_k,f}, f \in c$
Maximum	If the aggregation rule $AR(at)$ of attribute type at equals `maximum`, the overall aggregated attribute's instantiation value $iv(c,a)$ for configuration $c \in C$ is calculated as follows: $iv(c,a) = max(i(a_k)), \quad \forall a_k \in A$ such that $\exists ar_{a_k,f}, f \in c$
At least once	If the aggregation rule $AR(at)$ of attribute type at equals `at least once`, the overall aggregated attribute's instantiation value $iv(c,a)$ for configuration $c \in C$ is calculated as follows: $iv(c,a) = \begin{cases} 1 & \text{, if } \exists a_k = 1 \text{ such that } \exists ar_{a_k,f}, f \in c \\ 0 & \text{, else.} \end{cases}$

Table 4.3.: Overview of aggregation rules

The aggregation of attributes is dependent on the provision of aggregation rules, which is a major capability that attribute types add to service feature modeling. Listing 2 illustrates the procedure. It takes as input an SFM whose configuration set C is already determined. Initially, a *values* map is created that contains additional maps for every attribute type. The SFM's attributes are iterated and for every one of them, the feature they describe and their instantiation value $iv(f,a)$ are stored in the map of the corresponding attribute type. The *values* data structure thus represents a matrix whose rows are the SFM's attribute types and whose columns are the features contained in the SFM. The entries of this matrix are the instantiation values (if existent) that the column's feature has regarding the row's attribute type. The purpose of creating the *values* data structure is to speed up look-ups for instantiation values, which would otherwise require expensive iterations of the SFM. In consequence, the SFM's configuration are iterated per attribute type. Depending on the aggregation rule and using the *values* data structure, each configuration's instantiation value $iv(c, a)$ is calculated and stored.

After attribute aggregation, every configuration denotes exactly one attribute of each type, whose instantiation value $iv(c, a)$ is the result of the aggregation for that attribute type: $\forall c \in C \wedge at \in AT \ : \ \exists! a, atr(a, at), iv(c, a)$.

In the example from figure 3.4, the aggregated attributes for each configuration are described in columns 3 to 6 in table 4.2. For example, configuration c_6 contains instance features "REST" with an instantiation value for "price / 10k requests" of 80.00 and "real time quote updates" with an instantiation value for "price / 10k requests" of 40.00. In result, based on the aggregation rule of "price / 10k requests" being "sum", these values are added up, resulting in an instantiation value of $iv(c_6, \text{price / 10k requests}) = 120.00$.

4.3. Requirements Filtering

Requirements filtering allows decision-makers to dismiss configurations from a configuration set that do not fulfill certain minimum requirements. To realize this mechanism, we present a way to state and represent requirements in section 4.3.1. We then discuss how such statements are applied to the configuration set of an SFM in section 4.3.2.

4.3.1. Stating Requirements

Requirements $req \in Req$ can be stated within an SFM as we propose in previous work [WKM12]. Requirements $Req^f \subseteq Req$ concern the existence of features in configurations. Alternatively, requirements $Req^a \subseteq Req$ concern the instantiation values of configurations' attributes. These are the only two types of requirement: $Req = Req^f \cup Req^a$. They do not overlap: $Req^f \cap Req^a = \emptyset$. The number of all requirements is denoted as $|Req|$ and the number of feature and attribute requirements is, correspondingly, denoted as $|Req^f|$ and $|Req^a|$.

Requirements for features $req^f \in Req^f$ are represented by marking the corresponding features as *required*. This information can, for example, be captured

Algorithm 2 Attribute aggregation

```
procedure AggregateAttributes(SFM)
    values ← { }
    for all at ∈ AT do
        values.put(at, {})                      ▷ put empty hashmap per attribute type
    for all a ∈ SFM do
        f ← atr(f, a)                           ▷ obtain the feature containing attribute a
        values.get(type(a)).put(f, iv(f, a))    ▷ store f's instantiation value in attribute a in values
    for all Configuration c ∈ C do
        for all AttributeType at ∈ AT do
            switch AR(at) do
                case sum
                    v ← 0.0
                    for all Feature f ∈ c do
                        v ← v + values.get(at).get(f)
                case product
                    v ← 0.0
                    for all Feature f ∈ c do
                        v ← v * values.get(at).get(f)
                case maximum
                    v ← Double.MIN_VALUE         ▷ start with smallest value
                    for all Feature f ∈ c do
                        if values.get(at).get(f) > v then
                            v ← values.get(at).get(f)
                case minimum
                    v ← Double.MAX_VALUE         ▷ start with largest value
                    for all Feature f ∈ c do
                        if values.get(at).get(f) < v then
                            v ← values.get(at).get(f)
                case atleastonce
                    v ← 0.0
                    for all Feature f ∈ c do
                        if values.get(at).get(f) = 1.0 then
                            v ← 1.0
                            break
            iv(c, a) ← v                         ▷ assign calculated instantiation value
```

in a boolean property added to each feature. The following statements are possible:

- **Requiring an instance feature** A requirement regarding an instance feature $req(f^I) \in Req^f$ states that the instance feature f^I is required. Thus, only configurations containing this feature fulfill this requirement. The value $v(req(f^I), c)$ of such a requirement regarding a configuration c is calculated as follows:

$$v(req(f^I), c) = \begin{cases} 1 & \text{, if } f^I \in c \\ 0 & \text{, else.} \end{cases} \tag{4.1}$$

  Thus, $v(req(f^I), c) = 1$ means that the requirement is fulfilled while $v(req(f^I), c) = 0$ means that the requirement is not fulfilled by configuration c. Using this approach, for example, optional features can be required so that only configurations remain that denote this feature. Or, a certain instance feature within an XOR or OR grouping decomposition can be set as required. For example, in the SFM from figure 3.4, the instance feature "SOAP" can be required.

- **Requiring an abstract feature** A requirement regarding an abstract feature $req(f^A) \in Req^f$ states that it must be instantiated (in any way). Thus, at least one child instance features of the required abstracted feature must be present in a configuration to fulfill this requirement. The value $v(req(f^A), c)$ of such a requirement regarding a configuration c is calculated as follows:

$$v(req(f^A), c) = \begin{cases} 1 & \text{, if } \exists r | init(r) = f^A \wedge ter(r) = f^I, r \in R^{de}, f^A, f^I \in c \\ 0 & \text{, else.} \end{cases} \tag{4.2}$$

  Again, $v(req(f^A), c) = 1$ means that the requirement is fulfilled while $v(req(f^A), c) = 0$ means that the requirement is not fulfilled by configuration c. For example, in the SFM from figure 3.4, the abstract feature "data delivery options" can be required. In consequence, either the "real time data updates" or "inclusion of quote history" need to be present in requirements-fulfilling configurations.

Requirements for attributes $req^a \in Req^a$ can be set by defining the valid instantiation values of an attribute. Requirements for attributes always relate to the instantiation values of the aggregated attributes in configurations. The requirements can be modeled, for example, within a property "required values" added to each attribute type[1]. The following statements are possible:

[1] Note: after aggregation, each configuration denotes only one attribute per attribute type, expressing the aggregated instantiation value. Thus, attribute types are a suited place to state requirements valid for all configurations of an SFM centrally.

- **Requiring a specific value** A requirement regarding a specific attribute value $req(a, x) \in Req^a$ states that the attribute must denote value x. Configurations fulfill this requirement only if their value for attribute a equals x. The value $v(req(a, x), c)$ of such a requirement regarding attribute a and configuration c is calculated as follows:

$$v(req(a,x),c) = \begin{cases} 1 & \text{, if } iv(c,a) = x \\ 0 & \text{, else.} \end{cases} \tag{4.3}$$

  For example, in the SFM from figure 3.4, "WS-* specifications" can be required to equal 1 (= true) to delimit configurations that do not denote this qualitative characteristic.

- **Requiring a threshold for an attribute value** A requirement regarding a threshold for an attribute value $req(a, \diamond, x) \in Req^a$ states that the attribute's instantiation value must lie within the range specified by the threshold. The value $v(req(a, \diamond, x), c)$ of such a requirement regarding attribute a and configuration c is calculated as follows:

$$v(req(a,\diamond,x),c) = \begin{cases} 1 & \text{, if } iv(c,a) \ \diamond \ x, \quad \diamond \in \{<, \leq, \geq, >\} \\ 0 & \text{, else.} \end{cases} \tag{4.4}$$

  If a threshold is required, configurations fulfill this requirement if they denote an instantiation value within the interval specified by this threshold. For example, in the SFM from figure 3.4, "price / 10k requests" can be required to be smaller than 100.00 to delimit configurations that are more expensive.

A requirement is further specified with a weight w_{req} that expresses its importance. Weights lie between $w_{req} = 0$, meaning that the requirement req does not matter to the decision-maker at all, and $w_{req} = 1$, meaning that the requirement req denotes a hard constraint. Weights in between 0 and 1 thus express a relative importance. Similar to requirements, weights can be represented in dedicated properties of features and attribute types.

4.3.2. Matching Requirements to Variants

To process configuration sets against stated requirements, we propose a matchmaking approach. Our approach performs goal-based matchmaking to determine solutions that satisfy specified constraints [Aga07], in this case the requirements specified as described in section 4.3.1. It works by assessing every configuration in a configuration set regarding the stated requirements. The idea behind our matchmaking method is to be *fuzzy*. In fuzzy sets, elements are assessed gradually to be member of a set, typically by use of a membership function valued in the real unit interval [0, 1] [PSD13]. Instead of just denoting binary whether a configuration fulfills all requirements stated in *Req* or not, we aim to express their *degree of fulfillment*. The degree of fulfillment results from summing up the *fulfillment gaps* that express to what extend an individual requirement $req \in Req$ is not met. The algorithmic procedure of the requirements matchmaking method to achieve this goal is described in listing 3.

Algorithm 3 Filtering requirements

```
procedure FilterRequirements(SFM, Req)
    degList                                      ▷ list of deg(c, Req) values
    for all Configuration c ∈ SFM do
        fv                              ▷ map of non-fulfilled feature requirements
        aMap                            ▷ map of non-fulfilled attribute requirements
        deg(c, Req) ← 0       ▷ degree deg(c, Req) to which c differs from reqs.
        for all FeatureRequirement req^f ∈ Req do
            calculate v(req^f)
            if v(req^f, c) = 1 then
                gap(req^f) ← 0
            else
                gap(req^f) ← 1
            fv.add(req^f, w_{req^f} * gap(req^f))
        for all AttributeRequirement req^a ∈ Req do
            calculate v(req^a)
            if v(req^a, c) = 1 then
                gap(req(a, o, x), iv(c, a)) ← 0
            else
                calculate gap(req(a, o, x), iv(c, a))
            aMap.add(req(a, o, x), w_{req^a} * gap(req(a, o, x), iv(c, a)))
        calculate deg(c, Req)                    ▷ uses aMap and fv as input
        degList.add(deg(c, Req))
```

For all requirements for features, the requirements filtering algorithm checks the current configuration for the existence of required features, resulting in $v(req^f, c)$ being 0 or 1. Using this value, we define the fulfillment gap for requirement req^f as follows:

$$gap(req^f) = 1 - v(req^f, c) \tag{4.5}$$

Thus, $gap(req^f) = 1$ if the requirement req^f is not met and $gap(req^f) = 0$ if it is met. The fulfillment gap of every feature requirement is stored in a map multiplied by the weight w_{req^f} for that requirement.

Similarly, for all requirements for attributes, the requirements filtering algorithm checks the current configuration for the value of attributes regarding which requirements were specified, resulting in $v(req^a, c)$ being 0 or 1. The fulfillment gap $gap(req(a, o, x), iv(c, a))$ to which the required value x is not met by the actual value $iv(c, a)$ of configuration c in attribute a is calculated as follows:

$$gap(req(a, o, x), iv(c, a)) = \begin{cases} 0 & \text{, if } v(req^a, c) = 1 \\ \frac{|x - iv(c,a)|}{x} & \text{, else.} \end{cases} \tag{4.6}$$

For example, a requirement states that the attribute value for "development cost" needs to be equal or smaller than 800, so that $req(\text{"}developmentcost'', <, 800)$. A configuration has "development cost" of "700". In this case, because the requirement is met, the fulfillment gap is 0. Another configuration has "development cost" of "1000". In this case, the fulfillment gap equals $|(800 - 1000)|/800 = 0.25$. The fulfillment gap of every attribute requirement is stored in a map multiplied by the weight w_{req^a} for that requirement.

Having assessed every feature and attribute requirement for a configuration, the overall degree of fulfillment $deg(c, Req)$ is calculated and stored. The calculation of the degree of fulfillment uses *simple additive weighting (SAW)* [YH95]. In SAW, an evaluation score is calculated as a weighted average for each alternative. The evaluation score results from multiplying an alternative's value for a criteria with the weights of relative importance directly assigned by decision-maker to that criteria. The products are in consequence summed up. For every configuration c, the degree of fulfillment $deg(c, Req)$ results from summing up the fulfillment gaps for required features or attributes, multiplied by their weights. The resulting value is normalized by dividing it with the number of requirements. Subtracting this value from 1, one obtains the degree of fulfillment:

$$\begin{aligned} deg(c, Req) = \sigma\Bigg(1 - \frac{1}{|Req|}\Bigg[& \sum_{req^f \in Req^f} gap(req^f) * w_{req^f} \\ & + \sum_{req^a \in Req^a} gap(req^a, iv(c, a)) * w_{req^a}\Bigg]\Bigg) \end{aligned} \tag{4.7}$$

The factor σ denotes whether there exists a requirement req that is not fulfilled but that is weighted to be mandatory to the decision-maker, so that $w_{req} = 1.0$. If that is the case, the overall degree of fulfillment is set to 0.

$$\sigma = \begin{cases} 0 & \text{, if } \exists req \in Req : \ v(req, c) = 0 \ \wedge \ w_{req} = 1.0 \\ 1 & \text{, else.} \end{cases} \tag{4.8}$$

Factor σ acts as a safety mechanism to avoid consideration of infeasible configurations.

An advantage of our fuzzy approach is to avoid cases in which no configurations fulfill requirements. When no configuration fulfills all requirements, strict (or in terms of fuzzy logic *crisp* [PSD13]) matchmaking approaches produce no result. In contrast, fuzzy matchmaking reveals which configuration come closest to fulfilling requirements. Furthermore, decision-makers can be presented with the requirements that were not fulfilled (using fv and $aMap$ from listing 3), allowing them to revise and eventually lighten them. The decision-maker can also define a threshold for the degree of fulfillment stating until what point a configuration is still relevant enough to further consider it.

In the SFM from figure 3.4, consider requirements Req exist for abstract feature "data delivery options" to be realized, so that $req_1 := req($"data delivery options"$) \in Req$ with a weight of $w_{req_1} = 0.9$. A second requirement states that attribute "price / 10k requests" needs to be smaller than or equal to 60.00, so that $req_2 := req($"price / 10k requests"$, \leq, 60.00) \in Req$ with a weight of $w_{req_2} = 0.5$. For configuration c_3, the degree of fulfillment calculated with equation 4.7 results in $deg(c_3, Req) = 1 * \left(1 - \frac{1}{2}\left[1 * 0.9 + (|60.00 - 80.00|/60.00) * 0.5\right]\right) = 0.467$. For configuration c_5, the degree of fulfillment calculated with equation 4.7 results in $deg(c_5, Req) = 1 * \left(1 - \frac{1}{2}\left[0 * 0.9 + (|60 - 80|/60) * 0.5\right]\right) = 0.917$. This example illustrates that, while both configurations do not completely fulfill the stated requirements, c_5 does come much closer in doing so, because it fulfills the highly weighted requirement for a "data delivery options".

4.4. Preference-Based Ranking of Variants

Requirements filtering allows decision-makers to delimit configurations that do not meet what is needed. However, there may remain multiple configurations that all fulfill requirements and among which still a selection needs to be made. We aim to make use of the comparability of configurations that results from their annotation with attributes (cf. section 3.2.1). Given that each configuration is characterized by one attribute for every defined attribute type, *multi-criteria decision making (MCDM)* approaches can be applied. In them, multiple *decision alternatives* are compared and assessed in the presence of multiple, usually conflicting *criteria* or *objectives* [RZ13]. When applying MCDM approaches to service feature modeling, an SFM's configurations $c_1 ... c_n$ are the MCDM problem's decision alternatives, denoting the *problem space* $D := C = \{c_1, ..., c_n\}$. On the other hand, the SFM's attribute types $at_1 ... at_m$ are the MCDM problem's conflicting objectives or criteria, denoting the *solution space* $O := AT = \{at_1, ..., at_m\}$. Every decision alternative has a value regarding each criteria, which in service feature modeling is the instantiation value $iv(c, a)$ of configuration c regarding attribute a of type at_j (cf. section 3.2.4). As in any MCDM method, we aim to apply a mapping of the decision space to the solution space that allows for the assessment of every alternative regarding the value of every objective [RZ13]. For preference-based ranking of configurations, we use the *analytical hierarchy process (AHP)* [Saa90]. It is heavily researched [WDF+08] and frequently used in practice [VK06].

4.4.1. Ranking Overview

An overview of the preference-based ranking process's three steps is illustrated in figure 4.2.

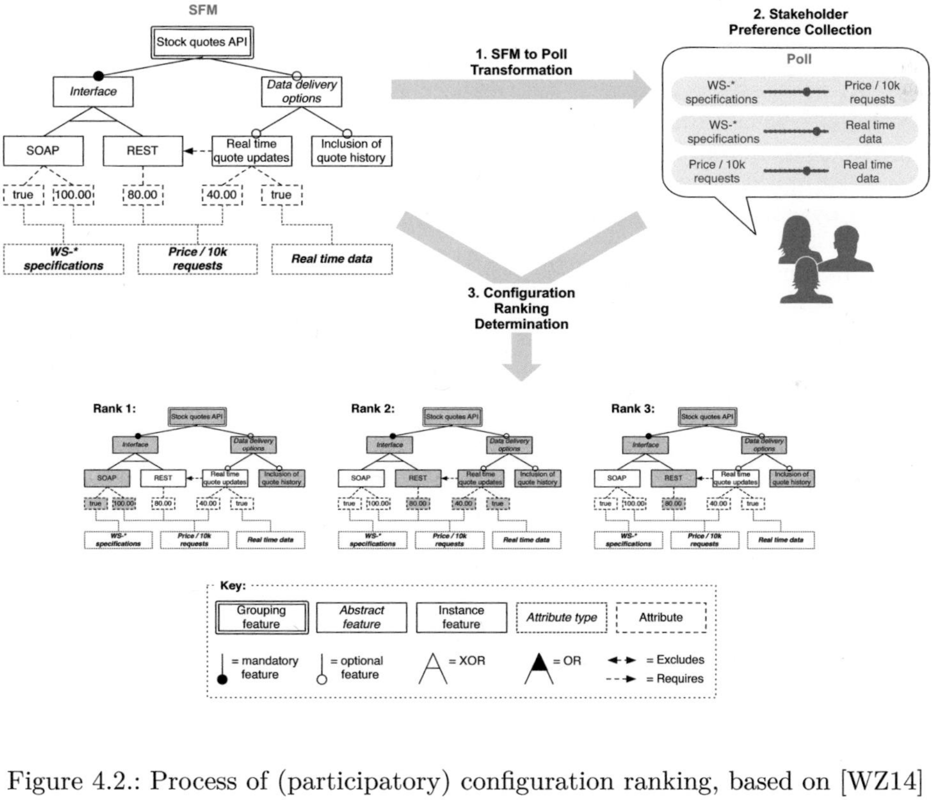

Figure 4.2.: Process of (participatory) configuration ranking, based on [WZ14]

The input for the method is a an SFM, including feature decompositions, cross-tree relationships, attribute types, and attributes. To derive decision alternatives from this SFM, its configuration set must have been determined. The configuration set may already have been released of configurations that do not fulfill requirements (cf. figure 4.1). To reduce the number of decision alternatives to consider in preference-based ranking, skyline filtering can be applied. It dismisses configurations that are dominated by others and can thus not achieve a high ranking in preference-based ranking. The first step of preference-based ranking is to transform the SFM into a *poll*. A poll consists of pairwise comparisons of the attribute types defined in the SFM. Polls thus provide an interface for preference-statement regarding an SFM. Using the poll, decision-makers state their preferences for the SFM's attribute types using the pairwise comparisons. Interaction with polls can be realized outside of SFM modeling tools, bearing potential to make polls accessible to non-experts and thus using them as a vehicle to enable participation (cf. section 4.4.6). Preferences stated by multiple stakeholders can be aggregated to obtain an insight into majority preferences. Using collected preferences, a ranking is determined reflecting how much the decision-maker(s) prefer the the attribute types relative to another. Similarly, rankings of configurations expressing their fulfillment of each attribute type are created. By combining these rankings, the relative fulfillment of the decision-maker's preferences for attribute types by configurations is determined. The higher the rank of a configuration, the better it meets the decision-maker's preferences as compared to all other configurations. The highest ranked configuration(s) can be selected for service development or delivery.

The following subsections outline the involved steps in detail. The content of the following subsections includes material currently under review [WZ14].

4.4.2. Skyline Filtering

Skyline filtering aims to reduce the number of alternatives to consider in preference-based ranking. It is based on the concepts of *dominance* [RZ13], which can be applied to service feature modeling in the following way: a configuration c_i dominates another configuration c_j if the following conditions both hold:

- Every instantiation value of c_i is equal or larger than the corresponding instantiation value of of c_j for all attribute types whose scale order is "higher is better" or "existence is better". Formally: $iv(c_i, a) \geq iv(c_j, a)$, $\forall a : \exists atr(a, at), scaleOrder(at) =$ "higher is better" $\vee$ $scaleOrder(at) =$ "existence is better".
- Every instantiation value of c_i is equal or smaller than the corresponding instantiation value of of c_j for all attribute types whose scale order is "lower

is better". Formally: $iv(c_i, a) \leq iv(c_j, a),\ \forall a : \exists atr(a, at), scaleOrder(at) =$ "lower is better".

We denote the dominance of configuration c_i over configuration c_j as $c_i \succ c_j$. If c_i is strictly larger/smaller (and not equal) in every instantiation value, the dominance is referred to as *strong*, otherwise it is referred to as *weak*. A decision alternative that is not dominated by any other decision alternative belongs to the *skyline* of the problem space D [SM09].

The most basic approach to determine the skyline, also referred to as basic loop [BKS01], is to perform complete enumeration by comparing each decision alternative against every other one with regard to every decision objective. To improve performance, *presorting* can be performed [CGGL03]. The assumption behind presorting is that decision alternatives with a high sum of normalized objective values are likely to dominate others, while decision alternatives with a low sum are likely to be dominated. Sorting based on the sums allows skyline filters to more easily dismiss dominated decision alternatives. Further approaches presort based on the number of objectives, in which decision alternatives dominate others [SM09]. Skyline filtering approaches apart from the basic loop one include block-nested loop (BNL) algorithms, divide and conquer algorithms, or binary tree algorithms [BKS01].

Algorithm 4 Block-nested loop skyline filtering for service feature modeling

procedure SKYLINEFILTERING(C) ▷ C is the list of configurations
    $window \leftarrow \emptyset$ ▷ window of objects not *yet* dominated
    for all $p \in C$ **do** ▷ go through all configurations, denoted as p
        $window$.add(p)
        for all $q \in window \setminus \{p\}$ **do**
            if $p \prec q$ **then**
                $window$.remove(p)
                break
            else if $p \succ q$ **then**
                $window$.remove(q)
    return $window$

We utilize a modified version of the BNL algorithm for service feature modeling as illustrated in listing 4. The algorithm works by defining a *window*, which stores not yet dominated configurations. Every additional configuration from the original configuration list is compared with the ones already in the window. If the new configuration is dominated by one from the window, the former is dismissed and comparison continues with the next configuration. If the new configuration dominates one from the window, the latter is dismissed and the comparison continues with remaining configurations in the window. If neither configuration dominates the other, both are kept in the window. In contrast to typical BNL algorithms, our algorithm refrains from writing results temporarily to disk [BKS01] because we assume memory of today's computers to be able to handle the required dataset sizes. The algorithm reveals the advantage of presorting: if configurations that are likely to dominate others are added early to the window, additional configurations from the original configuration list are likely to be dominated and dismissed early on. This reduces necessary comparisons.

The advantage of selecting skyline configurations is to reduce the problem size for subsequent preference-based ranking, which leads to two advantages: first, a reduced problem size results in more expressive results. In the configuration rankings determined in preference-based ranking, every configuration is ranked as compared to all other configurations. If the number of configurations is high, ranking values are likely to be similar. Additionally, the decision-maker has to assess a large number of ranking values. Second, reducing the number of decision alternatives has positive impact on the performance of preference-based ranking implementations, as our performance evaluation shows, presented in section 5.2.

Applying skyline filtering to the configurations of the example SFM presented in figure 3.4 (cf. table 4.2), 3 configurations are dominated: c_1 is dominated by c_2, which realizes "quote history provided" while having equal instantiation values for all other attributes. Additionally, c_5 dominates c_3 because the former has "quote history provided" information while having equal instantiation values for all other attributes. Finally, c_6 dominates c_4, again, based on the provision of quote history. Overall, skyline filtering emphasizes that providing quote history is beneficial in any case because the feature realizing this characteristic does not induce any negative impacts on the resulting service variant.

4.4.3. SFM to Poll Transformation

Taking as input an SFM whose configuration set is determined and potentially reduced through requirements and/or skyline filtering, the preference-based ranking requires a poll for stakeholders to state their preferences regarding the capabilities of the configurations. The idea of a poll is to enable stakeholders to rank criteria (= attribute types) based on their preferences, thus enabling to rank decision alternatives (= configurations) high that perform well with regard to important criteria. As proposed in the analytical hierarchy process (AHP), our polls make use of *pairwise comparisons* to order attribute types [Saa90]. Thus, for poll creation, each attribute type is opposed to every other attribute. We define the set of attribute types to consider in pairwise comparisons as:

$$AT^{eval} = \{at_1, ..., at_n\} \tag{4.9}$$

where at_i represents an individual attribute type to be evaluated. A poll considers only those $|AT^{eval}|$ attribute types of an SFM whose *to be evaluated* property is set to *true* (cf. section 3.2.4). The order of the pairwise comparisons is random. The resulting number K of pair-wise comparisons is:

$$K = \frac{|AT^{eval}| * (|AT^{eval}| - 1)}{2} \tag{4.10}$$

Being able to exclude attribute types from an evaluation using the *to be evaluated* property is useful considering that high numbers of comparisons likely discourage stakeholders from stating their preferences thoroughly.

In the example SFM presented in figure 3.4, only the 3 attribute types "WS-* specifications", "price / 10k requests", and "real time data" are considered in preference-based ranking. The *to be evaluated* property of "quote history provided" is set to "false", because the inclusion of quote history is without negative impacts, as already identified in the skyline filtering (cf. section 4.4.2). A poll of the selected attribute types results in the 3 comparisons "WS-* specifications" vs. "price / 10k requests", "WS-* specifications" vs. "real time data", and "price / 10k requests" vs. "real time data".

4.4.4. Stakeholder Preferences Collection

We use the *fundamental scale of absolute values* for stakeholders to compare their preference among attribute types [Saa08]. For each pairwise comparison of attribute type at_i and at_j ($at_i, at_j \in AT^{eval}$), a stakeholder's preference for one of the attribute types is expressed in terms of the *intensity of importance* $I(at_i, at_j)$. Values range from 1, meaning that attribute types a_i and a_j are considered equally important, to 9, meaning that attribute type at_i is considered extremely more important than attribute type at_j. A precise definition of the meaning of different values, following related work [Saa08], is given in table 4.4. Reciprocal values indicate reverse importance. A common validation of collected preferences is to evaluate their consistency. In a consistent preference statement, transitivity between statements holds. The typical approach to ensure consistency is to calculate and evaluate the consistency index (CI) [Saa13].

In the case that preferences of multiple stakeholders are of interest, an aggregation of their individual preferences is required. To do so, the *geometric mean* of the all stated intensity of importance values can be determined:

$I(at_i, at_j)$	**Definition**
-9	at_j is considered extremely more important than at_i
-7	at_j is considered very strongly more important than at_i
-5	at_j is considered strongly more important than at_i
-3	at_j is considered slightly more important than at_i
1	at_j and at_i are considered equally important
3	at_i is considered slightly more important than at_j
5	at_i is considered strongly more important than at_j
7	at_i is considered very strongly more important than at_j
9	at_i is considered extremely more important than at_j

Table 4.4.: Meaning of intensity of importance values, following the scale of absolute values [Saa08]

$$\overline{I(at_i, at_j)} = \left(\prod_{l=1}^{L} I(at_i, at_j)_l \right)^{\frac{1}{L}} \tag{4.11}$$

where $\overline{I(at_i, at_j)}$ is the resulting mean intensity of importance value for comparing attribute types at_i and at_j, $I(at_i, at_j)_i$ is a single intensity of importance value for stakeholder l, and L is the number of stakeholders.

In the example SFM illustrated in figure 3.4, sample intensity of importance values of a stakeholder who considers "WS-* specifications" to be very important, are:

I("WS-* specifications", "price / 10k requests") $= 5$,

I("WS-* specifications", "real time data") $= 3$,

I("price / 10k requests", "real time data") $= 3$.

4.4.5. Configuration Ranking Determination

The determination of the configuration ranking consists of three sub-steps. First, the *attribute type priority vector* w_{AT} is determined. It represents the order of attribute types by stating how much stakeholders value each attribute type if compared to all other attribute types. Because the attribute type priority vector is derived from the stakeholders' stated preferences, it needs to be recalculated each time a stakeholder submits new preferences. Second, *configuration comparison ranking vectors* are determined. They state how configurations perform compared to each other with regard to each attribute type. These vectors need only to be calculated once because they depend on the modeled configurations and not on the stated preferences. Third, the previously calculated vectors are aggregated to determine the configuration ranking based on the stakeholders' preferences. The following subsections present details on the three steps.

Determination of attribute type priority vector

To determine a ranking for the attribute types based on the received preference values, the following K by K matrix of pairwise comparisons is determined from the intensity of importance values that a stakeholder provides in a vote. K denotes the number of collected intensity of importance values:

$$MPC = \begin{pmatrix} 1 & \cdots & w_{1,j} & \cdots & w_{1,|AT|} \\ \vdots & \ddots & & \ddots & \vdots \\ \frac{1}{w_{1,j}} & & 1 & & w_{i,|AT|} \\ \vdots & \ddots & 1 & \ddots & \vdots \\ \frac{1}{w_{1,|AT|}} & \cdots & \frac{1}{w_{i,|AT|}} & \cdots & 1 \end{pmatrix} \tag{4.12}$$

where:

$$w_{i,j} = \begin{cases} I(at_i, at_j) & if \quad I(at_i, at_j) \geq 0 \\ \frac{1}{-I(at_i, at_j)} & if \quad I(at_i, at_j) < 0 \end{cases} \tag{4.13}$$

Matrix MPC has positive values everywhere and is reciprocal. Thus, for every entry $a_{i,j}$ the following is true: $a_{i,j} = \frac{1}{a_{j,i}}$. The principal eigenvector of matrix MPC corresponds to a priority vector that ranks the importance of each attribute type for the stakeholder [SH98]. The principal eigenvector can be calculated by first squaring the matrix MPC. For the squared matrix the rows are summed to result in an eigenvector whose elements are normalized to sum up to 1.0 by dividing them by the rows total. Starting with the squared matrix this process is repeated iteratively until the difference between the latest calculated eigenvector and the priorly calculated one is ϵ (= sufficiently close to 0).

In the example SFM illustrated in figure 3.4, and based on the sample intensity of importance values given in section 4.4.4, matrix MPC is:

$$MPC = \begin{array}{r} \\ \text{WS-* spec.} \\ \text{price/10k reqs.} \\ \text{real time data} \end{array} \begin{array}{c} \begin{array}{ccc} \text{WS-* spec.} & \text{price/10k reqs.} & \text{real time data} \end{array} \\ \begin{pmatrix} 1 & 5 & 3 \\ 1/5 & 1 & 3 \\ 1/3 & 1/3 & 1 \end{pmatrix} \end{array} \tag{4.14}$$

Calculating the normalized principal eigenvector w_{AT} of matrix MPC results in:

$$w_{AT} = \{\text{“WS-* spec.”} : 0.651, \text{“price/10k reqs.”} : 0.223, \text{“real time data”} : 0.127\} \tag{4.15}$$

Determination of configuration comparison ranking vectors

Next, for every attribute type at_i, a configuration comparison ranking vector w_{at_i} is determined based on a matrix $MPC(at_i)$ of pairwise comparisons for every attribute type. In matrix $MPC(at_i)$, the instantiation value of every configuration $c_l \in C$ as compared to another configuration $c_k \in C$ is captured for attribute type at_i. In the case of a continuous attribute type at_i (defined in the corresponding attribute type's domain property, see section 3.2.4) this matrix is obtained as follows:

$$MPC(at_i) = \begin{pmatrix} 1 & \cdots & v_{1,k} & \cdots & v_{1,|C|} \\ \vdots & \ddots & & \ddots & \vdots \\ \frac{1}{v_{1,k}} & & 1 & & v_{l,|C|} \\ \vdots & \ddots & 1 & \ddots & \vdots \\ \frac{1}{v_{1,|C|}} & \cdots & \frac{1}{v_{l,|C|}} & \cdots & 1 \end{pmatrix}, \text{ if domain}(at_i) \text{ is continuous} \tag{4.16}$$

where $v_{c_l,k}$ is a result of relating the instantiation values $iv(c_l, a)$ and $Iv(c_k, a)$ of configuration c_l and c_k with regard to attribute a of type $type(a) = at_i$ in the following way:

$$v_{l,k} = \begin{cases} \frac{iv(c_l,a)}{iv(c_k,a)} & \text{, if scaleOrder(type}(a)) = \text{“higher is better”} \\ \frac{iv(c_k,a)}{iv(c_l,a)} & \text{, if scaleOrder(type}(a)) = \text{“lower is better”} \end{cases} \tag{4.17}$$

In the above case, configurations can easily be related because of the comparability of attribute with numerical domain, for example “cost” or “throughput”. In the case of an attribute type with boolean domain, matrix $MPC(a_i)$ is obtained as follows:

$$MPC(at_i) = \begin{pmatrix} 1 & \cdots & v_{1,k} & \cdots & v_{1,|C|} \\ \vdots & \ddots & & \ddots & \vdots \\ \frac{1}{v_{1,k}} & & 1 & & v_{l,|C|} \\ \vdots & \ddots & 1 & \ddots & \vdots \\ \frac{1}{v_{1,|C|}} & \cdots & \frac{1}{v_{l,|C|}} & \cdots & 1 \end{pmatrix} \text{, if domain}(at_i) \text{ is boolean} \quad (4.18)$$

where $v_{l,k}$ depends on the instantiation values $iv(c_l, a)$ and $iv(c_k, a)$ of configuration c_l and c_k with regard to attribute a of type $type(a)$ and $cp(a)$ is the custom attribute type priority (see section 3.2.4) that defines how much better a service configuration is if $iv(c, a) = 1$ compared to a configuration where $iv(c, a) = 0$:

$$v_{l,k} = \begin{cases} 1 & \text{, if } iv(c_l, a) = iv(c_k, a) \\ cp(a_i) & \text{, if } iv(c_l, a) = 1 \wedge iv(c_k, a) = 0 \\ \frac{1}{cp(a_i)} & \text{, if } iv(c_l, a) = 0 \wedge iv(c_k, a) = 1 \end{cases} \quad (4.19)$$

For every attribute type, the priority vector for the configurations can be determined using the eigenvector method. As mentioned earlier, the determination of configuration comparison ranking vectors needs only to be performed once within a preference-based ranking process, even if attribute type ranking vectors are determined multiple times based on repeated statement of preferences by one or multiple decision-makers.

In the example SFM illustrated in figure 3.4, in the following, we only consider the skyline configurations c_2, c_5, and c_6 (cf. section 4.4.2). The matrix MPC("WS-* specifications"), given a custom attribute type priority for "WS-* specifications" is 3, is:

$$MPC(\text{“platform ind.”}) = \begin{matrix} & c_2 & c_5 & c_6 \\ c_2 & 1 & 3 & 3 \\ c_5 & 1/3 & 1 & 1 \\ c_6 & 1/3 & 1 & 1 \end{matrix} \quad (4.20)$$

Calculating the normalized principal eigenvector $w_{\text{WS-* specifications}}$ of matrix MPC("WS-* specifications") results in: $w_{\text{WS-* specifications}} = \{c_2 : 0.6,\ \ c_5 : 0.2,\ \ c_6 : 0.2\}$.

The matrix MPC("price/10k") is (consider: the domain of "price / 10k requests" is *lower is better*):

$$MPC(\text{"price/10k"}) = \begin{array}{c} \\ c_2 \\ c_5 \\ c_6 \end{array} \begin{array}{c} \begin{array}{ccc} c_2 & c_5 & c_6 \end{array} \\ \begin{pmatrix} 1 & 80/100 = 0.8 & 120/100 = 1.2 \\ 100/80 = 1.25 & 1 & 120/80 = 1.5 \\ 100/120 = 0.833 & 80/120 = 0.667 & 1 \end{pmatrix} \end{array} \tag{4.21}$$

Calculating the normalized principal eigenvector $w_{\text{price / 10k requests}}$ of matrix MPC("price / 10k requests") results in: $w_{\text{price / 10k requests}} = \{c_2 : 0.324, \quad c_5 : 0.405, \quad c_6 : 0.270\}$.

Finally, the matrix MPC("real time data"), given a custom attribute type priority for "real time data" is 5, is:

$$MPC(\text{"location-based inf."}) = \begin{array}{c} \\ c_2 \\ c_4 \\ c_6 \end{array} \begin{array}{c} \begin{array}{ccc} c_2 & c_5 & c_6 \end{array} \\ \begin{pmatrix} 1 & 1 & 1/5 \\ 1 & 1 & 1/5 \\ 5 & 5 & 1 \end{pmatrix} \end{array} \tag{4.22}$$

Calculating the normalized principal eigenvector $w_{\text{real time data}}$ of matrix MPC ("real time data") results in: $w_{\text{real time data}} = \{c_2 : 0.143, \quad c_5 : 0.143, \quad c_6 : 0.714\}$.

Calculation of overall configuration ranking

After calculating one attribute type priority vector and $|AT|$ configuration comparison ranking vectors for the attribute types, these vectors can be combined to determine the configuration ranking for the stated preferences. The ranking of a single configuration is calculated by summing up its ranking values from all configuration comparison ranking vectors, weighted by the corresponding attribute type priority within the respective vector. The rankings of all configurations sum up to 1. The configuration with the highest value relatively best matches the stakeholder preferences with regard to the attribute types in focus.

In the example SFM illustrated in figure 3.4, the ranking of c_2 for the exemplary preferences from section 4.4.4 results in $c_2 = 0.651 * 0.6 + 0.223 * 0.324 + 0.127 * 0.143 = 0.481$. The ranking of c_5 results in $c_5 = 0.651 * 0.2 + 0.223 * 0.405 + 0.127 * 0.143 = 0.238$. The ranking of c_6 results in $c_6 = 0.651 * 0.2 + 0.223 * 0.270 + 0.127 * 0.714 = 0.281$. As a result, configuration c_2 is most preferred compared to the other configurations. The result is driven by the high importance of "WS-* specifications" stated in the preferences, which is only addressed by configuration c_2.

4.4.6. Participatory Ranking

Preference-based ranking provides means for *participation* in selecting variants, addressing challenge 6 motivated in section 1.3.2. We understand participation as "[...] a set of behaviours or activities performed by users in the system development process" [BH89, page 53][2]. As this definition suggests, participation concerns the usage of SFMs for service development (cf. section 4.1). The goal of participatory preference-based ranking is to allow users to rank configurations based on their preferences. The ranking information drives the subsequent design, implementation, deployment, and operation of highly preferred service variants.

Advantages of user participation in early stages of service design have been proposed in related work [Mag03]. They include integration of more original ideas with greater value for the users. These ideas can be used directly to impact service design, they help to better understand user needs, and they provide inspiration for the experts concerned with designing the service. Participation in service design is additionally argued to increase the fit between service offer and consumer needs [SMDK11]. While user participation in service design leads to original, highly valued solutions, the realizability of participatory designs is simultaneously found to be lower than if services are designed by experts only [Mag03]. The here presented participatory preference-based ranking, rather than collecting novel ideas, focuses on receiving input from users on service variants that are actually realizable. It can be combined with other approaches that enable more open participation (cf. section 5.3.1).

In this section, we present how preference-based ranking is used to enable participation in service development. As described in the previous section, the concept of polls allows users to state their preferences regarding the characteristics of services variants, represented as attribute types. Polls thus abstract from concerns about a service's design, implementation, deployment, or operation, which are represented by features. Thus, polls enable also non-technical or non-experts to state their preferences. We introduce the concepts required for participatory preference-based ranking. We furthermore discuss the life-cycle of an evaluation, which is the main artifact of participatory ranking.

Concepts of Service Design Alternative Ranking

Participatory ranking incorporates different elements as illustrated in figure 4.3.

[2]We follow the authors' suggestion to differentiate participation from involvement, which is "[...] a subjective psychological state reflecting the importance and personal relevance of a system to the user" [BH89, page 53].

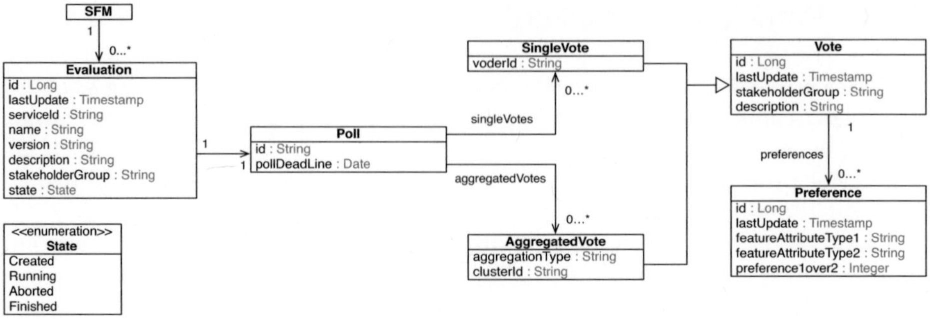

Figure 4.3.: Meta model of service feature modeling's participatory ranking concepts

An *evaluation* is the main artifact of the ranking approach. Semantically, an evaluation reflects the assessment of the service variants modeled in an SFM regarding one stakeholder group, for example consumers. Thus, an evaluation is associated with a single SFM and encompasses all further artifacts used throughout one ranking process. An evaluation is described by a set of properties, including its name, description, the stakeholder group it addresses or its current state. Details about the state of an evaluation are provided in section 4.4.6. An evaluation is associated to a single *poll*, which provides the interface for stakeholder participation. A poll is created from the SFM associated to the evaluation SFM as explained in section 4.4.3. The reason for separating the evaluation from the poll is that both can exist in and be controlled by different components (cf. section 5.1.3). A *vote* is a set of preferences regarding the importance of attribute types stated in a poll. A *single vote* is associated with a single stakeholder, whereas an *aggregated vote* results from the combination of multiple single votes. Aggregated votes, for example, reflect the preferences of all individual stakeholders belonging to a stakeholder group. Details about the collection of votes and their aggregation are presented in section 4.4.4. A *preference* is a statement made by a stakeholder about how much he values one attribute type if compared to another attribute type. Preferences thus reflect intensity of importance values. The set of preferences for all pairwise comparisons for one SFM's attribute types is combined in a vote.

Evaluation Lifecycle

An evaluation is created at the beginning of the participatory ranking process and typically ends with the decision-maker retrieving the evaluation results after the corresponding poll has completed. The existence of data objects representing evaluations is implementation-dependent. To control validity of the interactions that stakeholders can perform with an evaluation's poll, evaluations denote the four states *created*, *running*, *aborted*, and *finished*. The states and the transitions between them are illustrated in figure 4.4.

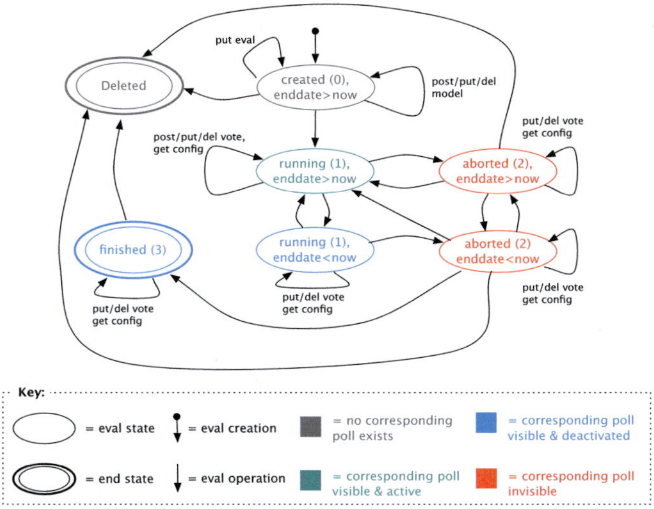

Figure 4.4.: States of an evaluation

After an evaluation has been created, its properties can be updated or an SFM corresponding to the evaluation can be created, updated or deleted without impacting the state. In addition, the evaluation can be deleted. During all these actions, no poll is created. By setting an evaluation's state to running, a poll corresponding to the evaluation is created and published, for example on an interaction platform (cf. section 5.1.3). This poll remains visible and active (meaning that stakeholders can state their preferences) as long as the evaluation is kept in state running. The poll becomes deactivated, meaning that stakeholders can no longer submit new votes but still view existing ones, if the end date specified in the evaluation's properties is reached. To reactivate an evaluation's poll, a new, future end date can be provided, thus extending the evaluation. While the evaluation is running, configuration rankings can be retrieved without changing the visibility or accessibility of the corresponding poll. If an evaluation's state is changed from running to aborted, the corresponding poll becomes invisible on the interaction platform. If the end date passes, an aborted evaluation can be reactivated by providing a new, future end date. In the aborted state, votes can be updated, retrieved, this is important to retrieve the latest aggregated vote, and deleted. However, no new votes can be created.

Configuration rankings can still be retrieved. To make a completed poll visible, its evaluation's state can be set to finished, thus allowing stakeholders to use it as illustrative material for future evaluations or to continue discussing the service variants. In the finished state, similar to the aborted state, votes can be updated or deleted and configuration rankings can be retrieved. The finished state is an end state that cannot be left without deleting the evaluation.

Overall, the presented concepts and lifecycle provide the basis for participatory ranking. An exemplary implementation of these concepts, defining for example how to present stakeholders with polls or how to retrieve evaluation results, is presented in section 5.1.3.

4.5. Usage with Multiple SFMs

The selection of service variants by consumers for delivery can be based not only on a single variable service, but also on multiple ones. In this case, the selection of a variant corresponds to two decision: 1) the selection of the variable service among a set of candidates and 2) the selection of a variant of the service selected in 1). To enable such selection with service feature modeling, multiple SFMs are required, each representing the variants of one candidate service.

A problem for using multiple SFMs is that they need to be comparable as motivated in challenge 5 in section 1.3.2. In section 3.3.3, we describe how comparability across SFMs is achieved by basing them on the same domain model. As a result, all derived models denote the same structure of grouping and abstract features as well as attribute types. The similarity of feature structure and names in SFMs based on the same domain model enables filtering regarding features requirements R^f across these SFMs. In this case, the requirements filtering procedure shown in listing 3 takes as input a combined list of all SFMs' configurations instead of a single ones. Abstract features are named and placed equally across SFMs based on the same domain model, making this approach feasible. On the other hand, instance features in multiple SFMs can follow different naming conventions, despite a shared domain model. Here, problems from semantically equal but syntactically different instance features may result. For example, the fulfillment of an instance feature requirement req("Encryption") by a configuration c may mistakingly be considered false, because c only contains a feature "encryption mechanism", which does not match syntactically. To avoid such pitfalls, vocabularies across SFMs can be prescribed, semantic technologies can be applied to detect synonyms, or implementations can promote naming conventions, for example through auto-completion mechanisms. The similarity of attribute types in SFMs based on the same domain model enables filtering regarding attribute requirements R^a across these SFMs. Again, the requirements filtering procedure needs to be provided with a combined list of configurations from multiple SFMs. The instantiation values for attributes are comparable across SFMs because they relate to the same attribute types specified in the domain model. For the same reason, skyline filtering and preference-based ranking can be performed across SFMs, given they as well receive a combined configuration list as input.

Ultimately, using domain models as basis and thus ensuring comparability, service feature modeling's usage methods can be applied to multiple SFMs at the same time.

4.6. Related Work on Variant Selection

In this section, we present work related to service feature modeling's usage methods. In standard feature modeling, multiple approaches have been presented for configuration, meaning in this context the selection of features. This part of related work is characterized by the similarity to service feature modeling's usage methods. We discuss feature modeling configuration approaches in section 4.6.1. In addition, we select related work based on similar intention. We consider approaches for selecting variants during service development in section 4.6.2. This related work includes requirements engineering approaches as well as service development methodologies. We also discuss selecting variants for service delivery in section 4.6.3, focusing on selection in service variability approaches. Finally, we present related work with regard to service selection in section 4.6.4.

4.6.1. Feature Model Configuration

The determination of a configuration is a common and well researched task in feature modeling. In software product line engineering, configuration is performed as an initial step in *application engineering*, which is about selection and reuse of the reusable artifacts to create a product [SD07]. The application of feature model configuration methods for services, thus, is best suited for variant selection during development. The here presented discussion of related work is based on and extends previous contributions [WZ14].

A widespread approach to determine a feature model configuration is *staged configuration* [CHE04]. It proposes step-wise specialization of a feature model by representing each specialized stage in a separate feature model. Specialization is performed by selecting features, which eventually causes further selections due to cross-tree relationships. One goal of staged configuration is to enable different decision-makers to participate in different stages of the configuration process.

Methods to support staged configuration through automated reasoning, for example utilizing constraint satisfaction problems, have been presented [WDSB09]. Staged configuration does not depend on determining the configuration set but rather derives a single configuration from a feature model. Our usage methods differ because they are not based on directly selecting features. Rather, the requirements and preferences of the decision-maker in conjunction with features and attributes in configurations drive selection. Service feature modeling's ranking approach selects features based on preferences for their characteristics, represented by attributes. This abstraction enables to hide complexity from the decision-maker who focuses solely on characteristics, thus also enabling less experienced or non-technical decision-makers to participate in the ranking process. Furthermore, we allow multiple decision-makers to perform configuration and to aggregate their preferences as described in section 4.4.4 to obtain an overall ranking of configurations.

Another approach for feature model configuration is *optimization* [BTRC05, TRC09]. In optimization a configuration is chosen that optimizes a given objective function, for example, minimizes cost or maximizes throughput. For optimization to be applicable, numeric characteristics about features or configurations needs be stored in a feature model. In consequence, optimization approaches address extended feature models that include attributes [BSRC10]. In this work we present some of the concepts also required for optimization, for example the aggregation of attributes and the specification of an objective function which we perform by means of pairwise comparison of attribute types to derive ranking vectors as discussed in section 4.4.5.

Multi-criteria decision making approaches have been proposed for feature model configuration [BAGS10]. Fuzzy linguistic variables are attached to features to state their impact on business concerns (for example, "security") being, for example, "high", "medium" or "low". Using *stratified analytical hierarchy process*, first, business objectives are ranked via pairwise comparisons and second, features are ranked with regard to their impact on the business concerns, again via pairwise comparisons. To reduce the number of pairwise comparisons, the second step only considers highly ranked business concerns. Similar to attributes in our approach business concerns abstract characteristics from features. The impact of features on these concerns is expressed linguistically. In contrast, we allow attributes to express capabilities quantitatively using numeric values and qualitatively using Boolean values. Doing so allows decision-makers to efficiently compare configurations against each other without additional pairwise comparisons of configurations and thus also without having to dismiss concerns. Building on staged configuration, the same authors present a semi-automatic configuration method [BNGR12]. Features are, again, annotated with their impact on concerns. Based on stakeholders' hard constraints, annotated feature models are configured, reducing variability. Configuration options remaining are then assessed in light of soft constraints, where the proposed method recommends a final feature selection, which can be revised by the decision-maker if desired. The authors motivate the problems of multiple experts aiming to select different, contradicting features (for example, selecting ones that exclude each other) and how to select features that maximize intended and minimizes unintended consequences. In service feature modeling's selection methods, the validity of configurations to consider is ensured by the automatic configuration set determination and selection of configurations best meeting requirements and preferences is ensured.

It has been proposed to allow stakeholders to collaboratively configure feature models [MC10]. The challenge here is to handle decision conflicts, which appear if locally valid configuration decisions are invalid globally. For example, configuring a branch of a feature model that has cross-tree relationships to another branch, which is configured by another stakeholder, can cause such conflicts. The proposed *collaborative product configuration* aims to avoid conflicts by planning the configuration process with work flows. The specified work flow avoids conflicts resulting from concurrent decisions by different stakeholders. Building upon a work flow definition, however, decreases flexibility in the configuration process. For example, already performed configurations of parts of the feature model might need to be revised in consequence of configurations in other parts. In service feature modeling, requirements can be stated as properties within an SFM (cf. section 4.3.1), allowing decision-makers to define requirements using service feature modeling's collaborative modeling approach presented in section 3.4. Service feature modeling's preference ranking allows for aggregation of different stakeholder preferences, resulting in an overall configuration ranking. However, we do not support the collaborative configuration where each stakeholder addresses only parts of an SFM.

4.6.2. Variant Selection in Service Development

The selection of software service variants during development is performed in **requirements engineering (RE)**. RE addresses the development of software under consideration of stakeholder requirements and preferences. RE, stemming from the systems engineering domain, is the process of identifying, analyzing, documenting, and checking the requirements (in the sense of capacities) and constraints for systems [Som11, page 101]. Requirements encompass needs and wishes of stakeholders on the one hand and detailed descriptions of a system's functionality on the other hand [HJD11]. RE is typically performed as an early activity in software development. The tasks of RE can be classified as elicitation, modeling, analysis, validation and verification, and management [CA09].

Elicitation is concerned with discovering the goals and motives behind the creation of a software system and identifying requirements that must be fulfilled to achieve these goals. Elicitation approaches aim to identify relevant stakeholders [SFG99] and support them in precisely and accurately stating their requirements, using, for example, use cases [Coc01] or specifying the intentions behind systems [Lev00]. Modeling aims to specify elicitated requirements more formally. While modeling techniques can also be used in elicitation, the modeling task focuses more at precision and completeness. For example, i* allows modelers to capture the domain of a system in terms of its stakeholders, their objectives and relationships, resulting in current processes that motivate the need for new systems [Yu97]. Analysis approaches (automatically) assess requirements with regard to trade-offs, conflicts, variability, ambiguity, completeness, or risks. Approaches aim, for example, to reveal potential interdependencies between requirements [CSL+01]. Validation aims to ensure at the more informal level that modeled / specified requirements reflect actual stakeholder needs. Verification aims to check that a developed system meets priorly stated requirements, using for example model checking approaches [CAB+98]. Finally, management is concerned with the evolution of requirements, their application to products of the same family, or dealing with very large numbers of requirements.

Within requirements engineering, multiple approaches address the selection of variants. The specification of software in requirements engineering has been described in a basic systems engineering process [Lev00]. It starts with the identification of objectives and criteria, based upon which alternative designs are generated. These alternative designs are then evaluated against objectives and criteria, resulting in the selection of one alternative to implement. While no specifics on how to perform the selection are provided, the process underlines the central role that alternative selection plays in requirements engineering. Goal-oriented analysis concerns the exploration and evaluation of system design alternatives regarding goals, for example, business or technical objectives [MCL+01]. The basis for goal-oriented analysis are goal models, in which functional goals and non-functional goals (softgoals) are decomposed into alternatives. For example, the non-functional requirements (NFR) framework allows modelers to capture and decompose non-functional requirements and to define design alternatives to meet them [CPL09]. Goals can be interrelated and the trade-offs between them can be made explicit. The positive or negative impact of alternatives on non-functional goals is expressed qualitatively, using "-" or "+" symbols (cf. section 3.5.3). In these approaches, the evaluation and subsequent selection of alternatives is informally described and is a manual process. Manual selection can become infeasible in light of large numbers of alternatives and delimits repeated variant selection for delivery. Other approaches propose to quantify the impact of alternatives on goals by numerical weights. They support selection of alternatives by assessing how they satisfy goals based on weighted average of the degree of satisfaction of subgoals [Rob90]. In more recent quantitative goal models, partial degrees of goal satisfaction are stated and the quantitative impact of alternatives on high-level goals can be derived [LVL04]. Selection support is based on computing objective functions of higher level goals for each alternative by bottom-up propagation of probabilistic distribution of non-functionalities. Similar ideas influenced service feature modeling's requirements filtering method that quantitatively measures the degree to which requirements with different weights are met by a service variant. Other techniques for selection from requirements engineering are, for example, feedback techniques to collect and elicit positive and negative statements about early system representations using models, animations, simulations, or storyboards [CA09].

The application of requirements engineering approaches, in general, for software service development is hindered by differences as compared to software products [LYM09, QP10, BELK10, BI10]. For example, means for selecting services, the notion of services being black-boxes from consumers' point of view, or the important role of quality attributes need to be addressed by dedicated approaches [FMÁ+10]. The requirements of providers, that deploy and operate services, need to be considered in addition to those of consumers [BELK10]. Or, for cloud services, RE approaches require a higher degree of automation and need to be remotely applicable [TSG13]. Considering the selection of variants, the manual effort required in requirements engineering approaches hinders their application for delivery in many scenarios. The manual utilization of more complex methods can be feasible only if the intended consumption of a service is long lasting.

Multiple **service development methodologies** consider the definition and selection of variants. The service-oriented design and development methodology defines a life-cycle model with different phases [PVDH06]. In the analysis and design phase, multiple business processes are defined. The methodology proposes to perform business case analysis to select the business process to implement. However, no specifics about the selection process are given. In the model for designing generic services, the modeling of design variants is motivated by faster derivation of service solutions from variants [DHJ09]. Again, no specifics about the variant selection process are provided. The design methodology for real services considers variability to be a key factor for service design methodologies [MNDF+10]. Variants address the different goals and preferences of stakeholders and are expressed in alternative control flows. The methodology mentions the expression of preferences in terms of soft goals to reason about and ultimately select variants as future work. It has been proposed to model and reason about Software as a Service reference architectures to faster derive new application architectures [TÖD11]. Feature modeling is used to represent the reference architecture. The derivation of an application feature model, and thus the selection of a architecture variant, is based on feature selection. The specifics of how to perform feature selection are not presented. In sum, we find that service development methodologies promote the definition of variants. However, we also find that they lack in supporting variant selection with concrete methods. Service feature modeling's selection process and methods address this gap.

4.6.3. Variant Selection in Service Delivery

In related work, service variability approaches address the realization of matching service delivery to stakeholder needs. Two fundamental approaches can be differentiated for dealing with varying consumer requirements [NC10]: in *design-time* approaches, multiple instances of the same service are deployed, each addressing a specific consumer's needs. For example, in Web services, customization options can be specified in customization policies [LSZJ06]. After the consumer customizes the Web service based on this policies, a corresponding service implementation is derived and deployed for consumption. Or, cloud services are redeployed in configurations that best match user experiences with regard to latency [KZZL11]. In *runtime-approaches*, service instances can be adapted to meet requirements and preferences. For example, in multi-tenancy cloud services, only one service instance is deployed that serves multiple consumers, each having a tenant-specific configuration [BKNT11, MMLP09, RA11]. Other approaches realize variability through exchanging the implementation of Web services at runtime [IFMW08]. Compositions of Web services can be formed based on requirements for Quality of Service [ASR10]. Or, the work flows underlying a service can be enhanced with configuration options [GVDAJVLR08, HBR10].

One challenge that service variability approaches need to address is how to select variants for delivery. Service variability approaches that make use of feature modeling frequently propose simple feature selection to derive variants, for example [LNSJ12, RA11]. The usage of optimization techniques has been proposed for selecting feature-based configurations of Infrastructure as a Service that minimize energy consumption [DWS12]. Overall, we notice a gap in service variability approaches with regard to the resolution of variability, i.e., variant selection. If variability modeling approaches are used, selection is frequently not addressed at all (cf. [RF03]), mentioned as a necessary step without providing details on how to perform it (cf. [NCH11]), or only discussed vaguely, stating for example that features need to be selected (cf. [NC10, SM10]).

4.6.4. Service Selection

Service selection is a field similar to service variant selection for delivery. Consumers perform service selection to chose a service that best matches their requirements and preferences from a set of candidates. Selection approaches assume candidate services as given input, being, for example, based on the same functionality. Service selection approaches are relevant related work because they apply methods comparable to those used in service feature modeling and because usage of multiple SFMs (cf. section 4.5) allows decision-makers to select service variants from different services.

In Web services, **matchmaking** is performed to select services for delivery by matching consumer requirements with service capabilities [WTM+04, LSZJ06]. Matchmaking approaches aim to apply a sorting to multiple service contracts, for example expressed as policies, regarding requested contractual terms [CPPP14]. Several approaches focus on Quality of Service (QoS) aspects expressed in numeric values. For example, a framework has been proposed that matches policies consisting only of generic as well as domain specific quality criteria against user requirements [LNZ04]. Similar to scale orders in service feature modeling's attribute types, the impact of rising values being positive or negative can be considered. Also similar to service feature modeling's requirements filtering, the fulfillment of requirements is not only binary but graded. Or, the QoS-based selection problem can be mapped to smaller sub-problems, which can be heuristically solved to increase performance [ARDN09]. Extending the so-far presented approaches, semantic technologies are used to correctly deal with differing vocabulary and data models [CPPP14]. However, these approaches take as input a single QoS vector for every service. In service feature modeling, different variants of a service are ranked and variants of multiple services can be considered given their SFMs are comparable (cf. section 4.5). Qualities of variants, expressed in SFMs using attributes, are furthermore aggregated from feature characteristics (cf. section 4.2.2), allowing modelers to model their origin fine-granularly. Overall, policies are typically designed to be used by computers and thus expressed in XML, making them difficult to utilize for human users. No means are presented that support humans in expressing their needs, which requires a higher level of abstraction. Service feature modeling's preference-based ranking, in contrast, abstracts from technical details and bases variant selection on characteristics represented by attributes.

Cloud service selection approaches typically make use of multi-criteria decision making methods. Cloud service selection can be formulated as a multi-criteria decision making problem [RHH11]. Cloud services are defined as alternatives, which are assessed regarding multiple criteria. Selection is based on requirements, stating thresholds on criteria if they are measurable, and weights, stating the importance of criteria. One proposed selection method compares cloud services regarding cost and gains, for example response time, traffic volume, or storage price [ZZZ09]. The approach uses simple additive weighting (SAW) to either minimize cost or maximize one gain. In other approaches, SAW is used to assess service candidates based on weights provided for criteria by the decision-maker [SP11]. Or, the analytical hierarchy process is utilized to support decision-makers in ranking criteria and consequently service candidates [GM09, GVB13]. Other cloud service selection frameworks combine multi-criteria decision making approaches with prior requirements filtering [MST11]. The filtering, however, considers requirements only to be mandatory constraints and excludes alternatives immediately given they do not fulfill a requirement. In contrast, service feature modeling's requirements filter allows decision-makers to define the importance of requirements and calculates a degree of fulfillment, allowing for more differentiated assessment of requirements. A comparison of cloud service providers based on monitored performance and cost has also been proposed [LYKZ10]. The authors propose various performance metrics, depending on the type of cloud service, and describe how to measure them. While no structured means are presented to select a service based on the measured criteria, the approach is relevant because it describes how attribute values can be obtained that can be integrated into SFMs through composition (cf. section 3.4). A methodology for cloud service selection that considers QoS history has been proposed [RHH13]. The underlying assumption is that qualities of cloud services change over time, weakening the validity of selection decisions that only consider qualities at a single point in time. Multi-criteria decision making approaches are used to rank service candidates based on decision-makers' preferences at different time periods. These approaches use parallel algorithms to increase performance. In the end, results for all periods are aggregated to obtain an insight into the long-term fulfillment of the consumer's preferences. The application of the outlined approaches to cloud service selection, most notably in the case of IaaS, can be explained by the difference in consumption as compared to Web services. While Web services, enabled by their uniform interface abstractions, can be re-selected or exchanged for each request, cloud service utilization is typically longer lasting. Exchanging infrastructure services causes considerable migration efforts, for example regarding re-deployment or data transfer [MR12]. The resulting consumption longevity makes the application of rather complex multi-criteria decision making approaches feasible. A hurdle of many multi-criteria decision making approaches is the required manual effort for performing pairwise comparisons. Approaches that purely based on such methods thus denote limitations with regard to the number of criteria that can be assessed with feasible effort. Service feature modeling's usage approach addresses this shortcoming by combining a set of methods. The problem size can be reduced using weighted requirements and skyline filtering before preference-based ranking, using as well pairwise comparisons, is applied.

4.7. Discussion

Service feature modeling's usage methods aim to support the selection of service variants, represented as configurations in an SFM. The methods can flexibly be combined in a usage process (cf. section 4.1.2), addressing challenge 4 motivated in section 1.3.2.

The automatic determination of configurations translates an SFM into a constraint satisfaction problem. Solving this problem produces the set of all valid feature combinations, or configurations, representing service variants. Constraint satisfaction problems are commonly used for feature models [BRN^{+}13] and our translation builds upon established rules [KOD10]. The subsequent attribute aggregation is based upon the aggregation rules defined in attribute types (cf. section 3.2.4). Denoting configurations with comparable characteristics that result from attribute aggregation is prerequisite for their subsequent selection. A drawback from determining all possible configurations upfront and then narrowing them down are large problem sizes if many configurations exist. To address this problem, skyline and requirements filtering aim to reduce configuration sets.

Service feature modeling's requirements filtering dismisses configurations that do not meet the decision-makers needs. While requirements filtering in related work is frequently understood binary (cf. [MST11, WTM^{+}04]), our method calculates a degree to which requirements are fulfilled. The degree allows decision-makers to be more flexible with regard to dismissing configurations, which is especially relevant if no configuration can completely fulfill requirements. Here, our method reveals configurations that come closest to meeting requirements, allowing to consider the revision of requirements. The requirements filter emphasizes the advantage of feature types in the service feature modeling language. Requiring an abstract feature means that any of its child instance features needs to be selected to fulfill this requirement. We are not aware of approaches to state such requirements based on the standard feature modeling language.

In skyline filtering, configurations that are dominated by others are dismissed from the configuration set. Dominance is based on the comparable characteristics of configurations determined in attribute aggregation. It has to be noted, though, that skyline filtering should be used with attention because it can dismiss configurations based on their attributes despite these configurations being desirable based on the features they contain.

While requirements filtering dismisses inadequate configurations, preference-based ranking orders configurations depending on how well they fulfill preferences. The multi-criteria decision making method it uses considers configurations' attributes as decision criteria. The preference collection is based on polls derived from SFMs, abstracting from their technicalities. Thus, preference-based ranking is an ideal candidate for including consumer preferences into variant selection, enabling participation in service development as motivated in challenge 6 in section 1.3.2. We support this approach with a set of concepts that drive participatory preference-based ranking. We furthermore present a method to aggregate preferences stated by multiple stakeholders (see section 4.4.4).

Enabled by the differentiation of feature types (cf. section 3.2.2), usage methods can be applied to multiple SFMs, given they are based on the same domain model. This capability paves the way to use service feature modeling for service selection and to compare variants across services as motivated in challenge 5 in section 1.3.2.

Comparing service feature modeling's usage methods and the complete usage process against related work, we find the following: some related approaches for feature-based variant selection focus on requirements (cf. [CHE04]) while others only consider preferences (cf. [BAGS10]). In contrast, service feature modeling's usage methods are combinable to address requirements and skyline filtering as well as preference-based ranking (cf. section 4.1). One of the most cited feature model configuration approaches, staged configuration, is a manual process that requires repeated input by the decision-maker [CHE04]. In contrast, service feature modeling's usage methods can be performed automatically and repeatedly given the required input in terms of requirements and preferences is available. This capability allows for variant selection to be performed, for example, to react to changes in context in service delivery. Or, when using service feature modeling's methods to incorporate dynamic attribute values (cf. section 3.4), reselections can repeated to consider latest values. Participation of non-technical stakeholders is basically enabled by the abstractions from feature models in some related work (for example, [BAGS10, BNGR12]), but not explicitly addressed or discussed. Service feature modeling thus provides a new perspective on the utilization of variability modeling for participatory service development. Existing service selection approaches (including policy-based approaches) consider each service to be a single alternative (cf. [ASR10, GVB13, LNZ04, MST11]). Service feature modeling's usage methods, in contrast, allow decision-makers to select individual variants from multiple services, each described by one SFM [WKM12]. In related work about considering variants in service development (for example, [DHJ09, MNDF+10]) and delivery (for example, [DWS12, LNSJ12]), selection is mentioned but no specifics on how to perform it are presented. Here, service feature modeling's usage methods provide a novel way of selecting service variants.

5. Evaluation

The evaluation of service feature modeling builds upon different elements as illustrated in table 5.1. We denote the evaluated contribution, the evaluation method, and the specific instrument used for the evaluation.

Contribution	Eval. method	Evaluation instrument & section
Modeling language	Proof of concept (POC)	Meta model (5.1.2), SFM designer (5.1.3)
	Use case	Public service development (5.3.2), IaaS consumption (5.4.2)
	Empirical	Service engineer survey (5.5)
Determining SFM configs.	POC	SFM designer (5.1.3)
	Performance	Benchmark (5.2)
	Use case	Public service/IaaS SFMs (5.4.3, 5.3.3)
SFM composition	POC	Collaboration server (5.1.3)
Skyline filtering	POC	SFM designer (5.1.3)
Requirements filtering	POC	Requirements filter component (5.1.3)
	Use case	IaaS consumption (5.4.3)
Preference-based ranking	POC	Preference-based ranking component (5.1.3)
	Performance	Benchmark (5.2)
	Use case	Public service development (participatory approach, 5.3.3), IaaS consumption (5.4.3)
	Empirical	Citizen survey (5.5)
Variant realization	POC	IaaS deployment middleware (interaction service component, 5.1.3)
	Use case	IaaS consumption (5.4.4)

Table 5.1.: How contributions of service feature modeling were evaluated

The evaluation is based on four methods, each addressing different aspects of the overall evaluation:

- **Proof of concept (POC):** We present the architecture and a prototypical implementation of a *service feature modeling tool suite* in section 5.1. It aims to illustrate the realizability of the envisioned concepts, showing that models based on the service feature modeling language can be created, that they can be composed from services, and that they can be used with the conceptualized usage methods. We thus denote the evaluation based on implemented components as *proof of concept (POC)*. Another reason for implementing a prototype is to enable further evaluation methods like the use cases or the empirical evaluation. It further, being developed early within our research, provided basis to assess design options for systems realizing service feature modeling and to collect knowledge about them [Som11, page 45].

- **Performance evaluation:** We evaluate the performance of the implementation for performance-critical tasks in section 5.2. The performance evaluation is based on benchmarks with SFMs from the use cases and synthetic models of varying sizes. The performance evaluation aims to show the applicability of the usage methods (cf. chapter 4) to models of varying sizes.

- **Use cases:** We use the prototypical implementation as a basis to apply service feature modeling to two use cases in sections 5.3 and 5.4. We define a use case, as proposed in software product line engineering, as "[...] a description of system behaviour in terms of scenarios illustrating different ways to succeed or fail in attaining one or more goals." [PuFvdL05, page 93]. We assume a scenario to be "[...] a concrete description of system usage which provides a clear benefit for the actor of the system." [PuFvdL05, page 93]. The service feature modeling evaluation is based upon two scenarios, namely the application to public service design within the COCKPIT project and the application for IaaS consumption. The use cases aim to show applicability of service feature modeling, in this context with regard to applying it in real-life contexts [WRH+12, page 14].

- **Empirical evaluation:** We present an *empirical* evaluation in section 5.5. It is based on surveys answered by users within the COCKPIT project, which is an established method to evaluate software [HPSVA95]. The intent of the empirical evaluation is to assess the perceived quality of exemplary targeted users of service feature modeling. Perceived quality is broken down into usability, expressiveness, and usefulness and interpretability, addressing the characteristics stated in this work's hypothesis. We thus use surveys in a descriptive manner, where they aim to assert the distribution of these characteristics based on the interviewers' perceptions [WRH+12, page 13].

Overall, the evaluation aims to assess the realizability of service feature modeling and its applicability, first with regard to models of different sizes and second with regard to two real use cases. The evaluation aims, furthermore, to draw inferences about the perceived quality of the characteristics of service feature modeling described in the hypothesis (cf. section 1.4).

5.1. Proof of Concept - Design and Implementation

The foundation for service feature modeling's evaluation is a proof of concept implementation. The proof of concept's purpose is to demonstrate the realizability of feature modeling's concepts. One main artifact created as part of the proof of concept implementation is the service feature modeling meta model described in section 5.1.2. It prescribes the syntax that SFMs, based on this meta model, have. The architecture of the service feature modeling tool suite is described in section 5.1.3. Its parts - the SFM designer, the valuation server, and the collaboration server - make use of the previously defined meta model to create or edit SFMs and perform usage methods. Finally, we discuss the prototypical implementation of the architecture in section 5.1.4. This section includes and extends previously published work about individual parts of the tool suite, presented in [WZR+11, WSKT12] and under review in [WZ14].

5.1.1. Requirements

We identify a set of requirements for the implementation of the service feature modeling tool suite. A functional requirement for the tool suite is to support all activities and methods foreseen in service feature modeling's methodology. On a high level, they include the modeling of SFMs as described in chapter 3 and the selection of variants as described in chapter 4. Modeling requires tools that support single modelers to create and edit SFMs. The tools need to support all elements contained in an SFM and be aware of the restrictions among them (cf. section 3.2). Modeling tools should support model persistence, copy and paste, model validation, and integration with version control tools. Graphical tools ease the modeling process. Modeling should further support the composition of SFMs from services (cf. section 3.4). The introduced coordination mechanisms need to be implemented and central supervision of their compliance needs to be guaranteed. To enable shared access to SFM results and asynchronous modeling, results need to be made available independent from whether their modelers are currently active. With regard to usage of SFMs, the configuration set determination is required, including attribute aggregation. It needs to be performed automatically because SFMs, similar to feature models, can become large, making manual reasoning on them infeasible [BSRC10]. Information about the configuration set, like the number of configurations and their aggregated attributes, should be made available to modelers on-demand to allow them to immediately react to this feedback. Skyline and requirements filtering need to be integrated with the modeling tools for modelers to apply these filters to determined configuration sets. Similarly, preference-based ranking needs to be integrated with the modeling tools. To enable participation, polls derived from SFMs need to be made available within evaluations (cf. section 4.4.6). Evaluations can potentially be long running so that they need to be made available independent from interactive modeling sessions. To support different types of participants, different user interfaces should be implementable. Further, retrieval of evaluation results back into the modeling tools needs to be enabled.

Apart from the outlined functional requirements, we identify further non-functional ones. The tool suite needs to be customizable and extensible. Customization allows the application of SFMs to different domains, while extensibility allows to add previously unforeseen capabilities. In addition, the integration with other service or software engineering artifacts needs to be enabled. Exemplary approaches to implement integration are model mappings or transformations. Finally, the performance of the implementation needs to be sufficient to handle realistically sized SFMs.

5.1.2. SFM Meta Model

A meta model is the model of another model [Küh06] and defines a diagrammatic language's syntax [HR04]. The term "meta" implies the double application of an operation (for example, a meta-discussion is a discussion about a discussion), in this case *modeling*. An SFM is an instance of the SFM meta model. Service feature modeling's meta model defines which elements are contained in an SFM and how they relate to another. The SFM meta model is illustrated in figure 5.1.

The meta model is specified as an *Eclipse Modeling Framework (EMF)* model [SBPM08]. EMF itself is a subset of UML. EMF models consist of *classes*, *attributes*[1] to describe these classes, and *references* between classes [SBPM08, page 124]. The parts of the SFM meta model which relate to basic feature modeling elements were inspired by related work [FFB02]. These parts are complemented on the one hand by service-specific elements and on the other

[1]We refer to them as "properties" in the following to avoid confusions with attributes in service feature modeling.

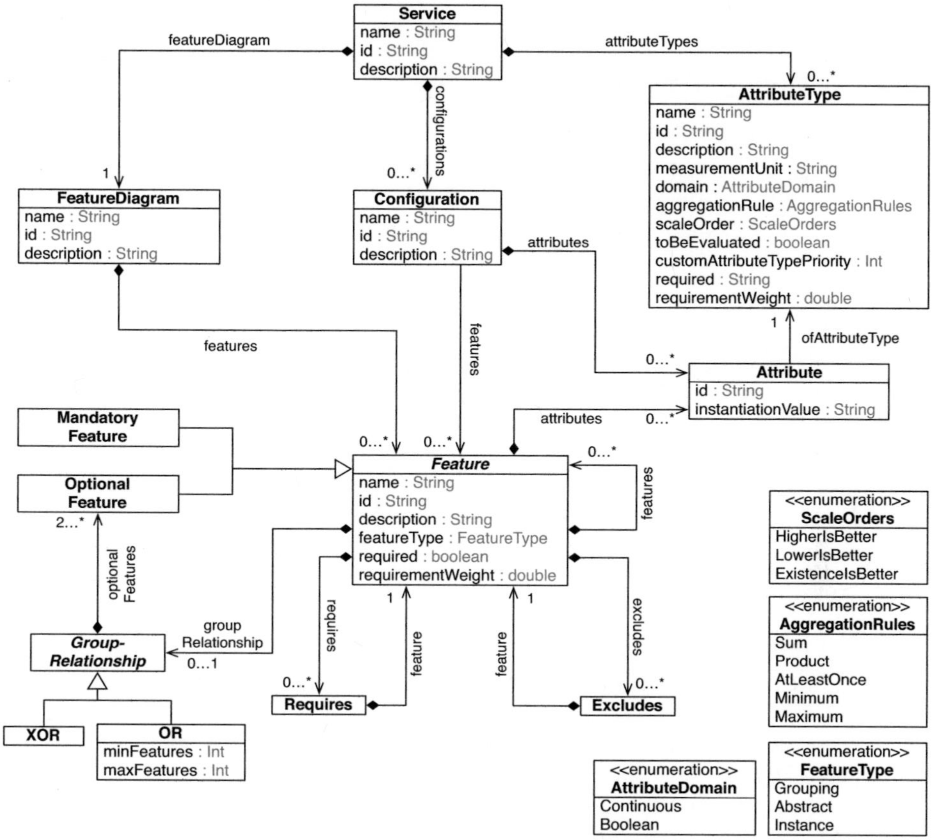

Figure 5.1.: The meta model underlying service feature modeling, based on [WZ14]

hand by service feature modeling's extensions, compared to standard feature modeling, presented in section 3.2.2 and 3.2.4.

The highest level element of each SFM is a single *service* element. It corresponds to the overall variable service that an SFM represents and groups all further elements of the SFM. The properties *name*, *id* and *description* capture corresponding details about the service. It possesses containment references to the feature digram, the configurations, and the attribute types.

The *feature diagram* contains all features of an SFM. As in standard feature modeling, feature diagrams are tree structures whose nodes are features and attributes. This structure is represented by the corresponding containment relationship. Differing from the diagram, the overall SFM contains additional information (cf. [CHE04]) like configurations.

Features are described, again, by the properties *name*, *id*, and *description*. Their type (grouping, abstract, or instance) is denoted by an enumerable property. Within an SFM, it can be stated that a feature is *required* and the weight of this requirement can be stated using *requirement weight*. Features possess a self-containment reference, which enables their decomposition into tree structures. They can further *require* or *exclude* other features, representing cross-tree relationships. The feature class itself is defined as abstract. The two concrete classes *mandatory feature* and *optional feature* inherit from it. This differentiation allows automated reasoners to assess whether the feature must be contained in each configuration or not.

Features may also contain a single *group relationship*, being either instantiated as *XOR* (an alternative group relationship) or *OR*. A group relationship contains at least two optional features. In the case of a XOR group relationship, exactly one of these features can be selected for a configuration. In the case of an OR group relationship, the minimum and maximum numbers of features to select for a configuration can be specified in corresponding properties.

Attributes are referenced from a feature. They denote a an *id* and an *instantiation value* property. All other information describing the attribute are defined in the referenced *attribute type*. It defines, as discussed in section 3.2.4, common properties of multiple attribute of the type. Correspondingly, information like the *name*, *description*, *measurement unit*, or *domain* are defined here. One of the *aggregation rules* predefined in a corresponding enumeration can be selected, corresponding to the description in table 4.3. The properties *scale order*, *to be evaluated*, and *custom attribute type priority* are used for preference-based ranking as described in section 4.4. As in the case of features, requirements regarding attributes can be stated in an SFM. The *required* property is of type String, allowing to state requirements regarding the range of attribute values, using for example "$<$ x" or "$=$ y". Again, the weight of a requirement can be stated using *requirement weight*.

The service node references to *configurations* with a containment reference. A configuration references to a selection of service features. Configurations further contain attributes, specifying characteristics that result from aggregating the attributes of the configuration's features.

The SFM meta model provides the basic structure to derive SFMs from. Additional constraints, restricting for example parent and child feature depending on the feature type, cannot easily be defined within the meta-model without cluttering it or creating ambiguity. These constraints are thus defined within the implemented logic. The meta model provides the basis for addressing the requirement to support all elements and their relations defined for service feature modeling as described in section 5.1.1.

5.1.3. Architecture

An overview of the service feature modeling tool suite's architecture is illustrated in figure 5.2.

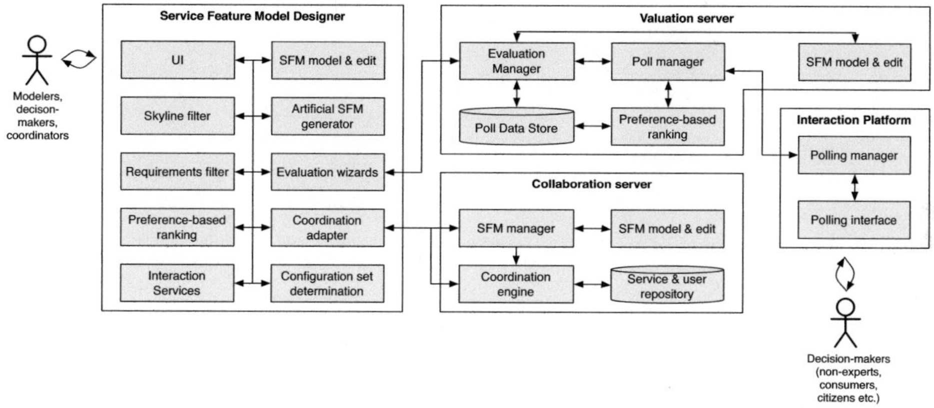

Figure 5.2.: Overview of the architecture of the SFM tool suite

The architecture consists of four parts marked by white boxes, namely the *SFM designer*, the *valuation server*, the *collaboration server*, and the *interaction platform*. Every part consists of further components marked by gray boxes, which contain subcomponents as illustrated in figures 5.3, 5.4, and 5.5. Arrows indicate communication between parts and components within them. Components that stand out from their containing parts indicate service interfaces or clients to such interfaces. We describe the SFM tool suite's four parts in the following subsections.

SFM Designer

The SFM designer is the modeling environment to create and edit SFMs. It further integrates service feature modeling's usage methods and provides means to interact with other parts of the tool suite. The SFM designer is intended to be used by technically skilled stakeholders who use it in the roles of modeler (cf. section 3.3.1) or decision-maker (cf. section 4.1.3). An overview of the SFM designer's architecture is provided in figure 5.3. Components are illustrated in gray and subcomponents in white. Subcomponents that stand out from their containing component, again, indicate service interfaces or clients of such interfaces.

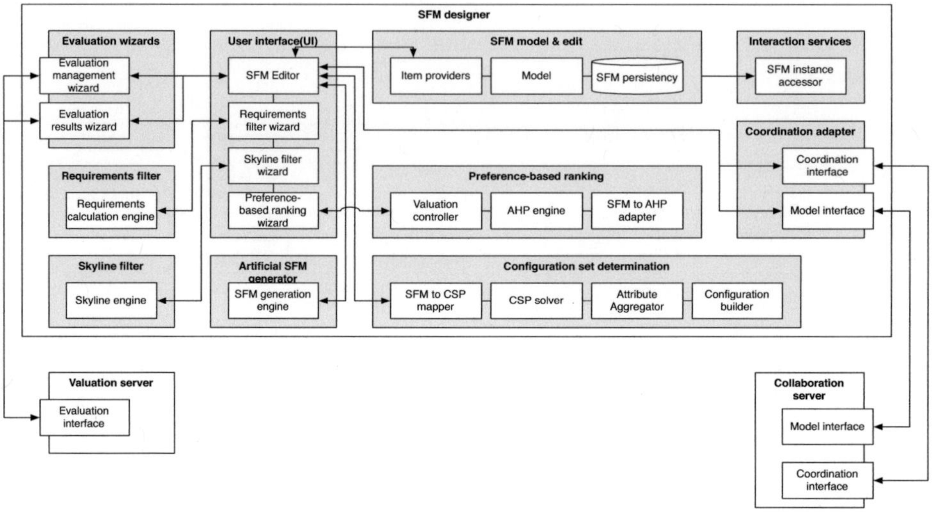

Figure 5.3.: Architecture of the SFM designer

The **SFM model & edit** component implements the meta model underlying service feature modeling described in section 5.1.2, thus providing the modeling facilities. The *model* subcomponent provides all classes with attributes and relationships as described in the meta model. *Item provider* classes enable access to a model instance's elements. The *SFM persistency* stores and retrieves SFMs on the hard disk. The SFM model & edit component is used in every part of the SFM tool suite. Furthermore, the item providers are used by every component or subcomponent that interacts with SFMs within the SFM designer. To keep the architecture diagrams readable, we do not illustrate all relationships between the item provider and all other components.

Driven by the modeling facilities, the **user interface (UI)** component provides means for modelers, decision-makers, and coordinators to interact with SFMs. The heart of the UI is the *SFM editor*, which provides capabilities for creating and editing SFMs. The editor is furthermore the starting point for invoking *wizards* for interacting with SFMs.

Invoking the **configuration set determination** component results in multiple actions: the *SFM to CSP mapper* transfers the SFM currently in focus into a constraint satisfaction problem as described in listing 1. A *CSP solver* component determines all valid solutions of the CSP. The *attribute aggregator* component determines attribute values for every CSP solution as described in listing 2. Finally, the *configuration builder* component uses the information resulting from the CSP solver and the attribute aggregator to create corresponding configuration elements and attributes (cf. meta model in figure 5.1) in the SFM.

The **requirements filter** component is invoked via the *requirements filter wizard.* The user selects the SFM to apply the filter to and another SFM stating the requirements as described in section 4.3.1. The requirements filter component implements the algorithm described in listing 3. Screenshots of the requirements filter component's user interface (UI) are presented in appendix B.

Similarly, the **skyline filter** component is invoked by the *skyline filter wizard.* The skyline filter component implements the block-nested loop algorithm described in listing 4. The user selects the SFM to apply the filter to and confirms the dismissal of dominated configurations.

The **preference-based ranking** component is invoked by the *preference-based ranking wizard.* The user, acting in the role of a decision-maker (cf. section 4.1.3), performs pairwise comparisons of attribute types in the wizard. The *valuation controller* initiates the *SFM to AHP adapter* to create a multi-criteria decision making problem from a given SFM as described in section 4.4.3. The *AHP engine* component determines the ranking of configurations for the stated preferences. Results are presented in the wizard and can be fed back into the SFM. Screenshots of the preference-based ranking wizard's user interface (UI) are presented in appendix B.

The **evaluation wizards** allow to interact with the valuation server part of the SFM tool suite. The *evaluation management wizard* allows users to create, retrieve, update, and delete evaluations on the valuation server. For example, the evaluation's state can be changed with this wizard. The *evaluation results wizard* allows to retrieve (aggregated) results form an evaluation and to display them to the decision-maker.

The SFM designer denotes a **coordination adapter** for composition of SFMs from services. The *coordination interface* allows users to define new results and assign them to services through interacting with the collaboration server's coordination interface. The *model interface* allows to post and retrieve model results to, and respectively from, the collaboration server.

The **artificial SFM generator** allows to create synthetic, randomized SFMs. Their purpose is primarily to drive performance evaluations with differently sized models (cf. section 5.2). The creation of the artificial SFMs is based on an algorithm described in related work [TBK09].

Finally, the **interaction services** component provides an *SFM interaction accessor*. It allows further editing tools, outside of the SFM designer, to access and eventually edit SFMs.

Collaboration Server

The collaboration server implements the logic required for composing SFMs from services as described in section 3.4, thus enabling collaboration in modeling SFMs. The description of the collaboration server is based on previously published work [WSKT12].

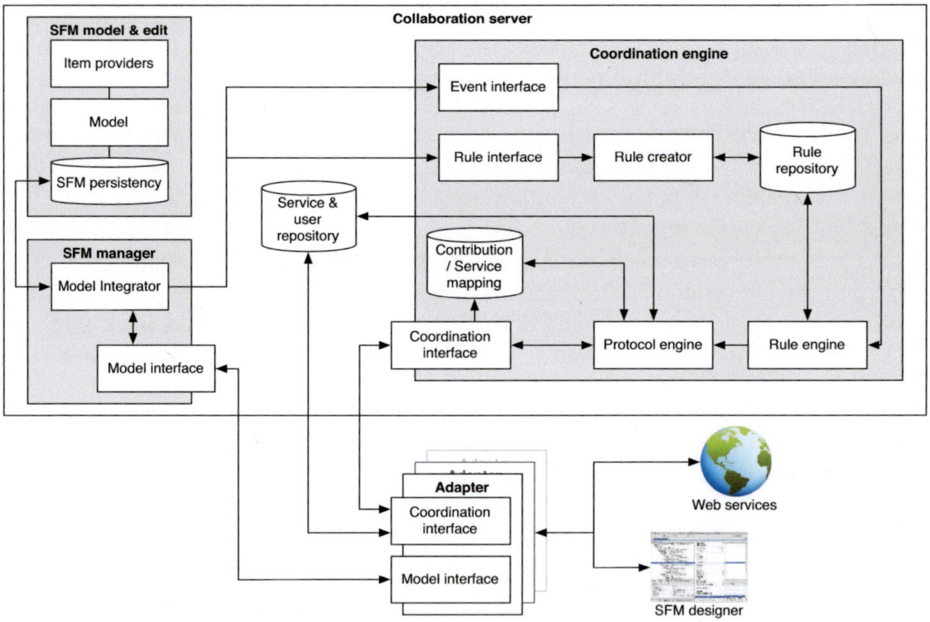

Figure 5.4.: Architecture of the collaboration server, based on [WSKT12]

Similar to the SFM designer, the collaboration server contains the **SFM model & edit** component. It allows all other components to interact with and persist SFMs to hard disk. Again, the relationships to all other components using it are not illustrated in figure 5.4 to keep it readable.

The **SFM manager** stores contributed results, namely SFMs and attribute values, in the *SFM persistency* component. Using the *model interface*, any service bound via adapters (cf. description below) can create, retrieve, update or delete results - thus, for both SFM and attribute value results, CRUD methods are provided. Results sent or requested pass through the *model integrator*. It checks committed results for a) model elements that require coordination rules to be defined - for example, attributes relating to attribute types outside of the result - and b) changes with regard to model elements that require coordination - for example, changes to cross-tree relationships. In such cases, the model integrator triggers the *coordination engine* to create rules or trigger events. Further, if a result from the collaboration server is requested, the model integrator composes it by integrating all sub results into one coherent SFM.

The **coordination engine** contains the coordination logic. The *coordination interface* allows services to participate in the coordination via adapters. A coordinator consults the *service & user repository* to find an adequate service to associate with a contribution. The association is stored in the *contribution / service mapping*. The *protocol engine* controls the binding and the service request / response protocol of the service based on information found in both the contribution / service mapping and the service & user repository. The *rule interface* triggers the *rule creator* when new model elements are contributed that require creation of a new coordination rule. Additionally, it can be used by any coordinator to manually define rules. Rules are stored in the *rule repository*. Through the *event interface*, events are sent to the *rule engine*. On receiving an event, the rule engine checks existing rules and, where appropriate, triggers an action. For example, if an attribute type is changed, the "AttributeType-Updated" event triggers a previously specified rule which notifies all depending modelers. Notifications are sent via the *protocol engine* that communicates with the respective service adapters via the coordination interface.

The collaboration server foresees numerous **adapters** that allow services to participate in the collaboration. Adapters ensure compatibility of the service interfaces and the collaboration server's interfaces - for example, they implement the coordination protocols described in section 3.4. For every service interface, a dedicated adapter is required. Adapters have two interfaces to communicate with our system: via the *coordination interface*, services are asked for binding and then are requested to contribute or update results. The *model interface* is used to retrieve existing results of the model in focus and to contribute (create, update, or delete) results. The adapter of the SFM designer, the coordination adapter, is described in section 5.1.3.

Valuation Server

The valuation server exposes preference-based ranking (cf. section 4.4) for participatory usage. Its architecture is illustrated in figure 5.5.

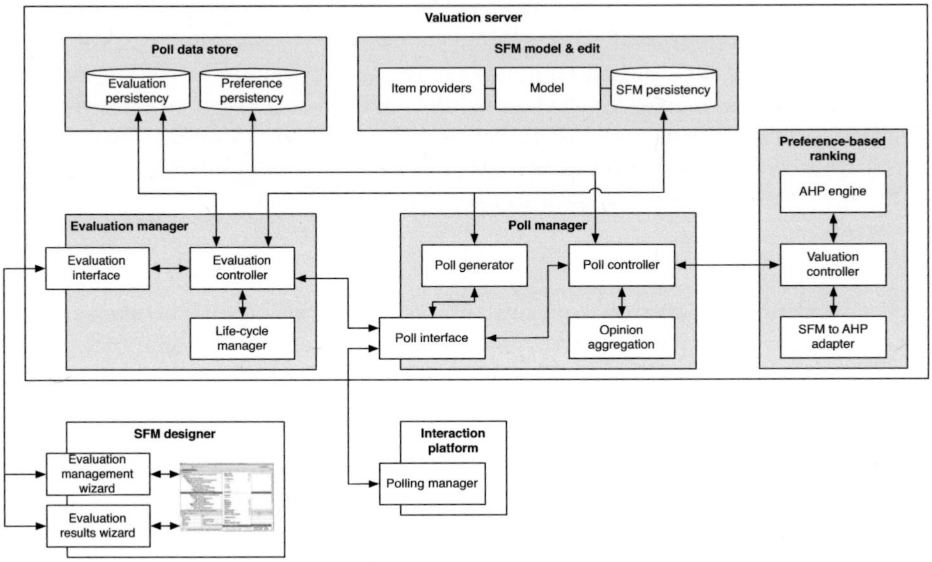

Figure 5.5.: Architecture of the valuation server

The **evaluation manager** is responsible for creating, controlling, accessing, and ultimately deleting evaluations (cf. section 4.4.6). SFM designers communicate with the valuation manager using the *evaluation interface* to create, update or delete evaluations or to retrieve their results. The evaluation interface is connected to the *evaluation controller*. It drives the valuation manager's logic in reaction to user commands received via the evaluation interface or due to events fired by the *life-cycle manager*. The life-cycle manager triggers actions in the evaluation controller based on events defined within the evaluation. These events are most notably state changes that are defined in an evaluation (cf. section 4.4.6). For example, if an end date is specified in an evaluation, the life-cycle manager will trigger the interaction manager to end the evaluation at the given date. The evaluation controller stores information about the evaluation in the poll data store component (cf. below) upon creation. If evaluation results are requested via the evaluation interface, the evaluation controller forwards this request to the poll manager and delivers the received results back through the evaluation interface.

The **poll data store** denotes a collection of persistence components to store artifacts required for evaluations. The *SFM persistence* is responsible for storing SFMs on the valuation server and accessing them if required. It uses the *EMF SFM meta model & edit* component also used within the SFM designer (cf. section 5.1.3) to process SFMs. The *evaluation persistence* stores meta information about evaluations. This information includes the stakeholder who initiated the evaluation, its creation date, its defined end-date, and its current state. A complete description of the information is provided in section 4.4.6. The *preference persistence* stores votes from stakeholders about their preferences and aggregated votes.

The **poll manager** is responsible for managing polls on the interaction platform (cf. section 5.1.3) and for reacting to requests for configuration rankings. The *poll interface* allows for communication with the interaction platform and the evaluation manager. The *poll generator* is responsible for creating the poll for a given SFM. It stores the poll to the poll data store. If triggered by the evaluation manager, the poll interface posts new polls to the interaction platform. The *poll controller* handles the logic required to determine a configuration ranking. If the poll interface receives a vote from the interaction platform or a request for evaluation results from the evaluation manager, the poll controller performs all actions necessary to provide the required configuration ranking using the preference-based ranking component (cf. below). The poll controller triggers the valuation service component to determine the ranking for the given vote and corresponding evaluation and returns the result to the poll interface. If the evaluation manager requests an aggregated configuration ranking (cf. section 4.4.4), the poll controller requests the *opinion aggregator* to derive an aggregated vote before triggering the valuation service with this vote.

The *preference-based ranking* component is responsible for determining the configuration ranking. It functions similar to the same component in the SFM designer (cf. section 5.1.3). The resulting ranking is fed back to the poll manager.

The collaboration server denotes, again, the **SFM model & edit** component to edit and persist SFMs.

Interaction Platform

The interaction platform provides user interfaces allowing stakeholders to express their preferences with respect to an SFM's attribute types. Stakeholders (most importantly consumers) express their preferences by means of interactive surveys that we refer to as polls.

The interaction platform includes a **poll manager** component that provides services for the valuation server to define and control polls. The poll manager also implements a protocol to send tentative poll results to the valuation server and in turn receive feedback information including a representation of the highest ranked configuration.

A *polling interface* is responsible for presenting valuation polls and interacting with stakeholders including input of their poll answers and output of feedback information. Different application scenarios pose different requirements on the realization of the user interface for service consumer participation. Likely variants include Web, desktop or mobile applications that can be stand-alone or integrated into other applications. For this reason, the SFM tool suite does not include a specific UI implementation.

5.1.4. Implementation

The SFM tool suite is implemented in Java. Thus, if not stated otherwise in the following, plain Java is used to implement components.

We implemented the SFM designer based on the Eclipse Modeling Framework (EMF), which is part of the Eclipse Modeling Project[2]. For a given data model - in this case the meta model underlying service feature modeling as described in section 5.1.2 - EMF generates Java classes for the model, adapter classes for viewing and command-based editing of the model (the item providers described in section 5.1.3), and a basic Eclipse-based editor (the SFM editor described in section 5.1.3). The generated model and adapter classes act as the SFM model & edit component used throughout the SFM tool suite's parts. The SFM persistency is XMI-based. The editor provides capabilities to create and edit SFMs within Eclipse, making use of many other capabilities provided in Eclipse like plug-ins for version control (cf. section 3.2.1) or for collaboration, thus addressing this requirement from section 5.1.1. Figure 5.6 illustrates a screenshot of the basic SFM designer's UI. Features are decomposed in tree structures and properties can be changed in dedicated property-views, illustrated at the bottom of the screen.

The user interface's wizards for invoking further components are implemented as JFace wizards[3]. All service interfaces and clients, for example, the evaluation wizards and the collaboration adapter, are implemented in a RESTful way, using the Jersey framework that implements the Java API for RESTful Services (JAX-RS API) specification[4]. Implementing service interfaces in a RESTful way

[2]`http://projects.eclipse.org/projects/modeling.emf`
[3]`http://wiki.eclipse.org/JFace`
[4]`https://jersey.java.net/`

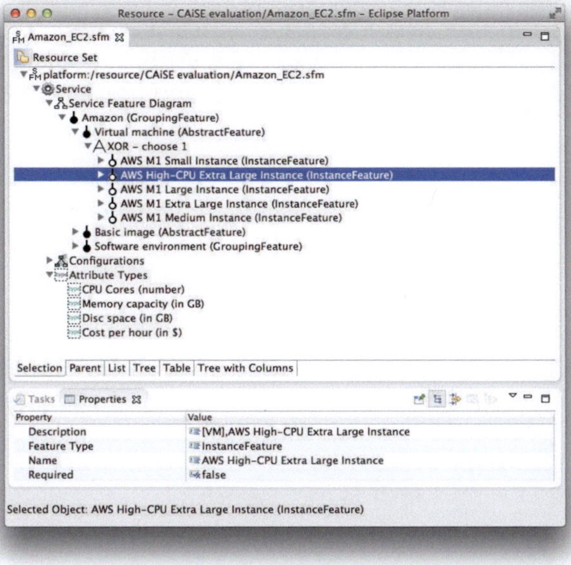

Figure 5.6.: Screenshot of the SFM designer

promotes the customizability and extensibility of the tool suite as required in section 5.1.1. The configuration set determination component uses the CHOCO solver as the CSP solver[5]. It has been used extensively in related work, for example, [DWS12, MC10, WDSB09], and has been found to perform well for feature model analysis [PLP11]. The preference-based ranking component uses the aotearoaLib for solving Analytical Hierarchy Process problems [6].

The collaboration server is implemented using Grails Web application framework[7] and RESTful design principles. The server components are implemented both with Java and Groovy[8]. The service repository, rule repository and contribution/service mapping persist data in a MySQL database. The rule engine is implemented using ESPER[9]. Correspondingly, the coordination rules described in section 3.4.3 are expressed with the ESPER Event Processing Language (EPL).

The valuation server is implemented as a set of RESTful Web services. The eval-

[5] `www.emn.fr/z-info/choco-solver/`
[6] `https://github.com/mugglmenzel/aotearoaLib/`
[7] `http://www.grails.org`
[8] `http://groovy.codehaus.org/`
[9] `http://esper.codehaus.org/`

uation manager and the poll manager are mapped on resource sets of evaluations, models and votes described in section 4.4.6. In terms of infrastructure, the server uses a JPA-based persistence layer on top of a Derby database[10]. Furthermore, it uses the JAX-RS API provided by Jersey[11] resulting in a servlet-based Web application hosted in a Tomcat container[12].

In terms of the interaction platform, the service feature modeling tool suite is technology agnostic. Different application scenarios are likely to pose very different requirements on the realization of the user interface for service consumer participation. Based on the service under consideration, the consumer group might differ in size and/or preferred interface style. Likely variants include Web, desktop or mobile applications that can be stand-alone or integrated into other applications. For this reason, the service feature modeling tool suite only contains a definition of the interaction platform service interface that is offered to the valuation server as well as its client API. This interface denotes RESTful Web service interfaces on poll resources. A concrete example of a Web-based interaction platform is presented in section 5.3.

5.1.5. Discussion

The here presented proof of concept implementation allows us to assert the realizability and functionality of the methods of the service feature modeling methodology. The meta model, representing the syntax of the service feature modeling language presented in section 3.2, and the SFM editor derived from it allow the modeling of SFMs as described in section 3.3.2. Using the collaboration server, the coordinated composition of SFMs as described in section 3.4 is equally feasible. The SFM designer's coordination adapters allow modelers to assign contributions to human-based and Web services. For SFM results, corresponding resources are created, updated, retrieved, and deleted by the SFM manager on the collaboration server. On updating SFMs, the model integrator triggers the creation of rules and triggers events with regard to existing rules as conceptualized in section 3.4.3. Notifications in case of detected inconsistencies are sent to humans acting as services services via e-mail. Thus, the SFM designer in combination with the collaboration server enables collaborative service feature modeling (cf. challenge 3) and the integration of dynamic or complex attribute values (cf. challenge 2). Regarding usage methods, all methods denoting the selection process (cf. challenge 4) were implemented. The proof of concept shows that the determination of configurations described in section 4.2 including the attribute aggregation described in section 4.2.2 is feasible (cf. challenge 1). A

[10] `db.apache.org/derby/`
[11] `https://jersey.java.net`
[12] `tomcat.apache.org`

more detailed analysis of the performance of this step is provided in section 5.2. The requirements filtering described in section 4.3 and the skyline filtering described in section 4.4.2 function as conceptualized. Preference-based ranking of configurations, using the transfer of SFMs to polls described in section 4.4.3 and the determination of rankings described in section 4.4.5, produces the expected results. For participatory ranking, the concepts and the corresponding evaluation life cycle, both described in section 4.4.6, were implemented in the valuation server. Polls can be made accessible with the interaction platform to stakeholders and results can be fed back to the SFM designer using the evaluation wizards. Thus, the participatory ranking of configurations is feasible.

In sum, the proof of concept implementation shows that all conceptualized methods of service feature modeling's methodology can be implemented and used. In the following sections, we present a performance evaluation, two use cases, and an empirical evaluation from one of the use cases to further assess the quality of service feature modeling.

5.2. Performance Evaluation

To assess the applicability of the implementation to SFMs of different sizes, we conduct a performance evaluation. It assesses the performance of parts of the implementation critical with regard to computation times using SFMs created within use cases (cf. section 5.3 and 5.4) and synthetic SFMs created with the artificial SFM generator (cf. section 5.1.3). The here presented performance evaluation is based upon and extends work currently under review in briefer form [WZ14].

5.2.1. Design of Performance Evaluation

We consider four main scenarios that depend on performance. Firstly, the automatic determination of an SFM's configuration set, i.e. the represented service variants, is time-critical. If this step takes too long, it impairs the modeling process, where the determination of the configuration set is a common task. Secondly and thirdly, the skyline and the requirements filter need to perform sufficiently because they are, again, eventually performed multiple times upon model changes. Fourthly, the determination of the configuration ranking needs to perform well, because we require to provide immediate feedback for stakeholders voting on the interaction platform.

The performance of configuration set determination depends on three steps: first, the SFM is translated from its EMF representation to a constraint satisfaction problem (CSP). In this step, all features in the SFM are iterated and corresponding constraints are created as described in related work [KOD10]. The performance of this step thus depends on the number of features and constraints in the SFM. Second, the CSP is solved. This step, as described above, is performed by the CHOCO off-the-shelf CSP solver. Its performance, again, depends on the number of features and constraints in the SFM. Third, based on the CSP's solutions, configurations are created, including the attribute aggregation. In this step, all solutions found for a CSP (corresponding to configurations of an SFM) are iterated and for each attribute type, an aggregation of the corresponding attributes is performed. Thus, the performance of this step depends on the one hand on the number of configurations and on the other hand on the number of attribute types in the SFM.

The skyline filter's single critical step is the block nested loop algorithm presented in listing 4. This algorithm's performance depends on the size of the configuration set that needs to be iterated. In addition, it depends on the number of attribute types because they are considered in every comparison of two configurations to check for dominance.

Similar to the skyline filter, the requirements filter's single critical step is the matching algorithm presented in listing 3. The algorithm depends on the number of configurations and on the number of requirements.

The performance of the configuration ranking depends on two steps: first, the SFM is translated to the domain model of the utilized AHP implementation aotearoaLib. The performance of this step depends upon the number of configurations and attribute types in the SFM. Second, aotearoaLib performs the actual ranking based on the input model and the preferences stated in form of a vote (see section 4.4.6). Again, this step's performance depends upon the number of configurations and attribute types in the SFM.

We ran the performance benchmarks on a notebook with a 2.4*Ghz* Core i5 Processor and 8*GByte* memory. Every run for every model was repeated 100 times and the mean values of these runs are presented in section 5.2.3.

5.2.2. Evaluation Models

Table 5.2 presents information about the SFMs created in the use cases ("GR01" and "IRIS01" as described in section 5.3.2 and "Amazon EC2" and "Rackspace" as described in section 5.4.2). This information indicates realistic dimensions of SFMs when used in practice. The comparatively small size of the SFMs "GR01" and "IRIS01" with regard to the number of configurations results from the model's focus on selected work flow variants which the decision-makers desired to select among.

Model ID	**Features**	**Cross-tree**	**Configurations**	**Attribute types**	**Attributes**
GR01	32	0	9	5	35
IRIS01	94	0	18	4	24
Amazon EC2	45	4	1280	4	20
Rackspace	32	2	896	4	28
Model 98 conf.	10	1	98	4	20
Model 952 conf.	20	2	952	4	20
Model 9450 conf.	30	3	9450	4	20
Model 21168 conf.	40	4	21168	4	20

Table 5.2.: Descriptions of use case and synthetic SFMs with rising number of configurations, based on [WZ14]

Additionally, we created artificial models of varying sizes. These models are designed corresponding to the considerations described in section 5.2.1 to test the limits of our implementation with regard to varying model dimensions that impact performance. The artificial models have a) an increasing number of configurations but fixed number of attribute types and attributes (described in table 5.2) and b) an increasing number of attribute types and attributes, while the number of configurations remains fixed (described in table 5.3). The models were defined based on the method proposed in [TBK09]. The probabilities for added child nodes being either mandatory, optional, XOR or OR nodes are each 25%. We defined a *maximum branch factor* of 5, meaning that every service feature has 5 children at most. Similar to [TBK09], we defined 1 cross-tree relationship per 10 service features. We also randomly defined attribute types and attributes, similar to the method described in [SGB+12]. The instantiation value per attribute is uniformly distributed between 0 and 100.

With regard to evaluating the requirements filter, we defined requirements in two ways. First, to assess the performance with regard to SFMs with rising configuration sets, we defined the same number of requirements for every SFM. We required 2 instance feature and 1 abstract feature to be required with weight 1.0. The features were selected randomly. In addition, we required for 2 attribute types to have values below or above a randomly selected value. Second, to assess the performance with regard to a rising number of requirements, we defined varying numbers of requirements for attribute types in SFM "Model 12 att.". Table A.3 provides details on the numbers of requirements for every model.

Model ID	Features	Cross-tree	Configurations	Attribute types	Attributes
Model 2 att.	20	2	952	2	10
Model 4 att.	20	2	952	4	20
Model 6 att.	20	2	952	6	30
Model 8 att.	20	2	952	8	40
Model 10 att.	20	2	952	10	50
Model 12 att.	20	2	952	12	60

Table 5.3.: Performance test models with rising number of attribute types and attributes [WZ14]

5.2.3. Results of Performance Evaluation

The processing times for **determining configurations** of the test models with rising numbers of configurations are illustrated in figure 5.7 (note: the axis scale is logarithmic for better visibility of the values). The results show that a higher number of features and constraints, resulting in more configurations in the test models, does not considerably impact processing times for transferring the SFM to a CSP. This step's very small impact on the overall performance of the configuration set determination renders it negligible. For both, the CSP solving and the attribute aggregation steps, the processing time increases approximately linear with an increasing number of configurations. Because the performance of the CSP solver lies outside our area of influence, we will not further discuss its performance. In general, we found that the performance of the CSP solving step corresponds to that reported in related work for this step [PLP11]. With regard to the aggregation of attributes, our findings are sensible because every configuration must be traversed to calculate its overall attribute value for every attribute type.

The processing times for determining configurations of the test models with rising attribute types and attributes are illustrated in figure 5.8. Attribute types and attributes neither play a role in the transfer of the SFM to a CSP nor in solving the CSP, which is also reflected in our findings. However, the processing times for attribute aggregation rises linear with an increasing number of attribute types and attributes. This finding is sensible because for each additional attribute type, an additional aggregation of its attributes has to be performed for every configuration.

Overall, the aggregation of attributes is the most expensive step of the configuration set determination. Its complexity is $\mathcal{O}(n * m)$, where n denotes the number of configurations and m the number of attribute types.

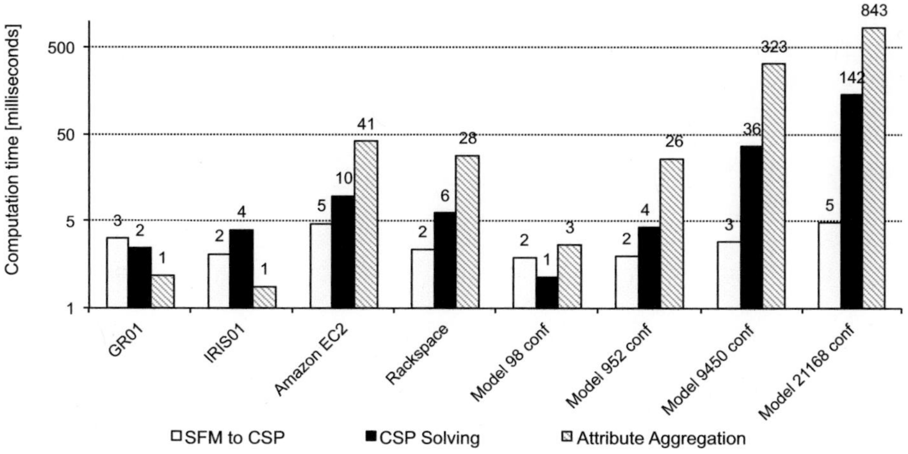

Figure 5.7.: Processing times for determining the configuration set of models with rising number of configurations, based on [WZ14]

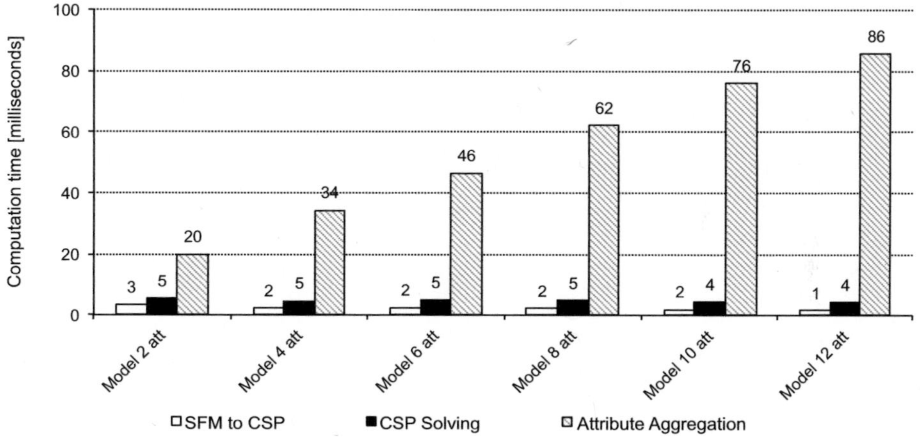

Figure 5.8.: Processing times for determining the configuration set of models with rising number of attribute types and attributes [WZ14]

The processing times for applying the **skyline filter** to the use case SFMs and ones with rising number of configurations is illustrated in figure 5.9. As can be seen, the computation time is highly dependent on the number of configurations. Our findings reflect discussions of the complexity of the block-nested loop algorithm in related work [BKS01]. The complexity ranges from $\mathcal{O}(n)$ to $\mathcal{O}(n^2)$, where n denotes the number of configurations. The best performance is achieved if the skyline is small, because in this case the window in the logarithm stays small and many configurations are immediately dismissed. Table A.2 in the appendix illustrates this case: models that denote a comparatively small skyline, for example "Model 952 conf." with only 4 configurations out of 952 in the skyline, require a small number of comparisons, thus resulting in comparatively small computation times. On the other hand, the models "Amazon EC2" and "Rackspace" do not denote any skyline configuration[13]. In consequence, $n * (n - 1)$ comparisons need to be performed, resulting in high computation times.

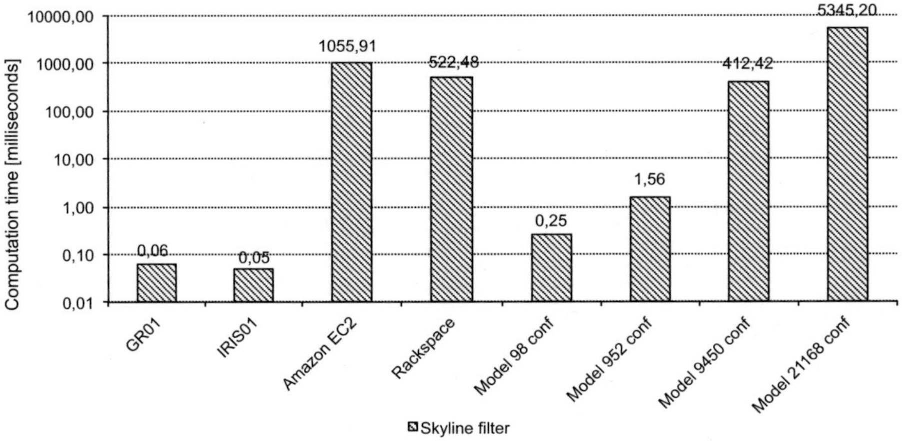

Figure 5.9.: Processing times for skyline filtering of use case models and ones with increasing numbers of configurations

The processing times for applying the skyline filter to SFMs with rising numbers of attribute types and attributes are illustrated in figure 5.10 (note: the axis scale is logarithmic for better visibility of the values). In general, there is a trend for computation times to increase with rising number of attribute types and attributes. This trend can be explained by each comparison between two configurations becoming more complex for every additional attribute type. Looking at table A.2 in the appendix, however, reveals also a reverse impact: more attribute types, in this case, result in a smaller skyline, thus reducing the

[13]This is caused by the pricing of the IaaS providers: VMs with high attribute values for "CPU cores", "memory", and "disk space" have equally higher "cost per hour".

number of comparisons. For example, “Model 2 att.” with a skyline including 48 configurations requires 3160 comparisons while “Model 12 att.” with a skyline including only 1 configuration requires just 951 comparisons. In this case, the increased complexity for each comparison in the latter model even overcompensates the gainings from the smaller number of comparisons.

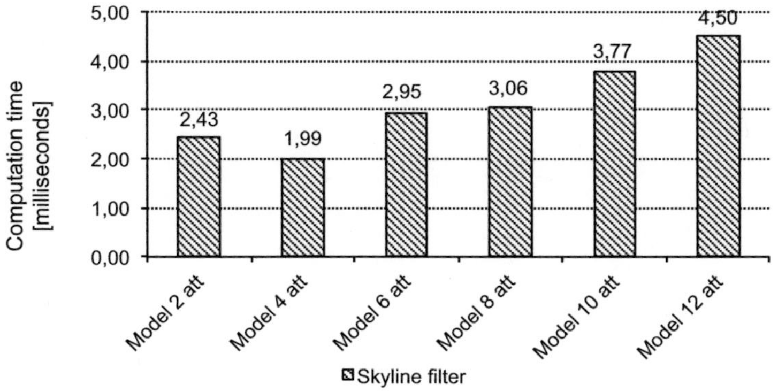

Figure 5.10.: Processing times for skyline filtering of models with rising numbers of attribute types and attributes

The processing times for applying the **requirements filter** to the use case SFMs and ones with rising numbers of configurations are illustrated in figure 5.11. The processing times grow roughly linearly with rising number of configurations. As illustrated in table A.3 in the appendix, the number of requirements was left fixed for this analysis.

On the other hand, figure 5.12 illustrates the processing times for applying the requirements filter to “Model 12 att.” with different numbers of attribute type requirements. The processing times rise linear with the rising numbers of requirements.

Overall, these findings confirm that the complexity of the requirements filter is $\mathcal{O}(n, m)$, where n denotes the number of configurations and m denotes the number of requirements.

The processing times for **ranking configurations** of the test models with rising configurations are illustrated in figure 5.13 (note: the axis scale is logarithmic for better visibility of the values). The results indicate that the biggest part of the processing time depends upon the transfer of the SFM to an AHP problem. Specifically, the creation of the matrices MPC and $MPC(a_i)$ is expensive. Every matrix $MPC(a_i)$ obtains an additional row and column for every configuration. In consequence, SFMs with many configurations result in very large

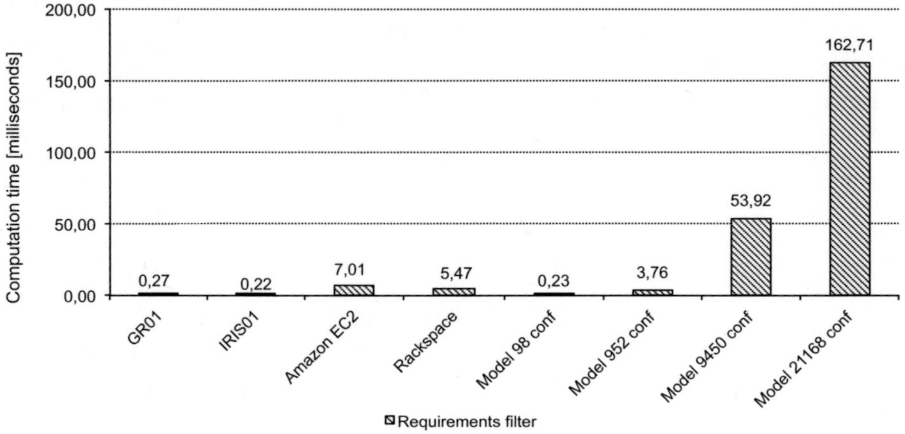

Figure 5.11.: Processing times for requirements filtering of use case models and ones with rising numbers of configurations

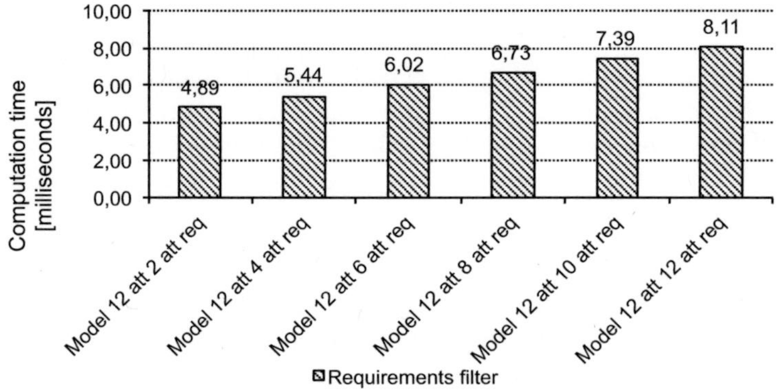

Figure 5.12.: Processing times for requirements filtering depending on different numbers of requirements

matrices. Thus, processing times for the model with 9450 configurations are just over two minutes, making it impossible to perform the complete calculation, for example, in Web applications where immediate response to user requests is important. In the case of the test model with 21168 configurations, a calculation was not possible due to memory limitations on the test machine. This performance bottleneck, however, can easily be addressed: the SFM to AHP translation needs only be performed once for every preference-based ranking process. The required times in the use of Web applications, thus, depends only on solving the AHP, which is sufficiently fast. Furthermore, also the determination of configuration comparison ranking vectors needs only to be performed once for every preference-based ranking process (cf. section 4.4.5). This calculation produces one vector for every attribute type, each of them having one element for every configuration. When pre-calculating them, only the attribute type priority vector needs to be determined repeatedly, which is comparatively small as it contains only one element for every attribute type. Considering these performance optimization potentials, preference-based ranking can be applied also to large SFMs to be used, for example, in Web applications.

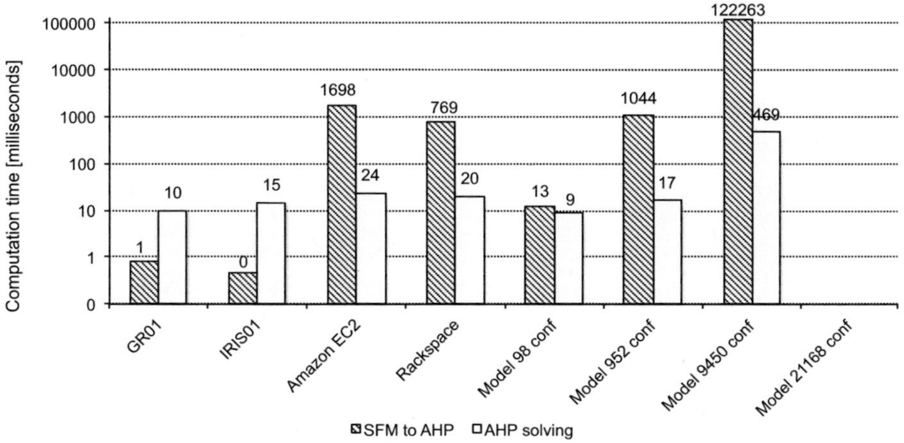

Figure 5.13.: Processing times for ranking configurations of use case models and ones with rising numbers of configurations, based on [WZ14]

The processing times for ranking configurations of the test models with rising numbers of attribute types and attributes are illustrated in figure 5.14. The processing time for the transfer of the SFM to an AHP problem increases linearly for increasing numbers of attribute types and corresponding attributes. This result is sensible because for each additional attribute type a_i, an additional matrix $MPC(a_i)$ needs to be created. The processing time for solving the AHP problem merely increases sublinearly for increased numbers of attribute types and attributes.

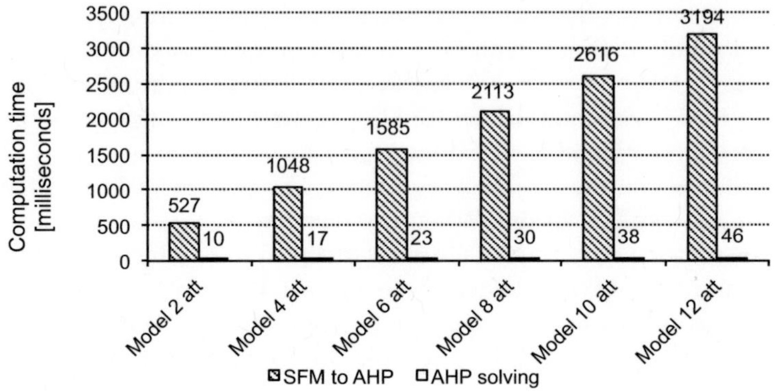

Figure 5.14.: Processing times for ranking configurations of models with rising numbers of attribute types and attributes [WZ14]

5.2.4. Discussion

The performance evaluation indicates the limits with regard to size of the SFMs to be applicable in real-life scenarios.

For determining the configuration set of an SFM, even the largest model with regard to configurations (21168) can be processed in under one second. While rising numbers of attribute types and attributes also increase processing times of the attribute aggregation, the impact is linear. We thus conclude that our approach is capable of handling considerably large models in a reasonable amount of time.

The performance of the skyline filter is hard to determine due to its dependence on the skyline size. Comparatively small skylines result in little numbers of comparisons while the other way round, large skylines can induce considerable performance impacts. Looking especially at the use case models, their skylines are all calculated in at most one second, with only the model with the most configurations requiring over 5 seconds. We thus consider the performance good enough to apply skyline filtering repeatedly during modeling.

The performance of the requirements filter is directly impacted, on the one hand, by the number of configurations and, on the other hand, by the number of requirements. In both cases, the processing time rises linearly with a linear increase in these numbers alone. For every assessed model, the processing times remained well under 200 ms, making the approach perform well even if it needs to be applied repeatedly.

For the configuration ranking, our evaluation shows that reasonable processing times are reachable for models with up to 1000 configurations. Beyond that, processing times and demand for memory increase disproportionately. While the impact of rising numbers of attribute types is linear, it can push processing times into unfeasible heights. We already presented potential optimization approaches, based on pre-calculating configuration priority vectors, in section 5.2.3. Alternatively, before applying preference-based ranking to an SFM's configurations, decision-makers should ensure appropriate model size. This argument is not only driven by performance considerations, but also by general usability of the approach: too many configurations will result in very similar ranking values, thus complicating the interpretation of results. Additionally, the number of attribute types should be low for the number of necessary pairwise comparisons to remain manageable (n attribute types result in $0.5*n*(n-1)$ comparisons). The realistic SFMs "GR01", "IRIS01", "Amazon EC2", and "Rackspace" generated in the use cases illustrate that service feature modeling is applicable despite the performance boundaries. Decision-makers can use the participatory approach to focus on specific aspects of the service on which to obtain preferences from stakeholders, thus keeping models reasonably sized. For larger models, approaches like the proposed skyline filter can be used to decrease model size.

5.3. Use Case - Public Service Design

To illustrate the applicability of modeling service variants with service feature modeling, we here present two use cases. The first use case addresses the design of public services considering variants, as motivated in section 1.1.1. Modeling SFMs was performed to represent service design alternatives for public services in the COCKPIT EU project [COC12]. The goal of COCKPIT is to enable citizens to participate in the (re-) design of public services. Public services, here, are not limited to mere software services but also include human actors performing manual tasks. This use case is part of work currently in review [WZ14].

5.3.1. Use Case Description

Service feature modeling was applied to two scenarios about public service design in the COCKPIT project [KKKP10].

The *redesigning social security record retrieval service* scenario was provided by the Greek Ministry of Interior. It aims to redesign the "Access extracts of insurance records in social security organization" service, abbreviated *GR01*. The background of the service is that in Greece, as in other EU countries, social security is paid for in part by employees and in part by employers. Employers retain part of their employees' income and pay it to the social security organization. Service GR01 allows employees to view their employer's payments. Doing so is needed on the one hand to ensure that employers perform the required payments. On the other hand, employees need statements about their social security fees being paid if they want, for example, to prove their work experience when applying for a job, to apply for permits to exercise professions that require work experience, or if they want to apply for loans. GR01 is provided to 6 Million employees across Greece. The existing service provides two variants: in the "conventional" service variant, citizens visit a department of the Social Security Institute, where they are provided with the latest excerpt from their social security record. Alternatively, citizens use the "electronic" service variant, where they have to register at a Social Security Office. Registration currently takes about 4 working days. Once registered, citizens can access their social security records on a Web site. The primary goal of the redesign is, for both service variants, to decrease execution times of the service.

The *Internet reporting information system* scenario was provided by the city of Venice. It aims to redesign the accordingly named service (abbreviated "IRIS"). IRIS allows citizens to submit and track civic issues, for example defect street lights, potholes, vandalism, or breaching of parking regulations. In IRIS, citizens use the Multimedia Messaging Service (MMS) from their smart phones or IRIS' portal to submit evidence of such issues. IRIS has to cope with approximately 3000 requests per year. One goal of the redesign is to improve the transparency on how the public administration processes submitted issues. Another goal is for the responsible public administration to react faster to submitted issues.

Service Feature Modeling in Public Service Design

We here outline the service engineering methodology in which service feature modeling was integrated. It has already been briefly introduced in section 1.1.1. The COCKPIT project's overall methodology, as illustrated in figure 5.15, encompasses a set of integrated methods. To illustrate the context in which service feature modeling was applied, we will roughly outline the different methods and their interactions.

Public service information abstraction aims to collect existing information relevant for the (re-) design of a public service. Policy and legal information is automatically extracted from corresponding Web sources, for example EUR-Lex[14] and national legal texts, for example the German "Gesetze im Internet"[15]. Citizens' stated opinions about the service are mined from Web 2.0 sources and structured, using for example sentiment analysis.

[14] `http://eur-lex.europa.eu/en/index.html`
[15] `http://www.gesetze-im-internet.de/`

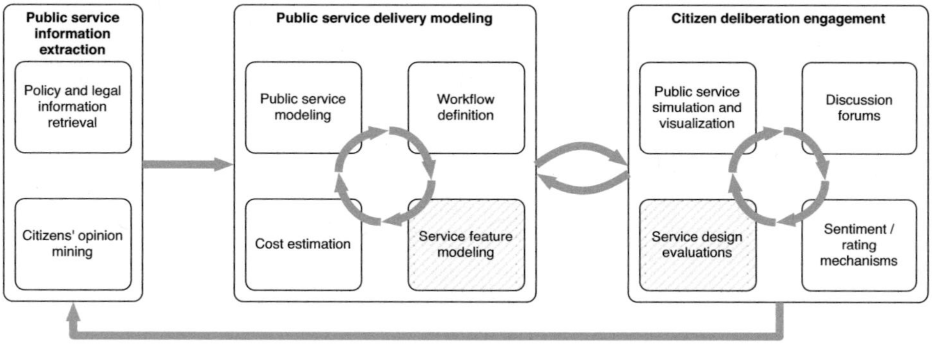

Figure 5.15.: Overview of COCKPIT's methodology, methods directly concerned with service feature modeling are marked in gray [WZ14]

Public service delivery modeling is concerned with conceptualizing the public service using modeling techniques. Generic public service modeling allows modelers to capture information like involved stakeholders, requirements, goals, involved resources, or cost figures of the service. Together with the generic modeling, work flows are defined that specify the actions performed by different stakeholders to deliver the service. Work flow definitions are specified in the Business Process Model and Notation (BPMN) [BPM10]. Work flow definitions make use of information contained in generic public service models. For example, defined stakeholders or resources are used as actors in the work flows. Cost estimation provides methods to determine the estimated mean cost of an individual service invocation for the service provider.

Citizen deliberation engagement aims at participation of citizens during the (re-) design process. Simulation and visualizations are used to communicate (preliminary) results of the public service design. Based on these findings, in discussion forums, citizens can state requirements or proposals on how to improve the service design. Sentiment and rating mechanisms allow for more formalized provision of feedback.

Service feature modeling is tightly integrated in this methodology in two ways: modeling is performed to capture design alternatives of the public service, and the modeled design alternatives are used in citizen deliberation engagement as a basis for citizens to evaluate service designs.

5.3.2. Modeling

Service feature modeling is tightly integrated with other methods of COCKPIT's public service design methodology, most notably with the method to define work flows. The work flow definition method provides two mechanisms to represent service design variants [Wit12]:

- **Inter-process variability** means that for a single request, multiple work flows exist describing the service delivery. As a design activity, one of these work flows is selected to deliver the service during operation.
- **Intra-process variability** means that within a single work flow, multiple flows are specified. To realize intra-process variability, *design-time decision gateways* extend the BPMN. A design-time decision gateway specifies more than one outgoing path, similar to standard BPMN decision gateways. However, as the name suggests, within a design activity, one of these paths is chosen to be implemented and only this path operates once the service is deployed. In contrast, standard BPMN decision gateways dynamically result in an outgoing path while the work flow is executed, based on the fulfillment of certain conditions.

A mapping between these two variability mechanisms and service feature modeling allows modelers to automatically create an SFM that represents the public service's work flow variants. Representing work flow variants with an SFM allows modelers to specify dependencies between them using cross-tree relationships (cf. section 3.2.1). Attributes can be used to specify characteristics of work flow variants. Finally, service feature modeling's usage methods can be used to select work flow variants to implement (cf. chapter 4).

An exemplary mapping between the described work flow variability and SFMs is illustrated in figure 5.16. Upon triggering the automatic creation of an SFM for a given work flow, a feature grouping all work flows is created. It contains all further features addressing work flow variability. Underneath, for every specified service request, an abstract feature is created. The abstract feature must be instantiated by one instance feature, each representing a work flow defined for the service request. Per work flow feature, for every design-time decision gateway within the work flow (if any), an abstract feature represents an alternative flow. In the alternative flow, a feature grouping all tasks within the flow, represented using instance features, is defined. Using this mapping, SFMs representing work flow variability can automatically, and thus repeatedly, be created. This capability is highly important to delimit the effort for creating SFMs.

Figure 5.17 illustrates an excerpt from the SFM modeled while redesigning the GR01 service. Within one of the work flows, a design-time decision gateway denoted "way of submission" is specified. Originating from it are flows that

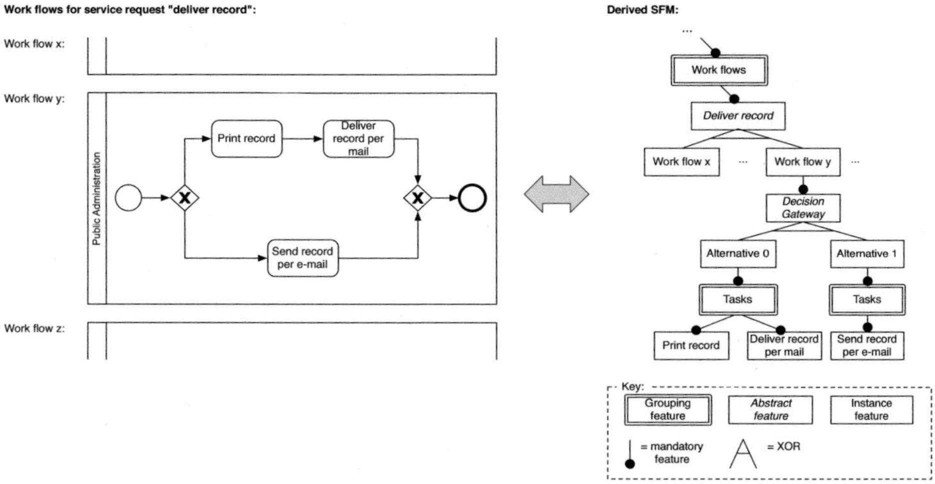

Figure 5.16.: Exemplary mapping of work flow elements to SFM

describe different ways of how citizens can request and obtain their social security records. Four flows originate, which are correspondingly denoted by the instance features "alternative 0" to "alternative 3". These alternatives, following the mapping between work flows and SFMs described above, contain features named "tasks", which group the flow's tasks. For example, one way is for citizens to request and obtain the record within the ERMIS portal[16], which acts as an unique access point for various public services in Greece. In an alternative service design, citizens contact an existing call center to request the record. The subsequent delivery of the record can either be performed by the Hellenic postal service (Greece's postal service) or by handing out the record to citizens in a service center. This structure is automatically created based on a previously defined work flow. As illustrated in figure 5.17, the modelers defined attribute types and associated corresponding attributes to the created features. Attribute types and attributes are the basis for using the SFM for selecting (a set of) service variants to implement (cf. chapter 4). A boolean attribute represents the capability for the citizens to submit the application for a social security record from home. Features (representing tasks) that realize this capability contain a corresponding attribute. Similarly, the capability to deliver the record to citizens' homes is represented with an attribute type and attributes. The "application time" denotes in minutes how long certain tasks approximately take. This attribute type is directly related to the main goal of the service

[16]Named after the Olympian god "Hermes" who acted as a messenger of the gods.

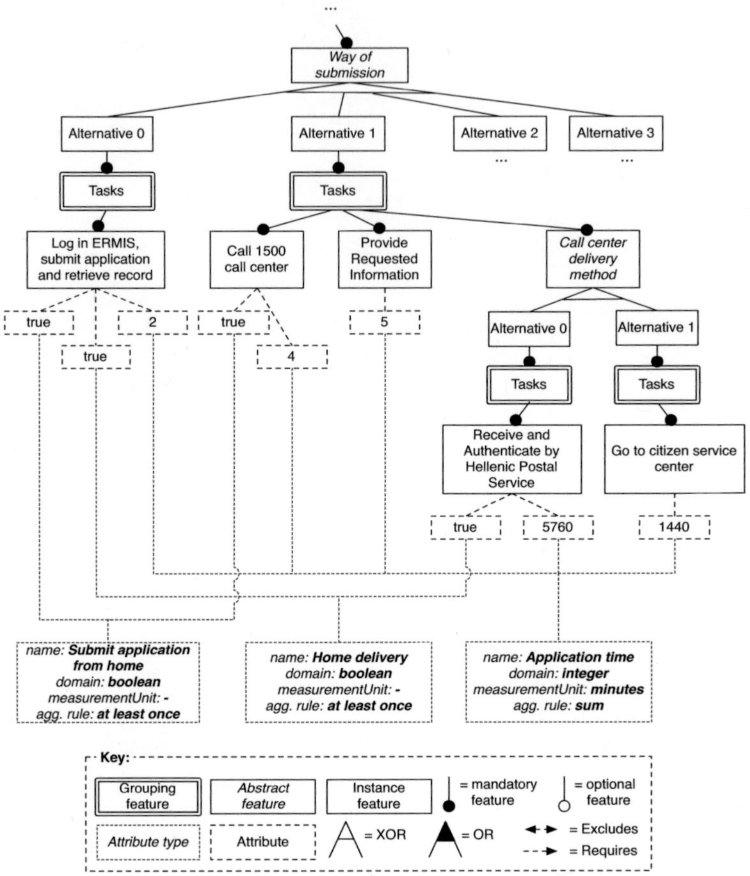

Figure 5.17.: Excerpt of SFM for service GR01 created in the public service use case, based on [WZ14]

redesign to reduce execution time (cf. section 5.3.1).

5.3.3. Usage

Within this use-case, participatory preference-based ranking was performed to obtain decision-makers' (in this case citizens') opinions about the alternative designs. On the implemented valuation server, evaluations were created for each of the two SFMs created in the use case scenarios by the corresponding public administrations. On the evaluation server, corresponding polls were automatically created as described in section 4.4.3. The public administrations, using SFM designers, activated the polls to make them accessible on the interaction platform. Figure 5.18 illustrates a screen shot of the poll for the GR01 service displayed on the evaluation platform.

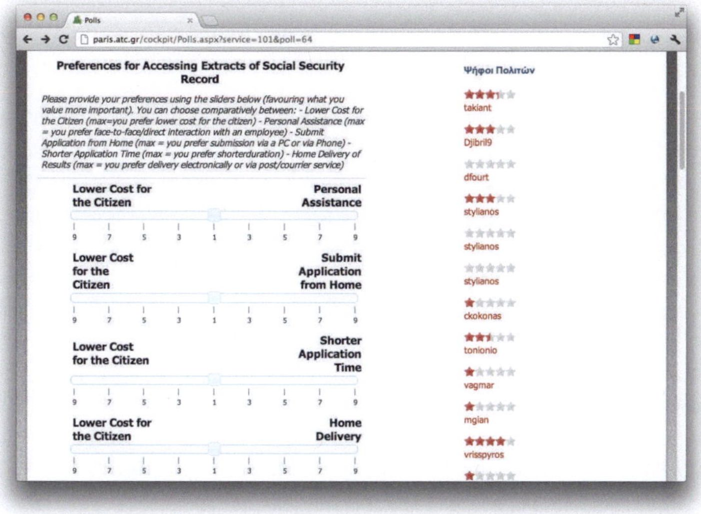

Figure 5.18.: Screenshot of the GR01 poll on the interaction platform [WZ14]

Using this poll, citizens stated their preferences regarding the attribute types defined in the SFMs. 59 citizens stated their preferences regarding GR01 and 43 regarding IRIS. The collected preferences were, at the end of the evaluation, aggregated using the method described in section 4.4.4 and retrieved from the valuation server via the SFM designer.

5.3.4. Realization

To realize service variants based on the ranked configurations, decision-makers of the public administrations assessed highly ranked ones. They ultimately manually selected a single configuration based on the evaluation's input, reflecting a work flow alternative of the public service in design. The decision-makers form the public administrations transferred this configuration to the work flow design by manually resolving the design time decision gateway: they removed 1) the gateway itself and 2) all flows originating from this gateway that were not present in the selected configuration. As a result, a work flow remains that only contains elements found in standard BPMN [BPM10]. This work flow was then used in further design activities, which in the COCKPIT methodology (cf. section 5.3.1) include simulation and visualization of the service design and ultimately implementing, deploying, and operating the service.

5.3.5. Discussion

The here presented modeling use case illustrates the applicability of service feature modeling to represent service variants during service development. The utilization of service feature modeling within a larger service engineering methodology and the presented mapping of features to work flow elements show how service feature modeling can be utilized in combination with established service engineering approaches. The mapping between features and work flow elements further enables automatic generation of SFMs for given work flow definitions, illustrating how automatic model creation can be performed. Representing work flow variants explicitly in SFMs allows to define dependencies between them or their elements (i.e., activities) or to specify their characteristics with attributes as motivated in challenge 1. Regarding the usage, this work flow shows the applicability of preference-based ranking, specifically in a participatory manner as motivated in challenge 6. In both scenarios, evaluations and corresponding polls were successfully created and operated and actual citizen preferences were selected. We discuss the assessment of the collected preferences and their impact on the latter service design activities in section 5.5.3. Regarding the realization of service variants in this use case, only manual methods were applied. The here presented use case further provided the basis for an empirical evaluation of service feature modeling, which is presented in section 5.5.

5.4. Use Case - IaaS Consumption

In the second use case, we use SFMs to configure Infrastructure as a Service (IaaS) for consumption and automatically deploy a Web application on top of it, as motivated in section 1.1.3. Configuration in this context refers to, as we describe in section 2.3.5, an approach to realize service variability through the provision of pre-determined information. This use case addresses the consumer of IaaS, who uses service feature modeling for IaaS configuration and subsequent automatic deployment of the Web application on top of IaaS. This use case further illustrates exemplarily the realization of service variants based on the variant selection made using an SFM. This use case is part of work currently under review [WLBB14].

5.4.1. Use Case Description

IaaS provides consumers with abstracted, virtualized hardware, for example for compute or storage purposes [BKNT11]. IaaS consists of *virtual machines (VMs)* that are hosted on the IaaS provider's physical infrastructure. Consumers rent VMs in different configurations (regarding, for example, number of CPU cores or memory size) and load *images* on them. Images can contain either only basic operating systems or include complete software stacks, depending on the intended use of the VM. On top of the image, consumers install additional software if required. These options result in a complex decision problem for consumers to solve when consuming IaaS. Descriptions of these options are currently provided in HTML (cf. [Ama, Rac]), impeding automated analysis and structured decision-making.

In this use case, SFMs represent the configuration options offered by different IaaS offers (also referred to as *clouds* in the following), for example the VM sizes and available images. The configuration options for each cloud are modeled in a single SFM. These SFMs can be modeled by the providers, to communicate their configuration options to consumers and allow them to select among them using the SFM, or by the consumers themselves. The SFMs are used by IaaS consumers in design activities to configure the IaaS based on their requirements and preferences. The requirements and preferences are driven by the intended use of the IaaS by the consumer, in this case the deployment of a Web application that consists of multiple *components*, each imposing unique requirements on the IaaS. The usage of SFMs is based upon the methods described in chapter 4. In this use case, we exemplarily show how actual service variants, selected through using SFMs, can be realized. Realization is performed though automatically consuming the selected IaaS configuration with the help of a deployment model and middleware and by deploying the Web application on top of it.

We perform the above-mentioned steps to ultimately deploy the Web application of the German start-up Barcoo[17] on IaaS. Barcoo provides community-enriched data on a plethora of products, for example, packaged groceries or cosmetics. Using a mobile application and the cameras of their smart phones, consumers scan the bar codes of products they are interested in. Barcoo provides information about the scanned product, including alternative prices, nutrition information, user ratings, and comments. Though only in operation since 2009, Barcoo reached 10 Million application downloads in April 2013 [Bar].

To provide their mobile applications with product information, Barcoo runs a Web application whose architecture with regard to the different components is illustrated in figure 5.19. The *load balancer* allocates requests to one of multiple

[17] `http://www.barcoo.com`

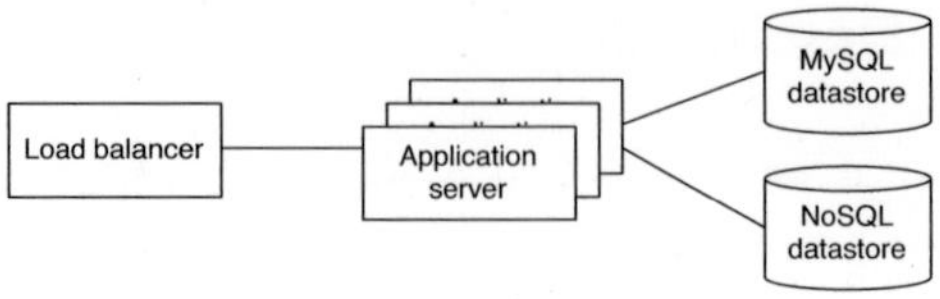

Figure 5.19.: Overview of Barcoo's architecture [WLBB14]

application servers. Barcoo's architecture enables horizontal scaling by switching application servers on and off in reaction to changing workloads. This is, for example, done every night because request amounts regularly drop at that time of day. The information to be sent to consumers is persisted in a *MySQL* database. For better performance, an additional in-memory *NoSQL* database caches the results of common queries to external services. These four components are currently hosted on Amazon Web Services. The motivation for Barcoo to model its Web application is to automatically re-deploy it, for example in case of a desaster. In such cases, Barcoo has to ensure fast delivery of a compensatory back-end to ensure ongoing service to avoid the loss of users.

5.4.2. Modeling

Modeling, in this use case, aims to represent the configuration options of IaaS offers. The configuration options of every IaaS offer to consider are represented by a single SFM. We first present a domain model for representing IaaS, enabling comparability between models as described in section 3.3.3. We then describe how we used this domain model to model the IaaS offers of two common providers.

IaaS Domain Model

We propose a domain model for IaaS feature models that captures the configuration options of IaaS to consider. An IaaS feature model represents the configuration options offered by one cloud, for example the AWS Elastic Compute Cloud [Ama]. A domain model serves multiple purposes: first, it prescribes the structure and relevant variation points to consider when modeling IaaS with service feature modeling. This decreases modeling effort because modelers use the structure as a starting point instead of beginning from scratch. Second, the domain model ensures comparability between different IaaS feature models as discussed in section 4.5. Comparability makes it easier to communicate different IaaS feature models and eventually allows for their (automatic) comparison.

The domain model is based on findings in previous work we performed to identify typical IaaS configuration options by assessing 11 IaaS offers [Bar13]. Initially, for every individual IaaS offer, all configuration parameters were collected and grouped. In the following, the collected parameters were filtered to contain only parameters that are present in at least two IaaS offers. Additionally, for every parameter, it was determined whether a) the parameter is controllable by the user, b) whether the user can select among variants for the parameter, c) what the range of the parameter is (alternative selection, interval, free choice), and d) whether the parameter is dependent on other parameters. In the following, every IaaS offer was described based on this scheme. Consolidating the 11 derived schemes provides an overview of the parameters in which IaaS offers are configurable and of the nature of the configuration options.

The thus obtained information was the basis for deriving two SFM domain models: one representing standard IaaS configuration options and one representing extended IaaS configuration options. The selection of configuration parameters to consider in every domain model is based on the frequency in which they are available in the assessed IaaS offers. To derive SFMs, mapping rules between the identified parameters and features were defined so that a) groups of parameters are represented by grouping features, b) independent parameters are represented by abstract features (with instance features representing the choices for the parameter), and c) dependent parameters are represented as feature bundles underneath a grouping feature. Additionally, for dependent parameters whose options are numeric, attributes and corresponding attribute types are created.

Figure 5.20 illustrates the proposed domain model for standard IaaS configuration options. The first configuration option concerns the *virtual machine*, which can be of different types, for example referred to as “small” or “large” [Ama]. Attributes characterize each virtual machine type, stating its *memory*, *disk size*, *cost / hour*, and *CPU cores*. These values are either added manually by the modeler or they could be provided dynamically through composition of SFMs (cf. section 3.4). The next configuration concerns the selection of a *basic image*. Prepacked software of the image is modeled in a mandatory abstract feature. Potential dependencies or incompatibilities between VMs and images are expressed using *requires* and *excludes* relationships. Potential costs of images are stored in attributes *cost / hour*. The *software environment* contains features representing *installation tasks* for software that can be installed on top of images. Both, images and installation tasks can be annotated with attributes stating *deployment times*, allowing decision-makers to consider these values in configuration.

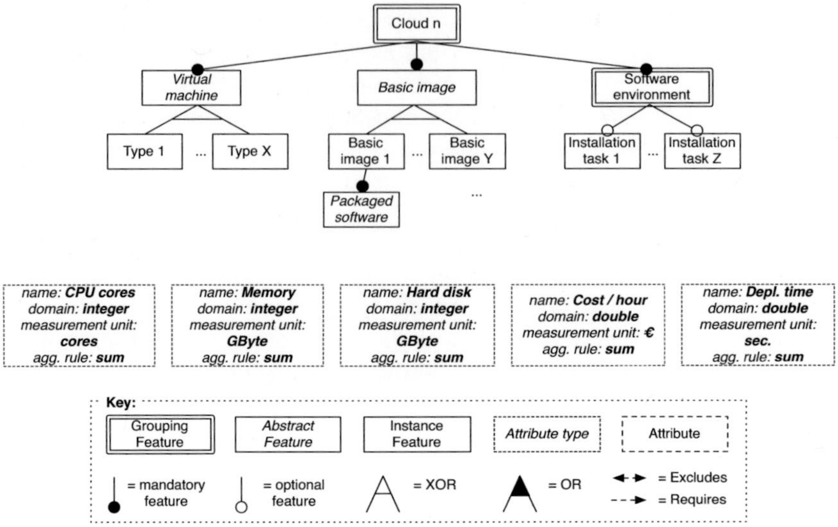

Figure 5.20.: Proposed domain model to represent IaaS [WLBB14]

Modeling IaaS Offers

Based on the presented domain model, we modeled two exemplary IaaS offers, namely those of Amazon EC2 [Ama] and Rackspace [Rac]. Figure 5.21 illustrates an excerpt for the SFM representing Amazon EC2.

In both SFMs, we modeled VMs of different sizes for the two IaaS providers, 6 for Amazon EC2 and 7 for Rackspace, as instance features. For each VM, we captured the number of CPU cores, the memory in GByte, the hard disk size in GByte, and the cost per hour in Euro using attributes associated with the attribute types defined in the domain model. The models values were derived from the publicly available descriptions of the IaaS services [Ama, Rac]. We further modeled basic images with correspondingly named instance features, 6 for Amazon EC2 and 3 for Rackspace. We use additional instance features to represent the prepacked software of the image, for example the operating system. In both SFMs, we modeled 6 software installation tasks, including MySQL, Git version control, or the Network Time Protocol (NTP). Cross-tree relationships are used to exclude redundant installation of software. For example, if an image is selected that already comes with MySQL installed, additional selection of the MySQL installation task is prohibited. Attributes represent the deployment time in seconds measured for starting VMs with selected images and for installing software on top of VMs. These attributes were derived from our own measurements of these times. Overall, the SFMs denote 1280 configurations

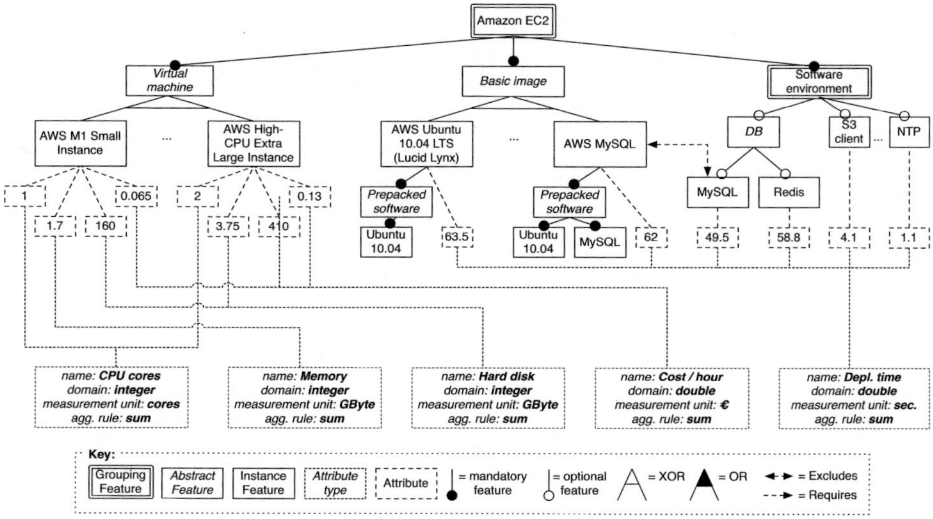

Figure 5.21.: Excerpt of the IaaS feature model representing Amazon EC2 [WLBB14]

for AWS and 896 for Rackspace. Details about the two models are provided in table 5.2.

5.4.3. Usage

The usage of the outlined SFMs followed the usage process described in section 4.1. The configurations for both SFMs were determined and narrowed down with requirements filtering, and ultimately preference-based ranking was used to select the configuration to consume. No skyline filter was applied because of how the IaaS offers are constructed: no configurations are dominated (cf. section 5.2.3). The Web application to deploy on IaaS, however, consists of multiple components as described in section 5.4.1. Every component requires a different configuration based on the functionalities it aims to fulfill and the non-functionalities. The usage methods are thus applied once for every component of the Web application, resulting possibly in different configurations for every component.

We defined exemplary requirements and preferences for the IaaS configuration for every component. In every case, we require the software responsible for delivering the required functionality to be present. For example, for the MySQL component, an instance feature "MySQL" is required. Additionally, for the application server and load balancer components, which are logic intensive, we required more than 8 CPU cores and for the two database components we required more than 1000 GByte disk space and more or equal to 8 GByte memory. The application server further requires installation of an Amazon Simple Storage Solution (S3) client, GIT for version control, and running the Network Time Protocol. All requirements have a weight of 1.0 assigned, indicating their non-negotiable nature. Filtering the configuration set for the stated requirements, we derived a reduced configuration set as depicted in column two in table 5.4. We stated exemplary preferences for the used attribute types. For the application server and load balancer components, we denoted the number CPU cores as most important, followed by low cost, memory, disk size, and lastly deployment time. For the database components, we prefer low cost, followed by CPU cores, memory, disk space, and lastly deployment time. Performing the preference-based ranking, we determined the highest-ranked configuration per component and fed it back into the IaaS deployment model.

Component	**Configurations meeting req.[#]**	**Mean deployment time [sec]** overall	inst. start	installation	**Depl. steps**
App. server	10 AWS, 0 Rack.	801	63	738	8
MySQL DB	96 AWS, 48 Rack.	122	62	60	3
NoSQL DB	64 AWS, 0 Rack.	135	65	70	3
Load balancer	160 AWS, 0 Rack.	93	63	30	3

Table 5.4.: Overview of characteristics for configuration and deployment use case [WLBB14]

5.4.4. Realization

In this use case, we exemplarily show the realization of selected service variants. Realization includes the automatic consumption of the selected VMs, loading the selected images on them, and installing software on top of these images, in this case resulting in the deployment of the Barcoo Web application. To automate these steps, we utilize an IaaS deployment model presented in previous work currently under review [WLBB14]. The deployment model's meta model is illustrated in figure 5.22.

The IaaS deployment model's application part models a *distributed system*, for example a Web application, to be deployed on IaaS. A distributed system consists of a set of *components*, representing, for example, a Web application's Web server or load balancer. A requires relationship models potential dependencies between components. Each component can be realized in multiple *instances*,

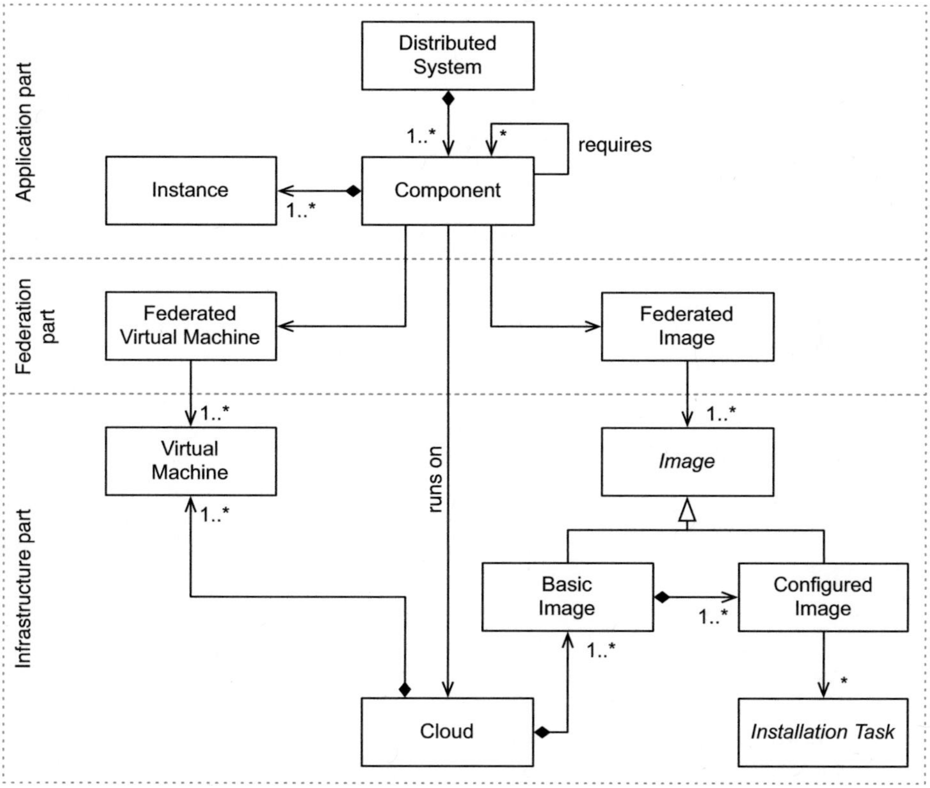

Figure 5.22.: Meta model of the IaaS deployment model [WLBB14]

running a configured operating system with predefined software stacks. Using the component element to group instances ensures they all have the same virtual machine type, image, and software stack. The varying numbers of instances deployable for each component results in horizontal scalability. The dynamic deployment or undeployment of instances in reaction to or in anticipation of changing load is outside of the scope of our approach and typically performed by a load balancer component.

The IaaS deployment model's federation part abstracts from underlying IaaS offers. This abstraction allows the modeler to specify that the distributed system's components run on different IaaS offers. Components are assigned to *federated virtual machines*, grouping similar VMs, and a *federated image*, grouping functionally equivalent images.

Finally, the infrastructure part contains information about different IaaS offers to run the application on. Each IaaS offer is represented by a *cloud*, which is operated by a single provider. Every component from the application part runs on a cloud. Clouds contain a set of *virtual machines* and a set of *basic images.* Basic images contain an operating system and packages software. A *configured image* represents a basic image with additional *installation tasks* to be executed during deployment. Configured images thus present increased deployment efforts, resulting in longer deployment times.

For our use case, we defined the application and the infrastructure part of the IaaS deployment model. As in the IaaS feature models, we defined 5 VMs and 6 basic images for Amazon AWS and 7 VMs and 3 basic images for Rackspace. We defined 6 software installation tasks to perform on top of basic images.

Having the IaaS deployment model in place and having obtained the information about the selected configuration for every component from the IaaS feature model, we defined the federation layer of the deployment model. Federated virtual machine elements were created for the selected VM and federated images were created for the selected basic image and additional software installation tasks for every component.

Using the thus completed deployment model, we ran the automatic deployment 10 times for every component to assert its proper functioning and reliably measure required times for the deployment. The deployment was performed using a *deployment middleware* as described in previous work [WLBB14]. It takes as input the completely modeled IaaS deployment models and performs deployment, including VM startup, image loading, and software installation via Secure Shell (SSH) commands. The measured mean times for deploying every component are illustrated in table 5.4.

5.4.5. Discussion

The application of model-based approaches to the configuration of IaaS and the deployment of a Web application on top of it has multiple advantages: the large number of configuration options (1280 for AWS and 896 for Rackspace) emphasizes the complexity of the decisions to be made, which we address with systematic support through requirements filtering and preference-based ranking. The application of service feature modeling and the IaaS deployment model allows users further to automate consumption of the selected IaaS configuration and deployment on top of it. This allows systems, for example, to deploy Web applications unexpectedly in reaction to a disaster. Given that requirements and preferences are stated, selection can automatically be re-performed on demand, based on service feature modeling's selection process, as motivated in challenge 4. If varying attributes are composed into the IaaS feature models (cf. section 3.4), re-selection of variants just before deployment might lead to different results and is thus desirable. Table 5.4 illustrates the many involved steps - for instance start up, updates, or installation of software - that produce effort and are error-prone if performed manually. Using the IaaS deployment model, we a) capture all relevant information for the deployment and b) perform it automatically with regard to starting selected VMs and images and installing the required software on top of them. While the measured execution times per component are high in some cases, we argue that the execution time of manual performance, requiring reactions and provision of input, is likely to be even higher.

In this use case, the representation of IaaS with SFMs allows the user to capture the many configuration options it offers. The use case does, though, also reveal limitations of applying service feature modeling [Bar13]: features and attributes are suitable to represent distinct concerns or values. However, when variable objects are very fine-granular and / or manifold, representation via features and attributes becomes cumbersome. For example, if memory or hard disk space is configurable on a megabyte level, an overwhelming and unfeasible number of features to represent the resulting variants is required. We discuss possible approaches to address this shortcoming in section 6.2.

This use case further exemplifies the role domain models play in service feature modeling. We want to make configuration decisions, regarding virtual machine types, images, and installed software, across clouds (cf. challenge 5). Thus, we require a common structure to make these decisions comparable among clouds. Furthermore, the domain model allows the user to map IaaS feature models to the IaaS deployment model. Using the mapping, IaaS feature models can automatically be created from an IaaS deployment model, given it already contains information about IaaS offers. This automatic SFM generation significantly decreases manual modeling efforts. It is enabled by a correspondingly designed *interaction service* within the SFM designer (cf. section 5.1.3). Based on the mapping, after using the IaaS feature model for configuration, the decisions made can be fed back into the IaaS deployment model. This results in the creation of *federated virtual machines* and *federated images* elements in the deployment model.

5.5. Empirical Evaluation

In addition to the so far outlined evaluation types, we performed an empirical evaluation. While the proof-of-concept implementation illustrates the realizability of service feature modeling and the use cases show its applicability to realistic scenarios, the empirical evaluation aims to provide insights into the perceived quality of our approach. The empirical evaluation was performed in the context of the use case presented in section 5.3. It consists of two surveys that address a) how the modelers and decision-makers from the public administrations (in the following denoted as *service engineers* for simplicity) who modeled and used SFMs perceived the approach and b) how the citizens participating in the preference-based ranking by answering the polls on the interaction platform perceived this method. Surveys of this kind are an established method to evaluate software or designs [HPSVA95]. In this section, we describe how we designed the surveys, we discuss the data we collected, and the results we draw from this data. The empirical evaluation is described in work currently in review [WZ14].

5.5.1. Design of Empirical Evaluation

The first survey was distributed to the **service engineers** from the use case partners. Its results thus provide a focused set of expert insights from a select group of highly suitable respondents (the backgrounds of the respondents can be seen in figure 5.5). A first set of attitude questions (with standardized ordinal scale of *strongly agree*, *somewhat agree*, *somewhat disagree* and *strongly disagree*), indicated with A in figure 5.23, addresses the *usability* of service feature modeling, namely, whether the approach was understood by the service engineer and what effort was required to adopt this new approach. A second set of attitude questions, indicated with B, addresses the *expressibility* of SFMs. Expressibility is addressed generically (is it possible to model all desired service alternatives?) and specifically with regard to attribute types for modeling properties of alternatives and dependencies for delimiting the set of valid alternatives. A third set of attitude questions, indicated with C, addresses the *interpretation* and *usefulness* of the rankings of service alternatives for the subsequent service design. The overall question addressed is whether the information on the ranking of service alternatives enables decision-makers to incorporate citizens' preferences into public service design. The individual questions aim to determine whether the presented rankings allow decision-makers to determine the preferences by the citizens. Further, it was asked whether properties of relevance for the citizens can be derived from the collected data. Finally, the comprehensibility and (from the service engineer's perspective) reasonableness of the determined suggestions is addressed. The service engineer survey further allowed service engineers to provide open feedback on service feature modeling to state concerns or comments that are not addressed by the attitude questions.

The second survey, consisting entirely of attitude questions, addresses the **citizens** who participated in the polls on the interaction platform. We have to note that, while addressing the SFM approach, these questions are biased by the created SFMs and by the design and implementation of the interaction platform, which in the COCKPIT project lay outside of our control area. However, the questions try to focus on those aspects that depend on the SFM approach per se and not its presentation on the interaction platform. A set of questions, indicated with D in figure 5.24, addresses the *usability* of the pairwise comparison method to state preferences on public service design variants. These questions address, on the one hand, how easy it was for citizens to perform these tasks, its effectiveness, and number of comparisons. A second set of questions, indicated with E, addresses the *usefulness* of stating preferences and evaluating public service design alternatives.

5.5.2. Data Collection

We collected 6 filled out service engineer surveys from the use case partners. Information on the background of the involved service engineers is provided in table 5.5. The collected data contained 6 missing values that we dealt with by *mean imputation*, meaning that we used the arithmetic mean to replace the missing value [Göt09].

We made the citizens survey available on the interaction platform. The survey was available in *English*, *Italian* and *Greek* to increase its reach. We collected overall 25 filled out surveys from citizens, 5 for the English, 11 for the Italian and 9 for the Greek version. The collected data contained 12 missing values that we dealt with, again, by mean imputation.

User	Experience in service design (years)	Experience with ICT tools (*)	Confidence w.r.t. the provided answers (*)
Greece 1	2	5	4
Greece 2	2.5	3	3
Greece 3	1	2	3
Greece 4	2	4	4
Greece 5	4	4	4
Venice	0	3	3
Mean	**1.92**	**3.5**	**3.5**

Table 5.5.: Information on service engineers participating in evaluation; *: 5=expert, 4=high, 3=medium, 2=low, 1=none [WZ14]

5.5.3. Results of Empirical Evaluation

The data collected from the **service engineers** hints, overall, at how useful service feature modeling is for usage in public service design. However, the data is, of course, the result of the individual experiences of the questioned service engineers. As table 5.5 illustrates, having on average around 1.9 years of experience in service design and self-assessing their experience with ICT tools and their confidence with regard to the provided answers both between medium and high, the consulted service engineers can be considered suitable for collecting data on service engineering.

With regard to the *usability* of service feature modeling, the service engineers found it takes getting used to the new approach - as indicated by the results for questions $A1$ to $A3$ that stagger between moderate agreement and moderate disagreement. The perception of how easy the modeling of SFMs is with the provided tools seems to depend on the experience with ICT tools: those service engineers that state to have "high" or "expert" experience with ICT tools found modeling of service alternatives rather easy, while those that assessed themselves as having lower ICT experience did not agree. To make service feature modeling usable also for service engineers with little ICT experience, its integration into larger service design methodologies, dedicated training, and strong user documentation, for example in the form of help mechanisms within the SFM designer, are fundamental.

The answers to questions $B1$ to $B3$ show in each case moderate to strong agreement with the claims that service feature modeling is *expressive* when it comes to capturing service design alternatives and their properties. The capability to delimit the set of alternatives using *requires* or *excludes* dependencies is considered

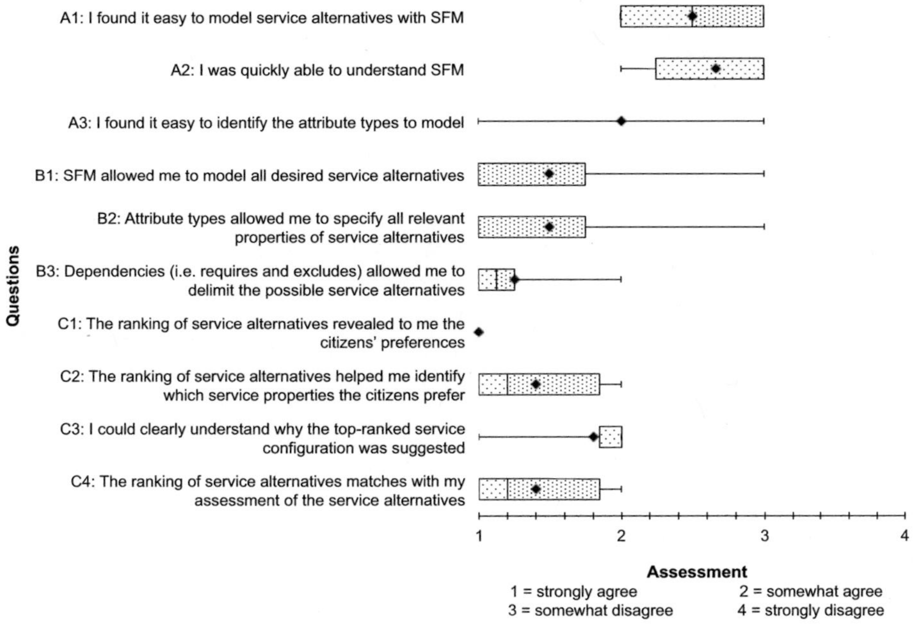

Figure 5.23.: Evaluation results of the service engineer survey [WZ14]

especially useful.

The answers to questions indicated with *C*, addressing the *interpretation* and *usefulness* of the ranking of service alternatives for the subsequent service design, are quite homogeneous. All 6 service engineers moderately to strongly agree that the provided information on ranking of service alternatives and attribute types is useful. Especially interesting is how the approach helped service engineers to determine not only the most preferred alternative, but also the subsequent ones in the form of a ranking. As one service engineer states in the open comments: "I think it is very useful indeed to be able to get the citizens' preferences automatically and sorted. It is not so much about the first choice as the order of the choices, especially if you have many votes.". Another service engineer agrees: "[...] it's not only the top ranked option but also all the order of the preferred configurations.". These answers indicate that it is advantageous to consider multiple service design alternatives, as advocated by service feature modeling. Again, a service engineer supports this notion: "I think the ability to have all alternatives in the same model is quite useful.".

The mean values for all answers indicate in all questions moderate agreement of the **citizens** with statements about the *usability* and *usefulness* of expressing opinions on service design alternatives with the service feature modeling approach. Figure 5.24 illustrates the results. These findings are not fully satisfactory and need to be taken seriously because they show how applicable service feature modeling's ranking approach is for participatory service design. It has to be noted, though, that the presented perceptions depend on how service feature modeling was utilized (for example, how well the meaning of attribute types was communicated to the citizens) and on the performance of the interaction platform in presenting the polls and their results.

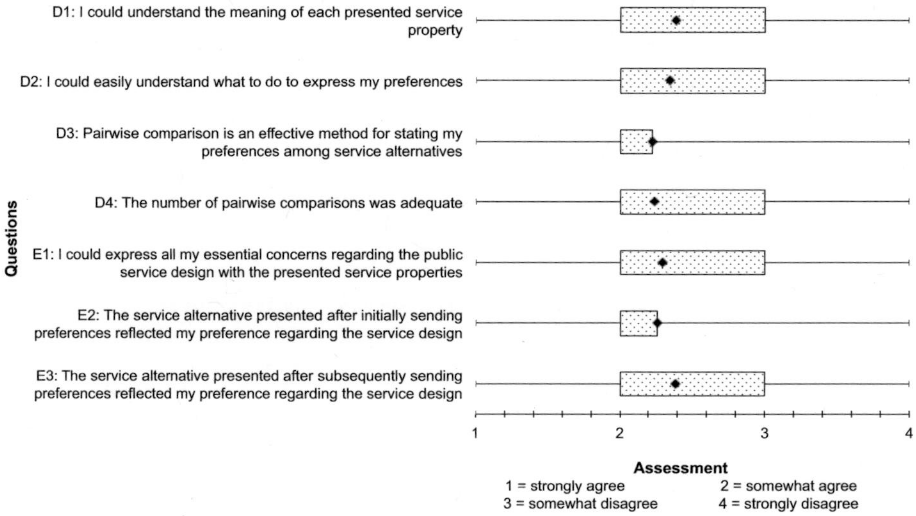

Figure 5.24.: Evaluation results of the citizen survey, based on [WZ14]

To improve the means of allowing citizens to state preferences on service design alternatives, more efficient statement techniques could be used, for example relying on *spider diagrams* [ABHV10] or by using *iterative AHP* to reduce the number of required pairwise comparisons [LS93]. Further, by means of checking hard constraints, for example that a certain budget threshold must be considered, the number of possible configurations could be reduced prior to evaluations on the interaction platform, thus allowing to present only very distinct service design alternatives.

5.5.4. Discussion

The results of the empirical evaluation have to be considered with caution, most notably due to the small sample size of answers by both service engineers and citizens. Due to this small size, the results should be perceived as indications or hints on how the utilized service feature modeling methods are perceived rather than as facts. We perceive the results relevant nonetheless in that they, especially the qualitative statements, hint on whether our original design goals were reached and what areas of future research might be of interest[18]. Another potential threat to the validity of the results is that the questioned service engineers may have been biased when providing their answers. This can be ruled out however, as they are affiliated with different institutions from different countries. Furthermore, the polled service engineers are unrelated to the authors of this thesis and were not part of the COCKPIT project in which this evaluation was performed.

Overall, service engineers with minor experience in ICT tools found service feature modeling rather demanding to get into, while those with more experience had less problems in this regard. All service engineers polled the approach good expressibility and rank the interpretation and usefulness of the information provided by service feature modeling as especially good, which supports corresponding claims in this work's hypothesis. This can be taken to show that service feature modeling was a valuable addition to established service design instruments in the context of public service design. Within the polled sample, citizens' assessment of usability and usefulness was only moderate. As discussed in section 5.5.3, these results may depend on the implementation of the interaction platform, which lay outside of our control. Thus, to obtain reliable results, further analyses need to be conducted, which we consider to be a relevant field for future work, as discussed in section 6.2.

[18]For example, in the course of the COCKPIT project, we received feedback that not only the participation of consumers through ranking in service design, but also the collaboration of experts in defining SFMs would be of value. This feedback largely motivated our approach to compose SFMs from services (cf. section 3.4).

6. Conclusion

To conclude this thesis, we summarize the presented contributions, especially with respect to the challenges presented in section 1.3 and the hypothesis presented in section 1.4. We furthermore provide an overview of future research directions that we identified throughout or work.

6.1. Summary

Within this thesis, we present our research regarding the modeling and selection of software service variants. Service feature modeling provides a modeling language and a set of methods to address the claims made in our hypothesis. The hypothesis consists of multiple parts that we address in the following:

- Service feature modeling provides an expressive and usable language to represent service variants, presented in chapter 3. To address this goal, feature modeling from software product line engineering acts as a basis for designing the service feature modeling language. Feature modeling is both well researched [BSRC10] and widely applied in practice [BRN+13]. This makes it more likely that users of service feature modeling feel already familiar with basic concepts of the language, for example the hierarchical decomposition into features and the types of relationships between them. Its foundation in feature modeling thus increases service feature modeling's usability. It furthermore allows modelers and decision-makers to make use of and build upon a broad set of related methods, addressing the extension of the language, for example with attributes [BTRC05] or cardinalities [CHE05], or related usage methods, for example staged configuration [CHE04] or the utilization of multi-criteria decision making methods [BAGS10]. Service feature modeling extends standard feature modeling via its addition of feature types. Feature types introduce more fine-grained semantics to features, which are generally understood in a solution-oriented way in service feature modeling. We specify how features of different types relate to service variants in section 3.2.3. The differentiated semantics of features based on their type positively impacts the understanding of SFMs and eases their creation. Feature types also play an important role for requirements filtering. They allow decision-makers to specify requirements regarding abstract features, whose fulfillment through the selection of a child instance feature cannot be expressed without differentiating between types. Finally, feature types allow to define domain models as described in section 3.3.3. They act as a common basis to derive similarly structured, comparable SFMs, enabling use cases like variant selection across SFMs, thus increasing the applicability of the language. Domain models thus address challenge 5 regarding comparability of variants from different services, which is motivated in section 1.3.2. We furthermore extended standard feature modeling with attribute types to capture information that is common to multiple attributes associated to that type. Attribute types increase the usability of modeling SFMs because they avoid redundant specification of information, which creates efforts and is error-prone. Attribute types furthermore increase the expressiveness of SFMs as compared to standard feature models, in that they allow the capturing of before unregarded information like standard aggregation rules or scale orders. Through the definition of aggregation rules, attribute types provide basis for expressing characteristics of service variants represented by configurations. Attribute types thus address challenge 1 regarding expressing characteristics of variants motivated in section 1.3.1. Overall, in contrast to languages from related work, service feature modeling is applicable to a broad set of services, makes use of advanced elements like attributes and even extends them with attribute types, and introduces feature types to differentiate the semantics of features and enable new usage methods.

- Service feature modeling enables experts to collaborate in specifying service variants. While service feature modeling is well capable of being used similarly to standard feature modeling (cf. section 3.3), it furthermore provides means to compose SFMs from services as presented in section 3.4. Through a composition model, specified roles, and coordination rules, this method allows services to contribute results to an SFM while detecting and triggering the resolution of conflicts. Dedicated service adapters allow humans to act as services in this process, being notified for example via e-mail about potential conflicts to resolve. Thus, composition of SFMs from services enables collaborative modeling, addressing the corresponding challenge 3 motivated in section 1.3.1. In addition, otherwise static elements of an SFM like attribute values can dynamically be provided on-demand through this method. For example, at the beginning of a usage process, up to date performance values describing service non-functionalities can be contributed. Composition of SFMs from service thus also addresses challenge 2 regarding the inclusion of dynamic or complex characteristics in SFMs as motivated in section 1.3.1. This composition method, in contrast to related work, does not only address the composition of SFMs but also the process of coordinating stakeholders in doing so.

- Service feature modeling provides a set of useful methods to use SFMs with the goal of (participatorily) selecting service variants, presented in chapter 4. The methods are subsumed by a service feature modeling usage process that allows to flexibly combine them for variant selection. The usage process addresses challenge 4 regarding a structured selection process motivated in section 1.3.2. Initially, the process starts with the determination of an SFM's configuration set. Each configuration represents a variant of the variable service modeled in the SFM. The mapping of SFMs to constraint satisfaction problems and their solving follow established approaches from related work [KOD10]. Extending existing approaches, attributes for each attribute type are aggregated for every configuration as defined by the corresponding aggregation rule. A novel requirements filter allows decision-makers to delimit the configuration set of configurations that do not fulfill desired functionalities or non-functionalities. Requirements can be stated regarding the existence of features in a configuration as well as regarding the values of the configuration's attributes. In contrast to many requirements filters presented in related work, this filter performs matchmaking between configurations and requirements in a fuzzy way. It determines the degree of fulfillment of configurations regarding weighted requirements. A fuzzy approach is especially useful where no configuration completely fulfills stated requirements. Service feature modeling furthermore provides a method for preference-based ranking of configurations. It applies a well-known multi-criteria decision making approach to service feature modeling. SFMs are transferred to polls consisting of pairwise comparisons among defined attribute types. Such comparisons result in a ranking of the importance of attribute types for stakeholders. In combination with a ranking of configuration performances regarding attribute types, an overall stakeholder preference ranking is derived. To decrease the number of configurations to consider in the preference-based ranking, prior skyline filtering dismisses dominated configurations from the configuration set. The description of the skyline filter, which is adapted from database systems, includes the mapping of SFMs to the skyline operator and the procedure on how to perform it. Preference-based ranking provides the basis for participatory service variant selection because it abstracts from (technical details defined in) SFMs. The concepts of evaluations, polls, votes, and preferences as well as an evaluation life-cycle lay the foundations for the participatory ranking of configurations. Participatory preference-based ranking addresses challenge 6 regarding user participation in variant selection as motivated in section 1.3.2. In contrast to approaches from related work, service feature modeling thus presents a comprehensive set of combinable methods for service variant selection.

To assess the outlined contributions, this thesis presents multiple evaluation methods in chapter 5. A proof-of-concept implementation of the SFM tool suite illustrates that the outlined methods, addressing in sum all challenges outlined in section 1.3, are realizable. The proof-of-concept includes the design of the SFM tool suite's architecture. It consists of an SFM designer that modelers and decision-makers use to create and edit SFMs and apply the different usage methods to it. Composition of SFMs from services is enabled by a collaboration server that stores results and ensures coordination of their contribution. The valuation server exposes polls for preference-based ranking to potentially non-technical stakeholders to allow them to participate in service variant selection. These parts of the architecture implement RESTful service interfaces, allowing their loose coupling and extension with novel, unforeseen components. A performance analysis of our implementation shows that it performs sufficiently to be utilized with SFMs of varying sizes. Both for realistic SFMs created in use cases as well as synthetic models of different sizes, configuration set determination, skyline and requirements filter, and preference-based ranking perform fast enough to be used in practice. Two use cases illustrate the applicability of service feature modeling, both regarding the modeling language and the selection methods. The first use case addresses the modeling and selection of variants during public service design. Here, modeling strongly builds upon a mapping between work flows defining the public service in design and SFM elements. Configuration set determination and participatory preference-based ranking are the usage methods applied in this use case. In participatory preference-based ranking, citizens state their preferences leading to the selection of a best-matching configuration and thus service variant. The second use case addresses the modeling, selection, and realization of IaaS variants. Multiple SFMs, based on the same IaaS domain model, are modeled to represent the configuration options offered by IaaS, which drive the realization of IaaS variants. The usage methods configuration-set determination, requirements filtering, and preference-based ranking are applied to select suitable IaaS configurations for every component of a Web application. This use case furthermore illustrates the realization of IaaS variants through automatic consumption of the configured variants and the subsequent automatic deployment of the Web application on top of them. Based on the first use case, an empirical evaluation presented in section 5.5 assesses how service feature modeling is perceived on the one hand by service engineers and on the other hand by citizens participating in variant selection through preference-based ranking. Results indicate that service feature modeling is easier to adopt for engineers with longer experience. The results underpin that the service feature modeling language is usable. Good expressibility of the service feature modeling language and usefulness of the preference-based ranking are attested both in survey ratings as well as in qualitative comments by the service engineers. The citizens on average judge the usability and usefulness of the preference-based ranking moderately positively. This is to be addressed in future work.

Overall, we find that service feature modeling is realizable with sufficient performance, is applicable to realistic scenarios, and is a strong method to model and select service variants. Service feature modeling thus constitutes a meaningful novel contribution that is beneficial to both modelers and decision-makers.

6.2. Future work

The research presented in this thesis can be extended into different directions.

- **Representing configuration parameters with a large range:** A shortcoming of feature-based representation is how to deal with configurable parameters that denote a large range, in the mathematical sense of the set of values a parameter may take. Representing every value of such a range with a dedicated instance feature and corresponding attributes would create an unfeasibly large SFM with an equally large configuration set. For example, IaaS offerings like that from ProfitBricks allow users to select IaaS configurations very fine-granularly. Users can, for a VM, select any number of CPU cores ranging from 1 to 48, any number of memory ranging from 1 up to 240 GBytes, and any number of GByte for storage up to 5000. Representing these options each with individual features would require 5288 features, and the resulting configuration set would include over 56 million configurations, considering these options alone. To address this expressibility issue, two solution strategies come to mind. On the one hand, solution approaches that aim to represent a reduced number of variants in an SFM have been presented [Bar13]. Here, experts are asked to delimit features and their combinations based on domain knowledge. For example, a VM with 48 cores but only 1 GByte of memory might be theoretically realizable but practically infeasible. A related approach is to narrow down variability based on profiles derived from best practices. For example, if a VM is intended to host a database, certain constraints on the variants might be deducible. Finally, clustering techniques or segmentation may be applied to combine multiple variants, thus reducing variability. On the other hand, different selection methods may be used that avoid having to represent every variant within an SFM. For example, parameters with a large range may be specified in artifacts used in conjunction with SFMs. Selection methods in this scenario, however, need to address potential dependencies between the parameter configuration and the SFM-based variant selection. This may lead to an iterative selection process that switches between parameter configuration and SFM-based variant selection. Both solution strategies are currently only roughly thought out and further research on their individual advantages and disadvantages, or even their combinability, needs to be conducted.

- **Representing complex attributes:** Attribute values in feature modeling as well as in service feature modeling are deterministic in nature and modeled independently from one another. In the variants of a variable service, however, dependencies between attribute values may exist. For example, attributes denoting "cost" induced by a feature may change in reaction to other features also being selected, in the case of discounts complex pricing functions. One approach to address dependencies between attributes are modify relationships [Kuh11]. Based on a generic definition of modify relationships [FFB02], in this context, they capture the effect that the change of an attribute value has on another feature's attribute value [Kuh11]. Modify relationships are cross-tree relationships that model value influences between features and attributes, allowing, for example, to state that the selection of a feature induces a linear transformation on a specific attribute value. Modify relationships have been formalized, a graphical syntax for them has been presented, analysis operations have been adapted to make use of them, and tool support exists in form of a proof-of-concept implementation. Existing shortcomings of the approach include dealing with cyclic modify relationships or representing influences that result from more complex triggers (for example, modifications are applied only if a set of features is selected). Another approach for dealing with dependencies between attributes is to make use of composing SFMs from services as presented in section 3.4. Rather than attempting to represent dependencies within an SFM, services are used to provide attribute values on demand, implementing arbitrary functionality to derive the required values. While this thesis lays the foundations for this approach, extensions can be considered in future work. For example, the contribution of results may be integrated into the determination of configurations as part of attribute aggregation. For every configuration, services could be invoked to provide configuration-specific, aggregated attribute values. Such an approach would lift configuration determination to be an orchestration of service invocations, driven by an SFM.

- **Aggregation of multiple preferences:** In participatory preference-based ranking, when multiple stakeholders state their individual preferences for attribute types, service feature modeling currently uses the geometric mean to aggregate the preferences. However, using mean values for the aggregation has limitations: in a worst case scenario, opposite opinions level each other out, producing a meaningless result. The utilization of alternative preference aggregation methods is thus future work. It has been proposed to verify that decision-makers have similar views as a precondition to aggregating individual preferences [O'L93]. However, given the potentially open nature of participatory approaches, including a diverse group of decision-makers, this precondition cannot necessarily be fulfilled. Another approach to deal with this problem is consensus voting, where every stakeholder needs to be present for all of them to agree to a shared set of preferences [Bol01]. Given the potentially long-running nature of evaluations, the required presence of all participating stakeholders cannot be guaranteed. Again another approach to look into when the assumption that preferences within a group are homogeneous does not hold is cluster analysis [Zah99]. Cluster analysis, as is its generic purpose [HK06, page 383], produces different sets (i.e., clusters) of stakeholders so that the preferences between any stakeholders within a set are similar to one another while the ones from stakeholders across sets are dissimilar. When using service feature modeling during development, depending on the size of clusters (relative to the overall number of stakeholders), cluster analysis provides insights into the number of variants that should be further developed and delivered. For example, if one cluster is significantly the largest, a single service variant might suffice, whereas multiple clusters of roughly the same size might correspondingly demand for delivering multiple variants.

- **SFM-based realization of service variants:** Service feature modeling is a prescriptive modeling approach, aiming to induce change in the subject (i.e., a variable service) it represents (cf. section 2.5). This thesis focuses on modeling and selection of service variants, two activities which are fundamental in a larger methodology before change can be applied. The actual realization of service variants is illustrated in a use case when it comes to automatically consuming IaaS variants and deploying a Web application on top of it (cf. section 5.4). In future work, further realization methods in conjunction with service feature modeling should be assessed. An overview of common service variant realization methods is provided in section 2.3.5. Various approaches from related work already address the realization of service variants based on feature models. They include the automatic deployment of Web service variants [NC10], the tenant-specific customization of SaaS [RA11], or the configuration of IaaS [LNSJ12]. These approaches, on the one hand, provide a basis for researching further variant realization techniques to use with service feature modeling. On the other hand, these approaches could benefit especially from service feature modeling's usage methods, as they currently address selection only peripherally (cf. section 4.6).

- **Implementation of own interaction platform:** As outlined in section 5.1.4, we did not within the scope of this thesis implement our own interaction platform. The results of the empirical evaluation provided by the citizens participating in polls through the interaction platform, however, indicates an only moderately positive assessment (cf. section 5.5.3). To obtain less biased results, an implementation controlled by us directly rather than a third party would allow for a better understanding of the reasons behind the assessment and for the iterative adaption of the implementation to improve it. Based on an own implementation, a rerun of this part of the empirical implementation would be desirable.

This thesis presents service feature modeling to model and select service variants. Modeling is based on an extend feature modeling language and includes means for expert collaboration and integration of results from services. Selection consists of a set of flexibly combinable methods that consider requirements and preferences of decision-makers. Thus, in sum, service feature modeling provides a set of contributions that would function on their own, but are here integrated into a comprehensive approach. The research directions outlined in this section, however, show that significant challenges remain to be addressed in future work. Solving these challenges will play an important role in further establishing the consideration of variants as a natural component in the development and delivery of software services.

Appendix

A. Appendix A

A.1. Sets of SFM elements

Table A.1 provides an overview of the sets of SFM elements:

Element	Set
Service Feature Model	$SFM = \{F, A, AT, C, R, AR\}$
Service feature diagram	$SFM^{diag} = \{V, E\}$
Vertices in a service feature diagram	$V = \{F, A\}$
Features	$F = \{F^G \cup F^A \cup F^I\} \| F^G \cap F^A \cap F^I = \emptyset$
Attribute types	AT
Attribute type relationships	AR
Attributes	$A \subseteq V, \forall a \in A : \exists ar(n, m) \mid n = a; m \in (F \vee C)$
Edges in a service feature diagram	$E = \{R, AR\}$
Relationships	$R = \{R^{de} \cup R^{cr}\} \| R^{de} \cap R^{cr} = \emptyset$
Decomposition relationships	$R^{de} = \{R^{man} \cup R^{opt} \cup R^{XOR} \cup R^{OR}\} \subset R$
Configurations	C

Table A.1.: Sets of SFM elements

A.2. Information about performance evaluation of the skyline filter

Table A.2 provides an overview of detailed information about the performance evaluation of the skyline filter.

Model ID	Configurations	Skyline configuration	Dominated configurations	Performed comparisons
GR01	9	5	4	54
IRIS01	18	6	12	42
Amazon EC2	1280	1280	0	1637120
Rackspace	896	896	0	801920
Model 98 conf.	98	2	96	112
Model 952 conf.	952	4	948	960
Model 9450 conf.	9450	288	9162	530538
Model 21168 conf.	21168	504	20664	12215844
Model 2 att.	952	48	904	3160
Model 4 att.	952	8	944	1000
Model 6 att.	952	4	948	960
Model 8 att.	952	1	951	951
Model 10 att.	952	1	951	951
Model 12 att.	952	1	951	951

Table A.2.: Information about the results of applying the skyline filter to the performance evaluation models

A.3. Information about performance evaluation of the requirements filter

Table A.3 provides an overview of detailed information about the performance evaluation of the requirements filter.

Model ID	**Configs.**	**Requirements**			**Degree of fulfillment** deg		
		req^I	req^A	req^{Att}	1.0	$1 > deg > 0$	0.0
GR01	9	2	1	2	0	1	8
IRIS01	18	2	1	2	1	10	7
Amazon EC2	1280	2	1	2	0	160	1120
Rackspace	896	2	1	2	80	0	816
Model 98 conf.	98	2	1	2	13	15	70
Model 952 conf.	952	2	1	2	44	220	688
Model 9450 conf.	9450	2	1	2	72	1818	7560
Model 21168 conf.	21168	2	1	2	864	5184	15120
Model 12 att 2 req	952	2	1	2	112	119	721
Model 12 att 4 req	952	2	1	4	0	231	721
Model 12 att 6 req	952	2	1	6	0	231	721
Model 12 att 8 req	952	2	1	8	0	231	721
Model 12 att 10 req	952	2	1	10	0	231	721
Model 12 att 12 req	952	2	1	12	0	231	721

Table A.3.: Information about the results of applying the requirements filter to the performance evaluation models

B. Appendix B

B.1. Screenshots requirements filter implementation

Screenshot B.1 shows the part of requirement filter's UI that displays an overview of requirements extracted from a given SFM.

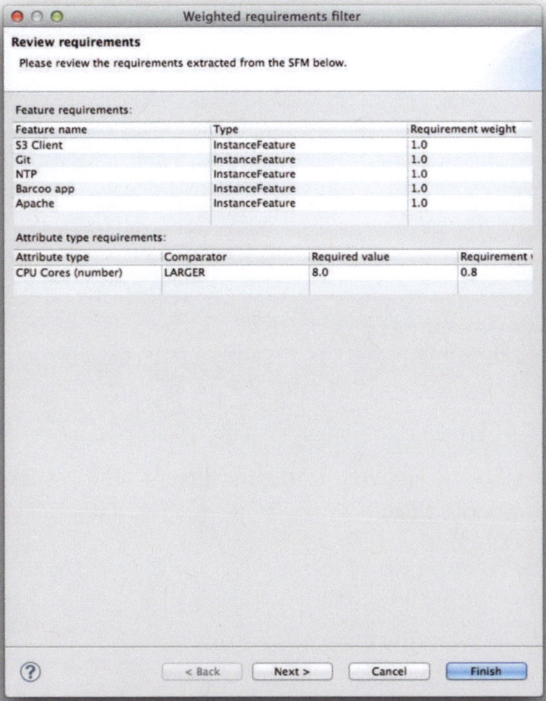

Figure B.1.: Screenshot of the requirements filter's UI - extracted requirements

Screenshot B.2 shows the part of requirement filter's UI that displays the results of applying requirements to narrow down a configuration set.

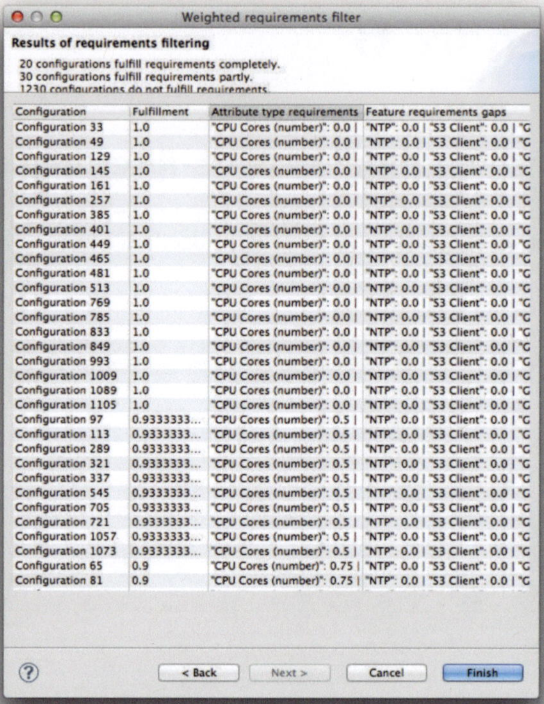

Figure B.2.: Screenshot of the requirements filter's UI - results of applying the requirements filter

B.2. Screenshots preference-based ranking implementation

Screenshot B.3 shows the part of preference-based ranking's UI that displays the input of preferences for attribute types.

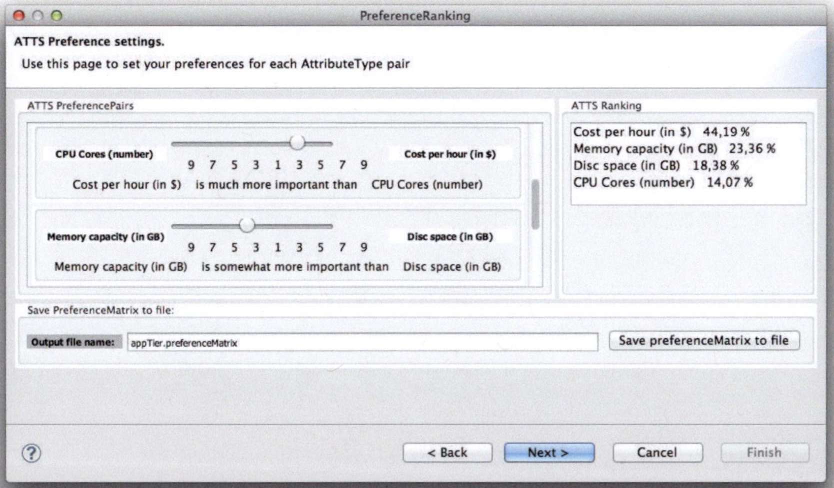

Figure B.3.: Screenshot of the preference-based ranking's UI - input of preferences for attribute types

Screenshot B.4 shows the part of preference-based ranking's UI that displays the results of applying the ranking to a configuration set.

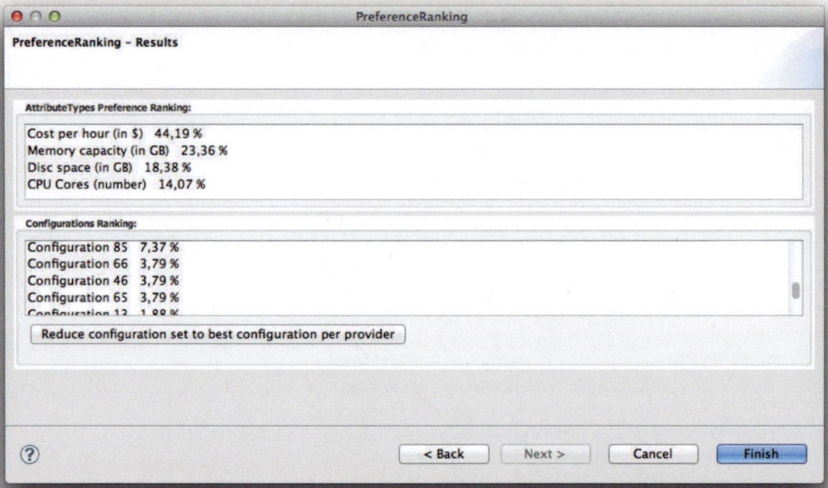

Figure B.4.: Screenshot of the preference-based ranking's UI - results

List of Figures

List of Tables

Bibliography

[ABHV10] Boris Agarski, Igor Budak, Janki Hodolic, and Dorde Vukelic. Multicriteria Approach for Assessment of Environmental Quality. *International Journal for Quality Research*, 4(2):131–137, 2010.

[ABKS13] Sven Apel, Don Batory, Christian Kästner, and Gunter Saake. *Feature-Oriented Software Product Lines: Concepts and Implementation.* Springer Berlin / Heidelberg, 2013.

[ACLF10] Mathieu Acher, Philippe Collet, Philippe Lahire, and Robert France. Composing Feature Models. In Mark van den Brand, Dragan Gaševic, and Jeff Gray, editors, *Software Language Engineering*, volume 5969 of *LNCS*, pages 62–81. Springer, Berlin / Heidelberg, 2010.

[AFR97] Eugene W Anderson, Claes Fornell, and Roland T Rust. Customer satisfaction, productivity, and profitability: Differences between goods and services. *Marketing Science*, 16(2):129–145, 1997.

[Aga07] Sudhir Agarwal. *Formal Description of Web Services for Expressive Matchmaking.* PhD thesis, Karlsruhe Institute of Technology (KIT), Karlsruhe, Germany, May 2007.

[AGGR07] Orlando Avila-García, Antonio Estévez García, and E. Victor Sánchez Rebull. Using Software Product Lines to Manage Model Families in Model-driven Engineering. In *Proceedings of the 2007 ACM Symposium on Applied Computing (SAC '07)*, pages 1006–1011, New York, NY, USA, 2007. ACM.

[Alt08] Steven Alter. Service system fundamentals: Work system, value chain, and life cycle. *IBM Systems Journal*, 47(1):71–85, 2008.

[Ama] Amazon Elastic Compute Cloud (Amazon EC2). `http://aws.amazon.com/ec2/`. (accessed January 11th, 2013).

[AP07] D. Ardagna and B. Pernici. Adaptive Service Composition in Flexible Processes. *Software Engineering, IEEE Transactions on*, 33(6):369–384, 2007.

[ARDN09] Mohammad Alrifai, Thomas Risse, Peter Dolog, and Wolfgang Nejdl. A Scalable Approach for QoS-Based Web Service Selection. In George Feuerlicht and Winfried Lamersdorf, editors, *Service-Oriented Computing – ICSOC 2008 Workshops*, volume 5472 of *Lecture Notes in Computer Science*, pages 190–199. Springer Berlin Heidelberg, 2009.

[ASR10] M. Alrifai, D. Skoutas, and T. Risse. Selecting skyline services for QoS-based web service composition. In *Proceedings of the 19th International Conference on World Wide Web (WWW '10)*, pages 11–20, 2010.

[BAGS10] Ebrahim Bagheri, Mohsen Asadi, Dragan Gaševic, and Samaneh Soltani. Stratified Analytic Hierarchy Process: Prioritization and Selection of Software Features. In *Software Product Lines: Going Beyond*, volume 6287 of *Lecture Notes in Computer Science*, pages 300–315. Springer Berlin / Heidelberg, 2010.

[Bar] Die Konsum-Revolution! barcoo durchbricht 10 Millionen-Marke bei Downloads. `http://www.barcoo.com/blog/2013/04/15/`. (accessed May 6th, 2013).

[Bar13] Sebastian Bartenbach. Einsatz von Variabilitäts-Modellen zur Absicherung von Cloud Infrastrukturen. Master's thesis, Karlsruhe Institute of Technology (KIT), Karlsruhe, Germany, June 2013.

[Bat05] Don Batory. Feature models, grammars, and propositional formulas. In *Proceedings of the 9th international conference on Software Product Lines*, SPLC'05, pages 7–20, Berlin, Heidelberg, 2005. Springer-Verlag.

[BB13] Anir Benlachgar and Fatima-Zahra Belouadha. Review of Software Product Line Models used to Model Cloud Applications. In *Proceedings of the ACS International Conference on Computer Systems and Applications (AICCSA)*, pages 1–4, 2013.

[BBB01] Rafael Bidarra, Eelco Van Den Berg, and Willem F. Bronsvoort. Collaborative Modeling with Features. In *Proc. of the 2001 ASME Design Engineering Technical Conferences (DETC '01)*, Pittsburgh, Pennsylvania, 2001.

[BC05] Felix Bachmann and Paul C Clements. Variability in Software Product Lines. Technical report, Software Engineering Institute, Carnegie Mellon University, September 2005.

[BD06] A.P. Barros and M. Dumas. The Rise of Web Service Ecosystems. *IT Professional*, 8(5):31 –37, September 2006.

[BEGB11] Ebrahim Bagheri, Faezeh Ensan, Dragan Gasevic, and Marko Boskovic. Modular Feature Models: Representation and Configuration. *Journal of Research and Practice in Information Technology*, 43(2):109–140, 2011.

[BELK10] Marina Berkovich, Sebastian Esch, Jan Marco Leimeister, and Helmut Krcmar. Towards Requirements Engineering for "Software as a Service". In *Multikonferenz Wirtschaftsinformatik (MKWI '10)*, pages 517–528, Göttingen, 2010.

[BH89] H Barki and J Hartwick. Rethinking the concept of user involvement. *Mis Quarterly*, 13(1):53, March 1989.

[BI10] Muneera Bano and Naveed Ikram. Issues and Challenges of Requirement Engineering in Service Oriented Software Development. In *Proceedings of the 5th International Conference on Software Engineering Advances (ICSEA '10)*, pages 64–69. IEEE Computer Society, 2010.

[BKNT11] Christian Baun, Marcel Kunze, Jens Nimis, and Stefan Tai. *Cloud Computing.* Web-Basierte Dynamische IT-Services. Springer-Verlag New York Incorporated, March 2011.

[BKS01] Stephan Börzsönyi, Donald Kossmann, and Konrad Stocker. The Skyline Operator. In *Proceedings of the 17th International Conference on Data Engineering*, pages 421–430, Washington, DC, USA, 2001. IEEE Computer Society.

[BLP04] S. Bühne, K Lauenroth, and K Pohl. Why is it not sufficient to model requirements variability with feature models. In *Proceedings of Workshop: Automotive Requirements Engineering (AURE04)*, pages 5–12, Los Alamitos, CA, USA, 2004. IEEE Computer Society Press.

[BNGR12] Ebrahim Bagheri, Tommaso Di Noia, Dragan Gasevic, and Azzurra Ragone. Formalizing interactive staged feature model configuration. *Journal of Software: Evolution and Process*, 24(4):375–400, 2012.

[Boe88] B. W. Boehm. A Spiral Model of Software Development and Enhancement. *Computer*, 21(5):61–72, 1988.

[Bol01] N. Bolloju. Aggregation of Analytic Hierarchy Process Models based on Similarities in Decision Makers' Preferences. *European Journal of Operational Research*, 128(3):499–508, 2001.

[Bos13] Jan Bosch. Software Product Line Engineering. In Rafael Capilla, Jan Bosch, and Kyo-Chul Kang, editors, *Systems and Software Variability Management: Concepts, Tools and Experiences*, chapter 1, pages 3–24. Springer Berlin / Heidelberg, Berlin / Heidelberg, 2013.

[BPE07] Web Services Business Process Execution Language (BPEL). `http://docs.oasis-open.org/wsbpel/2.0/OS/wsbpel-v2.0-OS.html`, 2007. (accessed September 19th 2013).

[BPM10] Business Process Model and Notation (BPMN). `http://www.omg.org/spec/BPMN/2.0/PDF/`, 2010. (accessed February 26th 2013).

[BRN+13] Thorsten Berger, Ralf Rublack, Divya Nair, Joanne M Atlee, Martin Becker, Krzysztof Czarnecki, and Andrzej Wąsowski. A survey of variability modeling in industrial practice. In *Proceedings of the Seventh International Workshop on Variability Modelling of Software-intensive Systems (VAMOS '13)*, page 7. ACM, 2013.

[BSCB13] Mathias Björkqvist, Sebastiano Spicuglia, Lydia Chen, and Walter Binder. QoS-Aware Service VM Provisioning in Clouds: Experiences, Models, and Cost Analysis. In Samik Basu, Cesare Pautasso, Liang Zhang, and Xiang Fu, editors, *Service-Oriented Computing*, volume 8274 of *Lecture Notes in Computer Science*, pages 69–83. Springer Berlin Heidelberg, 2013.

[BSRC10] D. Benavides, S. Segura, and A. Ruiz-Cortés. Automated analysis of feature models 20 years later: A literature review. *Information Systems*, 35(6):615–636, 2010.

[BTRC05] D. Benavides, P. Trinidad, and A. Ruiz-Cortés. Automated reasoning on feature models. In *Advanced Information Systems Engineering*, volume 3520 of *Lecture Notes in Computer Science*, pages 381–390. Springer Berlin / Heidelberg, 2005.

[BZ13] Muneera Bano and Didar Zowghi. User involvement in software development and system success: a systematic literature review. In *Proceedings of the 17th International Conference on Evaluation and Assessment in Software Engineering (EASE '13)*, New York, New York, USA, April 2013. ACM.

[CA09] Betty H C Cheng and Joanne M Atlee. Current and Future Research Directions in Requirements Engineering. *Design Requirements Engineering: A Ten-Year Perspective*, 14(Chapter 2):11–43, 2009.

[CA10] Yannis Charalabidis and Dimitris Askounis. eGOVSIM: A Model for Calculating the Financial Gains of Governmental Services Transformation, for Administration and Citizens. In *43rd Hawaii International Conference on System Sciences (HICSS)*, pages 1–10, 2010.

[CAB+98] William Chan, Richard J. Anderson, Paul Beame, Steve Burns, Francesmary Modugno, David Notkin, and Jon D. Reese. Model Checking Large Software Specifications. *IEEE Transactions on Software Engineering*, 24(7):498–520, July 1998.

[CABA09] Lianping Chen, Muhammad Ali Babar, and Nour Ali. Variability management in software product lines: a systematic review. In *Proceedings of the 13th International Software Product Line Conference*, pages 81–90. Carnegie Mellon University, 2009.

[Cap13] Rafael Capilla. Variability Scope. In Rafael Capilla, Jan Bosch, and Kyo-Chul Kang, editors, *Systems and Software Variability Management: Concepts, Tools and Experiences*, chapter 3, pages 43–56. Springer Berlin / Heidelberg, Berlin / Heidelberg, 2013.

[CGGL03] J. Chomicki, P. Godfrey, J. Gryz, and D. Liang. Skyline with Presorting. In *Proceedings of the 19th International Conference on Data Engineering (ICDE '03)*, pages 717–719, 2003.

[CGR+12] Krzysztof Czarnecki, Paul Grünbacher, Rick Rabiser, Klaus Schmid, and Andrzej Wąsowski. Cool features and tough decisions: a comparison of variability modeling approaches. In *Proceedings of the Sixth International Workshop on Variability Modeling of Software-Intensive Systems (VaMoS '12)*, pages 173–182, January 2012.

[CHE04] Krzysztof Czarnecki, Simon Helsen, and Ulrich Eisenecker. Staged configuration using feature models. In Robert Nord, editor, *Software Product Lines*, volume 3154 of *Lecture Notes in Computer Science*, pages 162–164. Springer Berlin / Heidelberg, 2004.

[CHE05] K. Czarnecki, S. Helsen, and U. Eisenecker. Formalizing Cardinality-Based Feature Models and Their Specialization. *Software Process: Improvement and Practice*, 10(1):7–29, 2005.

[CHS08] Andreas Classen, Patrick Heymans, and Pierre-Yves Schobbens. What's in a Feature: A Requirements Engineering Perspective. In *Fundamental Approaches to Software Engineering*, volume 4961 of *Lecture Notes in Computer Science*, pages 16–30. Springer, 2008.

[CK07] Soo Ho Chang and Soo Dong Kim. A Variability Modeling Method for Adaptable Services in Service-Oriented Computing. In *Proceedings of the 11th International Software Product Line Conference (SPLC '07)*, pages 261–268, Kyoto, Japan, 2007. IEEE Computer Society.

[CKM+03] Francisco Curbera, Rania Khalaf, Nirmal Mukhi, Stefan Tai, and Sanjiva Weerawarana. The next step in Web services. *Communications of the ACM*, 46(10):29–34, October 2003.

[Coc01] Alistair Cockburn. *Writing effective use cases.* Addison-Wesley Professional, 2001.

[COC12] COCKPIT Project. Citizens Collaboration and Co-Creation in Public Service Delivery, September 2012. (accessed September 9th, 2012).

[CPL09] Lawrence Chung and Julio Cesar Prado Leite. On Non-Functional Requirements in Software Engineering. In Alexander T. Borgida, Vinay K. Chaudhri, Paolo Giorgini, and Eric S. Yu, editors, *Conceptual Modeling: Foundations and Applications*, pages 363–379. Springer Berlin / Heidelberg, 2009.

[CPPP14] Marco Comerio, FlavioDe Paoli, Matteo Palmonari, and Luca Panziera. Web Service Contracts: Specification and Matchmaking. In Athman Bouguettaya, Quan Z. Sheng, and Florian Daniel, editors, *Advanced Web Services*, pages 121–146. Springer New York, 2014.

[CSFP04] Ben Collins-Sussman, Brian W. Fitzpatrick, and C. Michael Pilato. *Version Control with Subversion - Next Generation Open Source Version Control.* O'Reilly Media, 2004.

[CSL+01] P. Carlshamre, K. Sandahl, M. Lindvall, B. Regnell, and J. Natt och Dag. An industrial survey of requirements interdependencies in software product release planning. In *Proceedings of the 5th IEEE International Symposium onRequirements Engineering*, pages 84–91, 2001.

[CVW09] Jorge Cardoso, Konrad Voigt, and Matthias Winkler. Service Engineering for the Internet of Services. In Joaquim Filipe, José Cordeiro, Wil Aalst, John Mylopoulos, Michael Rosemann, Michael J. Shaw, and Clemens Szyperski, editors, *Enterprise Information Systems*, volume 19 of *Lecture Notes in Business Information Processing*, pages 15–27. Springer Berlin Heidelberg, 2009.

[CW98] Reidar Conradi and Bernhard Westfechtel. Version Models for Software Configuration Management. *ACM Computing Surveys (CSUR)*, 30(2):232–282, June 1998.

[CZZM05] Kun Chen, Wei Zhang, Haiyan Zhao, and Hong Mei. An approach to constructing feature models based on requirements clustering. In *Proceedings of the 13th IEEE International Conference on Requirements Engineering (RE '05)*, pages 31–40. IEEE, 2005.

[DB13] Jeffrey Dean and Luiz André Barroso. The Tail at Scale. *Commun. ACM*, 56(2):74–80, February 2013.

[DBM13] Valeria De Antonellis Devis Bianchini and Michele Melchiori. A Multi-perspective Framework for Web API Search in Enterprise Mashup Design. In Camille Salinesi, MoiraC. Norrie, and Óscar Pastor, editors, *Advanced Information Systems Engineering*, number 7908 in Lecture Notes in Computer Science, pages 353–368. Springer Berlin Heidelberg, May 2013.

[DD09] Tore Dyba and Torgeir Dingsoyr. What Do We Know about Agile Software Development? *IEEE Software*, 26(5):6–9, 2009.

[Dey01] Anind K. Dey. Understanding and Using Context. *Personal and Ubiquitous Computing*, 5:4–7, 2001.

[DGR+06] Islay Davies, Peter Green, Michael Rosemann, Marta Indulska, and Stan Gallo. How do practitioners use conceptual modeling in practice? *Data & Knowledge Engineering*, 58(3):358–380, September 2006.

[DHJ09] Ketki A Dhanesha, Alan Hartman, and Anshu N Jain. A Model for Designing Generic Services. In *2009 IEEE International Conference on Services Computing*, pages 435–442. IEEE Computer Society, 2009.

[DLFST07] A. De Lucia, F. Fasano, G. Scanniello, and G. Tortora. Enhancing collaborative synchronous UML modelling with fine-grained versioning of software artefacts. *Journal of Visual Languages and Computing*, 18(5):492–503, 2007.

[DNGM+08] Elisabetta Di Nitto, Carlo Ghezzi, Andreas Metzger, Mike Papazoglou, and Klaus Pohl. A journey to highly dynamic, self-adaptive service-based applications. *Automated Software Engineering*, 15(3-4):313–341, September 2008.

[DWS12] Brian Dougherty, Jules White, and Douglas C Schmidt. Model-driven auto-scaling of green cloud computing infrastructure. *Future Generation Computer Systems*, 28(2):371–378, February 2012.

[Fac] Facebook.com. Facebook.com. `https://www.facebook.com`. (accessed November 6th, 2013).

[FdSGdT07] M. Fantinato, I. de S Gimenes, and M. de Toledo. Supporting QoS negotiation with feature modeling. In *Proceedings of the 5th International Conference on Service-Oriented Computing (ICSOC '07)*, pages 429–434, 2007.

[FFB02] Dániel Fey, Róbert Fajta, and András Boros. Feature Modeling: A Meta-Model to Enhance Usability and Usefulness. In Gary J. Chastek, editor, *Software Product Lines*, Lecture Notes in Computer Science, pages 198–216. Springer Berlin / Heidelberg, 2002.

[FMÁ+10] Fernando Flores, Manuel Mora, Francisco Álvarez, Laura Garza, and Héctor Durán. Towards a Systematic Service-oriented Requirements Engineering Process (S-SoRE). In JoãoEduardo Quintela Varajão, MariaManuela Cruz-Cunha, GoranD. Putnik, and António Trigo, editors, *ENTERprise Information Systems*, volume 109 of *Communications in Computer and Information Science*, pages 111–120. Springer Berlin Heidelberg, 2010.

[GA13] Matthias Galster and Paris Avgeriou. Variability in Web Services. In Rafael Capilla, Jan Bosch, and Kyo-Chul Kang, editors, *Systems and Software Variability Management: Con-*

cepts, Tools and Experiences, chapter 18, pages 269–277. Springer Berlin / Heidelberg, Berlin / Heidelberg, 2013.

[Git] Git. `http://git-scm.com`. (accessed April 8th, 2014).

[GJNS13] S. Gudenkauf, M. Josefiok, O. Norkus, and U. Steffens. Cloud-Computing Referenzkontext. Technical report, acatec - Deutsche Akademie der Technikwissenschaften, 2013.

[GL09] Qing Gu and Patricia Lago. Exploring service-oriented system engineering challenges: a systematic literature review. *Service Oriented Computing and Applications*, 3(3):171–188, 2009.

[GM09] Manish Godse and Shrikant Mulik. An Approach for Selecting Software-as-a-Service (SaaS) Product. In *2009 IEEE International Conference on Cloud Computing*, pages 155–158. IEEE Computer Society, 2009.

[Goo] Google App Engine. `https://developers.google.com/appengine/`. (accessed March 1st, 2013).

[Göt09] Stephan Göthlich. Zum Umgang mit fehlenden Daten in großzahligen empirischen Erhebungen. In Sönke Albers, Daniel Klapper, Udo Konradt, Achim Walter, and Joachim Wolf, editors, *Methoden der empirischen Forschung*, pages 119–135. Deutscher Universitäts-Verlag, Wiesbaden, Germany, 3rd edition, 2009.

[GVB13] Saurabh Kumar Garg, Steve Versteeg, and Rajkumar Buyya. A framework for ranking of cloud computing services. *Future Generation Computer Systems*, 29(4):1012 – 1023, 2013.

[GVDAJVLR08] Florian Gottschalk, Wil MP Van Der Aalst, Monique H Jansen-Vullers, and Marcello La Rosa. Configurable workflow models. *International Journal of Cooperative Information Systems*, 17(02):177–221, 2008.

[HAT+13] Arnaud Hubaux, Mathieu Acher, Thein Than Tun, Patrick Heymans, Philippe Collet, and Philippe Lahire. Separating Concerns in Feature Models: Retrospective and Support for Multi-Views. In *Domain Engineering*, pages 3–28. Springer Berlin Heidelberg, Berlin, Heidelberg, May 2013.

[HBR10] Alena Hallerbach, Thomas Bauer, and Manfred Reichert. Capturing variability in business process models - the Provop approach. *Journal of Software Maintenance and Evolution: Research and Practice*, 22(6):519–546, 2010.

[Hes06] Wolfgang Hesse. More matters on (meta-) modelling: remarks on Thomas Kühne's "matters". *Software and Systems Modeling*, 5(4):387–394, October 2006.

[HJD11] Elizabeth Hull, Ken Jackson, and Jeremy Dick. *Requirements Engineering*. Springer, 2011.

[HJR+10] A. Hartman, A. Jain, J. Ramanathan, A. Ramfos, W.J. Van der Heuvel, C. Zirpins, S. Tai, Y. Charalabidis, A. Pasic, and T. Johannessen. Participatory design of public sector services. *Electronic Government and the Information Systems Perspective*, pages 219–233, 2010.

[HK06] Jiawei Han and Micheline Kamber. *Data Mining - Concepts and Techniques*. The Morgan Kaufmann series in data mangement systems. Morgan Kaufmann, San Francisco, 2nd edition, 2006.

[HKH05] Christian Homburg, Nicole Koschate, and Wayne D Hoyer. Do satisfied customers really pay more? A study of the relationship between customer satisfaction and willingness to pay. *Journal of Marketing*, pages 84–96, 2005.

[HL01] Hubert F Hofmann and Franz Lehner. Requirements engineering as a success factor in software projects. *IEEE Software*, 18(4):58–66, 2001.

[HPSVA95] R. Henderson, J. Podd, M. Smith, and H. Varela-Alvarez. An Examination of Four User-based Software Evaluation Methods. *Interacting with Computers*, 7(4):412–432, 1995.

[HR04] D. Harel and B. Rumpe. Meaningful modeling: what's the semantics of "semantics"? *Computer*, 37(10):64–72, 2004.

[IBM11] Getting cloud computing right. White paper, IBM Global Technology Services, Armonk, NY, US, April 2011.

[IFMW08] Florian Irmert, Thomas Fischer, and Klaus Meyer-Wegener. Runtime adaptation in a service-oriented component model. In *Proceedings of the 2008 international workshop on Software engineering for adaptive and self-managing systems (SEAMS '08)*, pages 97–104. ACM, 2008.

[ITI07] ITIL: Service Design. Technical report, The Stationary Office, 2007.

[IYE11] A. Iosup, N. Yigitbasi, and D. Epema. On the Performance Variability of Production Cloud Services. In *Cluster, Cloud and Grid Computing (CCGrid), 2011 11th IEEE/ACM International Symposium on*, pages 104 –113, may 2011.

[JFY09] Karuna P. Joshi, Tim Finin, and Yelena Yesha. Integrated Lifecycle of IT Services in a Cloud Environment. In *Proceedings of The Third International Conference on the Virtual Computing Initiative (ICVCI '09)*, Research Triangle Park, NC, 2009.

[JNS11] Christian Janiesch, Michael Niemann, and Ralf Steinmetz. The TEXO governance framework. Technical report, SAP Research, 2011.

[KaSSA09] M. Koning, C. a. Sun, M. Sinnema, and P. Avgeriou. VxBPEL: Supporting variability for Web services in BPEL. *Information and Software Technology*, 51(2):258–269, 2009.

[KCH+90] K C Kang, S G Cohen, J A Hess, W E Novak, and A S Peterson. Feature-oriented domain analysis (FODA) feasibility study. Software Engineering Institute, Carnegie Mellon University, Pittsburgh, Pennsylvania 15213, November 1990.

[KD08] Yukyong Kim and Kyung-Goo Doh. Adaptable Web Services Modeling Using Variability Analysis. In *Convergence and Hybrid Information Technology, 2008. ICCIT '08. Third International Conference on*, pages 700–705. IEEE Computer Society, 2008.

[KKKP10] Costas Koutras, Sotiris Koussouris, Panagiotis Kokkinakos, and Dimitris Panopoulos. COCKPIT Public Service Scenarios. COCKPIT project deliverable 1.1, National Technical University of Athens (NTUA), Athens, Greece, June 2010.

[KKP+12] P Kokkinakos, S Koussouris, D Panopoulos, D. Askounis, A. Ramfos, G Georgousopoulos, and Erik Wittern. Citizens Collaboration and Co-Creation in Public Service Delivery: The COCKPIT Project. *International Journal of Electronic Government Research*, 8(3):44–62, 2012.

[KOD10] Ahmet Karataş, Halit Oğuztüzün, and Ali Doğru. Mapping Extended Feature Models to Constraint Logic Programming over Finite Domains. In Jan Bosch and Jaejoon Lee, editors, *Software Product Lines: Going Beyond*, volume 6287 of *LNCS*, pages 286–299. Springer Berlin / Heidelberg, 2010.

[Kru04] Philippe Kruchten. *The Rational Unified Process: An Introduction.* Addison-Wesley, 3rd edition, 2004.

[KSB+10] Ajay Kattepur, S. Sen, B. Baudry, A. Benveniste, and C. Jard. Variability Modeling and QoS Analysis of Web Services Orchestrations. In *Web Services (ICWS), 2010 IEEE International Conference on*, pages 99–106, 2010.

[Küh06] Thomas Kühne. Matters of (Meta-) Modeling. *Software and Systems Modeling*, 5(4):369–385, July 2006.

[Kuh11] Jörn Kuhlenkamp. Service Feature Models: Conceptualization of and Automated Reasoning on Feature Attribute Relationships. Master's thesis, Karlsruhe Institute of Technology (KIT), Karlsruhe, Germany, September 2011.

[KZZL11] Yu Kang, Yangfan Zhou, Zibin Zheng, and M.R. Lyu. A User Experience-Based Cloud Service Redeployment Mechanism. In *IEEE International Conference on Cloud Computing (CLOUD '11)*, pages 227 –234, july 2011.

[Lev00] Nancy G Leveson. Intent specifications: an approach to building human-centered specifications. *IEEE Transactions on Software Engineering*, 26(1):15–35, 2000.

[LG10] Holger Luczak and Gerhard Gudergan. The Evolution of Service Engineering - Toward the Implementation of Designing Integrative Solutions. In *Introduction to Service Engineering*, pages 545–575. John Wiley & Sons, Inc., 2010.

[LK13] Jaejoon Lee and Gerald Kotonya. Service-Oriented Product Lines. In Rafael Capilla, Jan Bosch, and Kyo-Chul Kang, editors, *Systems and Software Variability Management: Concepts, Tools and Experiences*, chapter 19, pages 279–285. Springer Berlin / Heidelberg, Berlin / Heidelberg, 2013.

[LKL02] Kwanwoo Lee, Kyo C Kang, and Jaejoon Lee. Concepts and guidelines of feature modeling for product line software engineering. In *Software Reuse: Methods, Techniques, and Tools: Proceedings of the Seventh Reuse Conference (ICSR7)*, pages 62–77. Springer, 2002.

[LKN+09] Alexander Lenk, Markus Klems, Jens Nimis, Stefan Tai, and Thomas Sandholm. What's inside the Cloud? An architectural map of the Cloud landscape. In *Proceedings of the 2009 ICSE*

Workshop on Software Engineering Challenges of Cloud Computing (CLOUD '09), pages 23–31, Washington, DC, USA, 2009. IEEE Computer Society.

[LKSL13] Jaejoon Lee, Kyo C Kang, Pete Sawyer, and Hyesun Lee. A holistic approach to feature modeling for product line requirements engineering. *Requirements Engineering*, pages 1–19, 2013.

[LMLT11] Alexander Lenk, Michael Menzel, Johannes Lipsky, and Stefan Tai. What are you paying for? Performance benchmarking for Infrastructure-as-a-Service offerings. In *Proceedings of the 4th IEEE International Conference on Cloud Computing (CLOUD 2011)*, pages 484–491, Washington, D. C., Juli 2011. IEEE Computer Society.

[LNSJ12] Tam Le Nhan, Gerson Sunyé, and Jean-Marc Jézéquel. A Model-Driven Approach for Virtual Machine Image Provisioning in Cloud Computing. *Service-Oriented and Cloud Computing (ESOCC '12)*, pages 107–121, 2012.

[LNZ04] Yutu Liu, Anne H. Ngu, and Liang Z. Zeng. QoS Computation and Policing in Dynamic Web Service Selection. In *Proceedings of the 13th International World Wide Web Conference on Alternate Track Papers and Posters (WWW Alt. '04)*, pages 66–73, New York, NY, USA, 2004. ACM.

[LS93] Kai H. Lim and Scott R. Swenseth. An iterative procedure for reducing problem size in large scale AHP problems. *European Journal of Operational Research*, 67(1):64 – 74, 1993.

[LSZJ06] Haiqi Liang, Wei Sun, Xin Zhang, and Zhongbo Jiang. A Policy Framework for Collaborative Web Service Customization. In *Proceedings of the 2nd IEEE International Symposium on Service-Oriented System Engineering (SOSE'06)*, pages 197–204. IEEE, October 2006.

[Lud03] Jochen Ludewig. Models in software engineering - an introduction. *Software and Systems Modeling*, 2(1):5–14, March 2003.

[LVL04] Emmanuel Letier and Axel Van Lamsweerde. Reasoning about partial goal satisfaction for requirements and design engineering. In *Proceedings of the 12th ACM SIGSOFT twelfth international symposium on Foundations of software engineering (SIGSOFT '04)*, volume 29, pages 53–62. ACM, 2004.

[LYKZ10] Ang Li, Xiaowei Yang, Srikanth Kandula, and Ming Zhang. CloudCmp: comparing public cloud providers. In *IMC '10: Proceedings of the 10th annual conference on Internet measurement.* ACM, November 2010.

[LYM09] Lin Liu, Eric Yu, and Hong Mei. Guest Editorial: Special Section on Requirements Engineering for Services - Challenges and Practices. *IEEE Transactions on Services Computing*, 2(4):318–319, October 2009.

[Mag03] Peter R. Magnusson. Benefits of involving users in service innovation. *European Journal of Innovation Management*, 6(4):228–238, 2003.

[MBJ+09] B. Morin, O. Barais, J.M. Jézéquel, F. Fleurey, and A. Solberg. Models@ run. time to support dynamic adaptation. *Computer*, 42(10):44–51, 2009.

[MC10] Marcilio Mendonca and Donald Cowan. Decision-making coordination and efficient reasoning techniques for feature-based configuration. *Science of Computer Programming*, 75(5):311–332, May 2010.

[McB] Gary McBride. The Role of SOA Quality Management in SOA Service Lifecycle Management. `http://www.ibm.com/developerworks/rational/library/mar07/mcbride/`. (accessed February 22nd, 2013).

[MCL+01] John Mylopoulos, Lawrence Chung, Stephen Liao, Huaiqing Wang, and Eric Yu. Exploring alternatives during requirements analysis. *IEEE Software*, 18(1):92–96, 2001.

[MD89] D. McCarthy and U. Dayal. The Architecture of an Active Database Management System. In *Proceedings of the 1989 ACM SIGMOD International Conference on Management of Data (SIGMOD '89)*, pages 215–224, May 1989.

[MFBC10] Pierre-Alain Muller, Frédéric Fondement, Benoît Baudry, and Benoît Combemale. Modeling modeling modeling. *Software and Systems Modeling*, 11(3):347–359, August 2010.

[MHGA13] Sara Mahdavi-Hezavehi, Matthias Galster, and Paris Avgeriou. Variability in quality attributes of service-based software systems: A systematic literature review. *Information and Software Technology*, 55(2):320–343, 2013.

[MMLP09] R. Mietzner, A. Metzger, F. Leymann, and K Pohl. Variability modeling to support customization and deployment of multi-tenant-aware Software as a Service applications. *Proceedings of the 2009 ICSE Workshop on Principles of Engineering Service Oriented Systems*, pages 18–25, 2009.

[MNDF+10] Alessandro Marchetto, Cu D Nguyen, Chiara Di Francescomarino, Nauman A Qureshi, Anna Perini, and Paolo Tonella. A Design Methodology for Real Services. In *Proceedings of the 2nd International Workshop on Principles of Engineering Service-Oriented Systems*, pages 15–21. ACM, 2010.

[MR12] Michael Menzel and Rajiv Ranjan. CloudGenius: Decision Support for Web Server Cloud Migration. In *Proceedings of the 21st International Conference on World Wide Web (WWW '12)*, pages 979–988, Lyon, France, March 2012.

[MST11] M. Menzel, M. Schönherr, and S. Tai. (MC2) 2: criteria, requirements and a software prototype for Cloud infrastructure decisions. *Software: Practice and Experience*, 43(11):1283–1297, 2011.

[MTW+12] H. Moens, E. Truyen, S. Walraven, W. Joosen, B. Dhoedt, and F. De Turck. Developing and managing customizable Software as a Service using feature model conversion. In *IEEE Network Operations and Management Symposium (NOMS)*, pages 1295–1302. IEEE Computer Society, 2012.

[NC10] Tuan Nguyen and Alan Colman. A Feature-Oriented Approach for Web Service Customization. In *Proceedings of the 2010 IEEE International Conference on Web Services*, ICWS '10, pages 393–400, Washington, DC, USA, 2010. IEEE.

[NCH11] Tuan Nguyen, Alan Colman, and Jun Han. Modeling and Managing Variability in Process-Based Service Compositions. In G. Kappel, Z. Maamar, and H.R. Motahari-Nezhad, editors, *Service-Oriented Computing*, pages 404–420. Springer Berlin / Heidelberg, 2011.

[NCH14] Tuan Nguyen, Alan Colman, and Jun Han. Comprehensive Variability Modeling and Management for Customizable Process-Based Service Compositions. In Athman Bouguettaya, Quan Z. Sheng, and Florian Daniel, editors, *Web Services Foundations*, pages 507–533. Springer New York, 2014.

[NCTH11] Tuan Nguyen, Alan Colman, Muhammad Adeel Talib, and Jun Han. Managing Service Variability: State of the Art and Open Issues. *Proceedings of the 5th Workshop on Variability Modeling of Software-Intensive Systems*, pages 165–173, 2011.

[Net] Netflix Inc. Netflix - Watch TV Shows Online, Watch Movies Online. `http://www.netflix.com/`. (accessed November 6th, 2013).

[OBB+09] Daniel Oberle, Dipl-Ing Nadeem Bhatti, Saartje Brockmans, Dipl-Wirtsch-Ing Michael Niemann, and Christian Janiesch. Countering service information challenges in the internet of services. *Business & Information Systems Engineering*, 1(5):370–390, 2009.

[Obj] Object Management Group. UML Resources Page. `http://www.uml.org/`. (accessed March 13th, 2013).

[O'L93] Daniel E O'Leary. Determining Differences in Expert Judgment: Implications for Knowledge Acquisition and Validation*. *Decision Sciences*, 24(2):395–408, 1993.

[Pap03] M.P. Papazoglou. Service-oriented computing: concepts, characteristics and directions. In *Web Information Systems Engineering, 2003. WISE 2003. Proceedings of the Fourth International Conference on*, pages 3 – 12, 2003.

[PBP06] Kai Petersen, Nadine Bramsiepe, and Klaus Pohl. Applying Variability Modeling Concepts to Support Decision Making for Service Composition. In *Service-Oriented Computing: Consequences for Engineering Requirements (SOCCER '06)*, pages 1–1, Los Alamitos, CA, USA, 2006. IEEE Computer Society.

[PC12] Lawrence Pizette and Toby Cabot. Databse as a Service: A Marketplace Assessment. Technical report, The MITRE Corporation, 2012.

[PCP+12] Luca Panziera, Marco Comerio, Matteo Palmonari, Flavio De Paoli, and Carlo Batini. Quality-driven extraction, fusion and matchmaking of semantic web API descriptions. *Journal of Web Engineering*, 11(3):247–268, September 2012.

[PLP11] Richard Pohl, Kim Lauenroth, and Klaus Pohl. A performance comparison of contemporary algorithmic approaches for automated analysis operations on feature models. In *Automated*

Software Engineering (ASE), 2011 26th IEEE/ACM International Conference on, pages 313–322. IEEE Computer Society, 2011.

[PS00] Linda Peters and Hasannudin Saidin. IT and the mass customization of services: the challenge of implementation. *International Journal of Information Management*, 20(2):103 – 119, 2000.

[PSD13] Costas P. Pappis, Constantinos I. Siettos, and Thomas K. Dasaklis. Fuzzy Sets, Systems, and Applications. In Saul I. Gass and Michael C. Fu, editors, *Encyclopedia of Operations Research and Management Science*, pages 609–620. Springer US, 2013.

[PuFvdL05] Klaus Pohl and Günter Bockle und Frank von der Linden. *Software Procut Line Engineering*. Springer-Verlag Berlin Heidelberg, 2005.

[PVDH06] Michael P Papazoglou and Willem-Jan Van Den Heuvel. Service-oriented design and development methodology. *International Journal of Web Engineering and Technology*, 2(4):412–442, 2006.

[QDH+12] C. Quinten, L. Duchien, P. Heymans, S. Mouton, and E. Charlier. Using Feature Modelling and automations to select among cloud solutions. In *Proceedings of the 3rd International Workshop on Product Line Approaches in Software Engineering (PLEASE)*, pages 17–20, 2012.

[QP10] N.A. Qureshi and A. Perini. Requirements Engineering for Adaptive Service Based Applications. In *Proceedings of the 18th IEEE International Requirements Engineering Conference (RE)*, pages 108–111. IEEE Computer Society, 2010.

[Quo] QuoteMedia, Inc. Stock Quotes and Market Data Provider > QuoteMedia. `http://www.quotemedia.com/`. (accessed March 4th, 2014).

[RA11] Stefan T. Ruehl and Urs Andelfinger. Applying Software Product Lines to Create Customizable Software-as-a-Service Applications. In *Proceedings of the 15th International Software Product Line Conference, Volume 2*, SPLC '11, pages 1–4, New York, NY, USA, 2011. ACM.

[Rac] Cloud Servers by Rackspace. `http://www.rackspace.com/cloud/servers/`. (accessed November 5th, 2013).

[RC06] Roland T. Rust and Tuck Siong Chung. Marketing Models of Service and Relationships. *Marketing Science*, 25(6):560–580, November 2006.

[RF03] S. Robak and B. Franczyk. Modeling Web Services Variability with Feature Diagrams. In *Web, Web-Services, and Database Systems*, volume 2593 of *Lecture Notes in Computer Science*, pages 120–128. Springer Berlin / Heidelberg, 2003.

[RHH11] Zia ur Rehman, Farookh K Hussain, and Omar K Hussain. Towards Multi-Criteria Cloud Service Selection. In *Proceedings of the 5th International Conference on Innovative Mobile and Internet Services in Ubiquitous Computing (IMIS)*, pages 44–48. IEEE Computer Society, 2011.

[RHH13] Zia ur Rehman, Omar Khadeer Hussain, and Farookh Khadeer Hussain. Parallel Cloud Service Selection and Ranking Based on QoS History. *International Journal of Parallel Programming*, pages 1–33, October 2013.

[Rob90] W.N. Robinson. Negotiation behavior during requirement specification. In *Proceedings of the 12th International Conference on Software Engineering (ICSE '90)*, pages 268–276, 1990.

[Rot89] J. Rothenberg. The Nature of Modeling. In Lawrence E. Widman, Kenneth A. Loparo, and Norman R. Nielsen, editors, *Artificial Intelligence, Simulation & Modeling*, pages 75–92. John Wiley & Sons, Inc., New York, NY, USA, 1989.

[Roy70] Winston W. Royce. Managing the Development of Large Software Systems. In *Proceedings of IEEE WESCON*, pages 1–9, August 1970.

[RvdA07] Michael Rosemann and Wil MP van der Aalst. A configurable reference modelling language. *Information Systems*, 32(1):1–23, 2007.

[RZ13] Ramaswamy Ramesh and Stanley Zionts. Multi-Criteria Decision Making (MCDM). In SaulI. Gass and MichaelC. Fu, editors, *Encyclopedia of Operations Research and Management Science*, pages 1007–1013. Springer US, 2013.

[Saa90] T Saaty. How to Make a Decision: The Analytic Hierarchy Process. *European Journal of Operational Research*, 48(1):9–26, September 1990.

[Saa08] Thomas L. Saaty. Decision making with the analytic hierarchy process. *International Journal of Services Sciences*, 1(1):83, 2008.

[Saa13] Thomas L. Saaty. Analytic Hierarchy Process. In *Encyclopedia of Operations Research and Management Science*, pages 52–64. December 2013.

[Sal] Salesforce.com, inc. CRM and Cloud Computing To Grow Your Business. `http://www.salesforce.com/`. (accessed November 6th, 2013).

[SAP] SAP AG. Cloud Suite. `http://www.sap.com/pc/tech/cloud/software/cloud-applications/enterprise-suite.html`. (accessed November 6th, 2013).

[SBPM08] Dave Steinberg, Frank Budinsky, Marcelo Paternostro, and Ed Merks. *EMF - Eclipse Modeling Framework*. Addison-Wesley Professional, 2nd edition, December 2008.

[SBRCT08] Sergio Segura, David Benavides, Antonio Ruiz-Cortés, and Pablo Trinidad. Automated Merging of Feature Models Using Graph Transformations. In *Post-proceedings Summer School on Generative and Transformational Techniques in Software Engineering (GTTSE'07)*, volume 5235 of *LNCS*, pages 489–505, Braga, Portugal, 2008. Springer.

[SC04] Daniela Sangiorgi and Brendon Clark. Toward a Participatory Design Approach to Service Design. In *Proceedings of the Participatory Design Conference (PDC '04)*, pages 148–151, 2004.

[Sch06] Douglas C Schmidt. Model-Driven Engineering. *IEEE Internet Computing*, 39(2):25–31, 2006.

[SD07] Marco Sinnema and Sybren Deelstra. Classifying variability modeling techniques. *Information and Software Technology*, 49(7):717–739, 2007.

[SDNB04] Marco Sinnema, Sybren Deelstra, Jos Nijhuis, and Jan Bosch. COVAMOF: A Framework for Modeling Variability in Software Product Families. *Software Product Lines*, pages 197–213, 2004.

[Sel03] Bran Selic. The Pragmatics of Model-Driven Development. *IEEE Software*, 20(5):19–25, 2003.

[SFG99] H. Sharp, A. Finkelstein, and G. Galal. Stakeholder identification in the requirements engineering process. In *Proceedings of the 10th International Workshop on Database and Expert Systems Applications*, pages 387–391. IEEE Computer Society, 1999.

[SGB+12] Sergio Segura, José A Galindo, David Benavides, José A Parejo, and Antonio Ruiz-Cortés. BeTTy: benchmarking and testing on the automated analysis of feature models. In *Proceedings of the Sixth International Workshop on Variability Modeling of Software-Intensive Systems*, VaMoS '12, pages 63–71, New York, NY, USA, January 2012. ACM.

[SH98] T.L. Saaty and G. Hu. Ranking by eigenvector versus other methods in the analytic hierarchy process. *Applied Mathematics Letters*, 11(4):121 – 125, 1998.

[Sha12] Mary Shaw. The Role of Design Spaces. *IEEE Software*, 29(1):46–50, 2012.

[SM09] Md. Anisuzzaman Siddique and Yasuhiko Morimoto. K-dominant skyline computation by using sort-filtering method. In Thanaruk Theeramunkong, Boonserm Kijsirikul, Nick Cercone, and Tu-Bao Ho, editors, *Advances in Knowledge Discovery and Data Mining*, volume 5476 of *Lecture Notes in Computer Science*, pages 839–848. Springer Berlin Heidelberg, 2009.

[SM10] M. Stollberg and M. Muth. Service customization by variability modeling. In *Proceedings of the 2009 international conference on Service-oriented computing*, pages 425–434, Stckholm, Sweden, 2010. Springer.

[SMBG07] J. Spohrer, P.P. Maglio, J. Bailey, and D. Gruhl. Steps toward a science of service systems. *Computer*, 40(1):71–77, 2007.

[SMDK11] Marc Steen, Menno Manschot, and Nicole De Koning. Benefits of co-design in service design projects. *International Journal of Design*, 5(2):53–60, 2011.

[SMML12] Julia Schroeter, Peter Mucha, Kay Jugel Muth, and Malte Lochau. Dynamic configuration management of cloud-based applications. In *Proceedings of the 16th International Software*

Product Line Conference (SPLC '12), pages 171–178. ACM, 2012.

[Som11] Ian Sommerville. *Software Engineering*. Addison-Wesley, 9th edition, 2011.

[SP11] P. Saripalli and G. Pingali. MADMAC: Multiple Attribute Decision Methodology for Adoption of Clouds. In *Proceedings of the 4th International Conference on Cloud Computing (CLOUD '11)*, pages 316–323, 2011.

[Spo] Spotify USA Inc. Music for every moment - Spotify. `https://www.spotify.com/`. (accessed November 6th, 2013).

[Spo08] Jim Spohrer. Services Sciences, Management, and Engineering (SSME) and Its Relation to Academic Disciplines. In Bernd Stauss, Kai Engelmann, Anja Kremer, and Achim Luhn, editors, *Services Science*, pages 11–40. Springer Berlin / Heidelberg, 2008.

[SRS$^+$10] Chang-ai Sun, Rowan Rossing, Marco Sinnema, Pavel Bulanov, and Marco Aiello. Modeling and managing the variability of Web service-based systems. *Journal of Systems and Software*, 83(3):502–516, March 2010.

[STD08] Daniel Schall, Hong-Linh Truong, and Schahram Dustdar. Unifying human and software services in web-scale collaborations. *IEEE Internet Computing*, 12(3):62–68, May 2008.

[SVGB05] Mikael Svahnberg, Jilles Van Gurp, and Jan Bosch. A Taxonomy of Variability Realization Techniques. *Software: Practice and Experience*, 35(8):705–754, 2005.

[SZG$^+$08] Wei Sun, Xin Zhang, Chang Jie Guo, Pei Sun, and Hui Su. Software as a Service: Configuration and Customization Perspectives. In *IEEE Congress on Services Part II (SERVICES-2)*, pages 18–25. IEEE Computer Society, 2008.

[SZS11] N. Schuster, C. Zirpins, and U. Scholten. How to balance flexibility and coordination? Service-oriented model and architecture for document-based collaboration on the Web. In *Service-Oriented Computing and Applications (SOCA), 2011 IEEE International Conference on*, pages 1–9. IEEE Computer Society, 2011.

[TBD07] Salvador Trujillo, Don Batory, and Oscar Diaz. Feature oriented model driven development: A case study for portlets. In *29th International Conference on Software Engineering (ICSE '07)*, pages 44–53. IEEE Computer Society, 2007.

[TBK09] T Thum, D. Batory, and C. Kästner. Reasoning about edits to feature models. In *Software Engineering, 2009. ICSE 2009. IEEE 31st International Conference on*, ICSE '09, pages 254–264, 2009.

[Tic03] Walter F. Tichy. Software Configuration Management. In *Encyclopedia of Computer Science*, pages 1601–1604. John Wiley and Sons Ltd., Chichester, UK, 2003.

[TMW+05] V Talwar, D Milojicic, Qinyi Wu, C Pu, W Yan, and G Jung. Approaches for Service Deployment. *IEEE Internet Computing*, 9(2), 2005.

[TÖ13] Bedir Tekinerdogan and Karahan Özturk. Feature-Driven Design of SaaS Architectures. In Zaigham Mahmood and Saqib Saeed, editors, *Software Engineering Frameworks for the Cloud Computing Paradigm*, Computer Communications and Networks, pages 189–212. Springer London, 2013.

[TÖD11] Bedir Tekinerdogan, Karahan Özturk, and Ali Dogru. Modeling and Reasoning about Design Alternatives of Software as a Service Architectures. In *Proceedings of the 9th Working IEEE/IFIP Conference on Software Architecture (WICSA)*, pages 312–319. IEEE Computer Society, 2011.

[TRC09] Pablo Trinidad and Antonio Ruiz-Cortés. Abductive Reasoning and Automated Analysis of Feature Models: How are they connected? In *Proc. of the 3rd Int. Workshop on Variability Modelling of Software-Intensive Systems (VAMOS '09)*, pages 145–153, 2009.

[Tri] TripAdvisor LLC. Reviews of Hotels, Flights and Vacation Rentals - TripAdvisor. `http://www.tripadvisor.com`. (accessed November 6th, 2013).

[TSG13] Irina Todoran, Norbert Seyff, and Martin Glinz. How cloud providers elicit consumer requirements: An exploratory study of nineteen companies. In *Proceedings of the 21st IEEE International Requirements Engineering Conference (RE '13)*, pages 105–114, Rio de Janeiro, Brasil, 2013. IEEE Computer Society.

[UML11] Unified Modeling Language (OMG UML), Superstructure. http://www.omg.org/spec/UML/2.4.1/, 2011. (accessed February 4th, 2014).

[U.S] U.S. government. Get It Done Online! U.S. Government Online Services. http://www.usa.gov/Citizen/Services.shtml. (accessed November 6th, 2013).

[VK06] Omkarprasad S. Vaidya and Sushil Kumar. Analytic hierarchy process: An overview of applications. *European Journal of Operational Research*, 169(1):1 – 29, 2006.

[VMA08] Stephen L Vargo, Paul P Maglio, and Melissa Archpru Akaka. On value and value co-creation: A service systems and service logic perspective. *European Management Journal*, 26(3):145–152, 2008.

[W3C04] W3C Working Group. Web Services Glossary. http://www.w3.org/TR/ws-gloss/, 2004. (accessed Februrary 21st, 2013).

[WDF+08] Jyrki Wallenius, James S. Dyer, Peter C. Fishburn, Ralph E. Steuer, Stanley Zionts, and Kalyanmoy Deb. Multiple Criteria Decision Making, Multiattribute Utility Theory: Recent Accomplishments and What Lies Ahead. *Management Science*, 54(7):1336–1349, 2008.

[WDSB09] Jules White, Brian Dougherty, Doulas C. Schmidt, and David Benavides. Automated reasoning for multi-step feature model configuration problems. In *Proceedings of the 13th International Software Product Line Conference (SPLC '09)*, pages 11–20, Pittsburgh, PA, USA, 2009. Carnegie Mellon University.

[Wee08] Sanjiva Weerawarana, editor. *Web services platform architecture: SOAP, WSDL, WS-policy, WS-addressing, WS-BPEL, WS-reliable messaging, and more.* Pearson Education, Upper Saddle River, NJ, 5. print. edition, 2008.

[WF13] Erik Wittern and Robin Fischer. A Life-Cycle Model for Software Service Engineering. In *Proceedings of the 2nd European Conference on Service-Oriented and Cloud Computing (ESOCC '13)*, LNCS 8135, pages 164–171. Springer Berlin / Heidelberg, 2013.

[Whi07] Jim Whitehead. Collaboration in Software Engineering: A Roadmap. *Future of Software Engineering (FOSE '07)*, pages 214–225, 2007.

[Wit12] Erik Wittern. Public Service Cost and Valuation Model, 2nd Version. COCKPIT project deliverable 3.2.2, Karlsruhe Institute of Technology (KIT), Karlsruhe, Germany, January 2012.

[WKM12] Erik Wittern, Jörn Kuhlenkamp, and Michael Menzel. Cloud Service Selection Based on Variability Modeling. In *Proceedings of the 10th International Conference on Service Oriented Computing (ICSOC '12)*, Lecture Notes in Computer Science, pages 127–141. Springer Berlin / Heidelberg, 2012.

[WLBB14] Erik Wittern, Alexander Lenk, Sebastian Bartenbach, and Tobias Braeuer. Feature-based Configuration and Cloud-independent Deployment on IaaS. In *Proceedings of the 18th International Enterprise Distributed Object Computing Conference (EDOC '14), short paper*, pages 128–135, 2014.

[WLS+05] Hai Wang, Yuan Fang Li, Jing Sun, Hongyu Zhang, and Jeff Pan. A semantic web approach to feature modeling and verification. In *Workshop on Semantic Web Enabled Software Engineering (SWESE'05)*, 2005.

[Wor07] World Wide Web Consortium (W3C). Web Services Policy 1.5 - Framework. `http://www.w3.org/TR/ws-policy/`, September 2007. (accessed October 1st, 2013).

[WRH+12] Claes Wohlin, Per Runeson, Martin Höst, Magnus C. Ohlsson, Björn Regnell, and Anders Wesslén. *Experimentation in Software Engineering.* Springer Berlin / Heidelberg, 2012.

[WSKT12] Erik Wittern, Nelly Schuster, Jörn Kuhlenkamp, and Stefan Tai. Participatory service design through composed and coordinated service feature models. In *ICSOC'12: Proceedings of the 10th international conference on Service-Oriented Computing.* Springer-Verlag, November 2012.

[WTM+04] E. Wohlstadter, S. Tai, T. Mikalsen, I. Rouvellou, and P. Devanbu. GlueQoS: Middleware to sweeten quality-of-service policy interactions. *Proceedings of the 26th International Conference on Software Engineering (ICSE '04)*, pages 189–199, 2004.

[WWMQ10] Guangping Wang, Jianling Wang, Xiaoqin Ma, and Robin G Qiu. The effect of standardization and customization on service satisfaction. *Journal of Service Science*, 2(1):1–23, June 2010.

[WZ11a] Erik Wittern and Christian Zirpins. On the use of feature models for service design: the case of value representation. *Towards a Service-Based Internet. ServiceWave 2010 Workshops*, pages 110–118, 2011.

[WZ11b] Erik Wittern and Christian Zirpins. Validating Service Value Propositions Regarding Stakeholder Preferences. In *2011 IEEE Fourth International Conference on Software Testing, Verification and Validation Workshops (ICSTW)*, pages 294–297, Berlin, May 2011. IEEE.

[WZ14] Erik Wittern and Christian Zirpins. Service Feature Modeling: Modeling and Participatory Ranking of Service Design Alternatives. *Software and Systems Modeling (SoSyM)*, pages 1–26, May 2014.

[WZR$^+$11] Erik Wittern, Christian Zirpins, Nidhi Rajshree, Anshu N Jain, Ilias Spais, and Konstantinos Giannakakis. A Tool Suite to Model Service Variability and Resolve It Based on Stakeholder Preferences. In *The 9th International Conference on Service Oriented Computing (ICSOC)*, pages 1–2, 2011.

[Xig] Xignite, Inc. Market Data Feed and API - Financial Web Service - On-Demand. `http://www.xignite.com`. (accessed March 4th, 2014).

[YBCD08] Jin Yu, Boualem Benatallah, Fabio Casati, and Florian Daniel. Understanding Mashup Development. *IEEE Internet Computing*, 12(5):44–52, September 2008.

[YdPLLM08] Yijun Yu, Julio Cesar Sampaio do Prado Leite, Alexei Lapouchnian, and John Mylopoulos. Configuring features with stakeholder goals. pages 645–649, March 2008.

[YH95] K. P. Yoo and C-L. Hwang. *Multiple Attribute Decision-Making: An Introduction.* Sage University Publications, California, 1995.

[Yu97] Eric S.K. Yu. Towards modelling and reasoning support for early-phase requirements engineering. In *Proceedings of the Third IEEE International Symposium on Requirements Engineering*, pages 226–235. IEEE Computer Society, 1997.

[Zah99] Sajjad Zahir. Clusters in a group: Decision making in the vector space formulation of the analytic hierarchy process. *European journal of operational research*, 112(3):620–634, February 1999.

[ZKL+09] Olaf Zimmermann, Jana Koehler, Frank Leymann, Ronny Polley, and Nelly Schuster. Managing Architectural Decision Models with Dependency Relations, Integrity Constraints, and Production Rules. *Journal of Systems and Software*, 82(8):1249–1267, August 2009.

[ZMZ06] Wei Zhang, Hong Mei, and Haiyan Zhao. Feature-driven requirement dependency analysis and high-level software design. *Requirements Engineering*, 11(3):205–220, June 2006.

[ZZZ09] Wenying Zeng, Yuelong Zhao, and Junwei Zeng. Cloud Service and Service Selection Algorithm Research. In *Proceedings of the First ACM/SIGEVO Summit on Genetic and Evolutionary Computation (GEC '09)*, pages 1045–1048, New York, NY, USA, 2009. ACM.

Index